Sandwich
Soldiers, Sailors, Sons

A Cape Cod Town in the Civil War

Stauffer Miller

Copyright 2019
Stauffer Miller

ISBN Number 9781699926741

Contents

Maps vii

Acknowledgements ix

Introduction 1

Chapter One:
A Pre-War Town 3

Chapter Two:
A Pre-War Heritage 16

Chapter Three:
To Virginia's Sacred Soil—April to December 1861 28

Chapter Four:
Not Much of a Celebration—January to July 1862 44

Chapter Five:
Reinforcements Now Arriving—July to December 1862 56

Chapter Six:
Hard Tack and Mule Beef—January to May 1863 73

Chapter Seven:
Only Son of a Widow—Draft of Summer 1863 85

Chapter Eight:
Do You See the End—June to December 1863 90

Chapter Nine:
John, Did You Catch it Bad—January to May 1864 106

Chapter Ten:
My Greatest and Best Friend—June to December 1864 119

Chapter Eleven:
It Seemed Like a Dream—End of War 1865 136

Epilogue 148

Appendix A: Military Roster of Sandwich Soldiers 153

Appendix B: Personal Roster of Sandwich Soldiers 160

Appendix C: Roster of Sandwich Sailors 168

Notes. 171

Bibliography. 195

Index 202

Maps

1. Town of Sandwich Circa 1860 3

2. Sandwich Village Circa 1860 5

3. Southeast Virginia May 1861-July 1862 50

4. Virginia and Maryland August and September 1862 64

5. South Carolina, Georgia and Florida 1862-1865 109

6. Route of 18th Corps May 27-June 1, 1864 120

Acknowledgements

Logistics—getting the goods of war to troops when and where they need them—is as crucial to the success of a military operation as are sound battle tactics. Author/historian Walter R. Borneman underscored that point in his recently published *MacArthur at War: World War II in the Pacific* when he wrote that for every combat division deployed in that war's Pacific theater there were twice as many personnel supporting it.

I was fortunate to have equally strong support as I researched and wrote Sandwich's Civil War story. Most supportive was my "team" of Barbara Gill, Fran MacPhail and Susan Hanson. No one knows Sandwich families better than Barbara, the town's former archivist. To my many requests, she replied promptly and productively. Fran came aboard when I was struggling with Colin Shaw's Prince Edward Island-Sandwich connection and stuck with me finding countless relevant newspaper articles. Susan, who has helped me with my past books, found and corrected my family relationship errors. For some curious reason, she relishes untangling confusing nineteenth-century household and family connections.

I owe much to the staff of the North Baker Research Library in San Francisco who sent me photocopies from their Allyne collection. The kindness of Mike Widener of the Yale Law Library afforded me a pleasant New Haven afternoon of perusing Attorney Eben Whittemore's 1862 diary. Emma Hawker and Diana Bachman of the University of Michigan's Bentley Library photocopied letters that allowed me to trace the movements of Sandwich prisoner of war Horace Lovell.

Several people forwarded useful scans and microfilms. From Joan Barney of New Bedford, Massachusetts came the richly informative obituary of George Lloyd while Diane Parks of Boston Public Library sent issues of the *Boston Pilot* newspaper. Mark Procknick of New Bedford Whaling Museum chipped in with the microfilmed log of the Sandwich whaling brig *Ocean*. Donna Howard of my local Gordon Library in Charlottesville, Virginia cheerfully handled my numerous interlibrary loan requests.

Civil War battlefields can be both moving and educational. At Fort Donelson, Tennesseee, park ranger Deborah Austin helped me understand how and where Sandwich and Illinois soldier Thomas F. White was killed. Park rangers at Manassas, Virginia Battlefield Park provided similar information for soldier Thomas Wheeler Jr. Historian Bob Krick of Richmond National Battlefield Park patiently fielded my many questions about where this or that event took place near that city.

I could not have written this book without the help of the marvelous research staff of the National Archives in Washington. They do all in their power to assist the public. Anyone with an unfavorable attitude about government or government workers would do well to see the professionalism of these men and women. Equally helpful was Jennifer Fauxsmith of the Massachusetts Archives.

In an almost unimaginable show of kindness, Margaret and Bill Ryan of Sandwich went to Barnstable County Courthouse, photocopied court cases and mailed them to me. Bill Daley of Sandwich worked closely with me on soldier/sailor rosters while town clerk Taylor White granted me access to Sandwich Civil War register books. Dorothy G. Hogan-Schofield, curator at the Sandwich Historic Society, made its Civil War materials available.

My talented step-daughter Connie Soja assisted me with maps and rosters. Charles Thorne of Winchester, Virginia ably and patiently formatted text and images. Tom Jones, a Kansas City friend, who understands the confusing Civil War situation in Missouri about as well as anybody, brought me some clarity regarding that theater of the war.

Several other persons merit mention. Scott D. Hann sent me copies of the few extant pages from the Samuel W. Hunt diary which sadly has disappeared. I am hopeful it may turn up some day. Pat Deal and Susan Steele of the Irish Ancestral Research Association encouraged me to cover as fully as possible in my project Sandwich's Irish population, and this I have tried to do. Susan Greendyke, curator of collections in the Massachusetts State House in Boston, facilitated use of the handsome flag images that adorn the book's covers.

A special thanks goes out to two women I have never met, Pat Nygren of Sioux City, Iowa and Gloria Oberg of nearby Dixon County Nebraska. I contacted Pat in 2014 because I had no record of date and place of death of Sandwich Irish soldier James Ball. Pat not only found that Ball died in 1904 in Dixon County, but also that he had no grave marker. Gloria worked with Veterans Affairs and now Ball has a stone at Calvary Cemetery in Newcastle, Dixon County. I take pleasure and pride in thinking I, and all who aided my project, helped put up Ball's marker. All of us in a sense have a piece of us in that corner of Nebraska where Missouri River bluffs meet the Great Plains.

Now, as I rest my pen and keyboard, I think of the many times over the course of my project when "writer's cramp" set in, I began to struggle like a weary soldier on the march and I thought seriously of shelving the whole thing. But then, thinking of all the people who had supported me, I steadied myself and pressed on. I can only hope that the finished product befits and vindicates all who gave me their much-needed support.

Introduction

Curling into the Atlantic Ocean like an unclasped necklace is the Cape Cod peninsula. Adorning this necklace are jewels, the Cape's towns and villages, each special in its own way. Chatham glitters for its fine shopping; Eastham excels for its beaches; Truro takes honors for its natural beauty. And the Town of Sandwich, in particular its principal community of Sandwich Village, stands out for its remarkable preservation of houses, public buildings and streetscapes in a space compact enough to allow easy exploration on foot.

Still standing from Sandwich Village's earliest century, the seventeenth, is the Hoxie house, built around 1675, or about forty years after the first European settlers arrived. Located along Water Street, its saltbox shape and tiny casement windows readily call to mind the Puritan period of our nation's history.

More conventional in shape are the Village's eighteenth-century houses, characterized by stout center chimneys and symmetrical two and a half-story gable ends. Several of these colonial period houses can be seen in a walk north along Water Street from the Hoxie house. Continuing north, the Sandwich Town Hall comes into view. One of Massachusetts's first such edifices, this substantial building was built around 1835. A growth spurt had begun in Sandwich when a glassworks arrived ten years earlier, making this building necessary. The large fluted columns framing the main entrance convey a confident spirit that representative government was becoming well rooted in the new nation and state, and in Sandwich too.

The growth beginning in 1835 in Sandwich Village continued apace for the next thirty years. That flowering can be seen in the many Greek Revival and Cape Cod style houses of those years that line side streets of Sandwich Village and the adjoining Irish community of Jarvesville. Plaques on many of these houses give a year of construction that falls within that time span.

A walk down one of these side streets, perhaps Liberty Street, plays tricks with the mind. The houses are so little changed it is easy to be transported back in time. Save for the utility poles and the street, now paved with asphalt rather than packed with dirt, you are in the nineteenth century. It is April 1861, an April like many before. The verdure of spring is emerging from the long winter. Song sparrows and towhees are singing in wood lots.

But this April is different. War has been declared between two regions of the country. Men in silk hats gather at the post office to read the latest news from Boston. Bonneted women converse over picket fences and garden gates. Concern fills the air. And young men of Liberty Street and Jarvesville, on outlying farms, in settlements along Cape Cod and Buzzard's Bay, even Sandwich's sailors at sea, hear and contemplate their country's call for their service. These are the stories of those young men, their family situations and the small Cape Cod town from which they came.

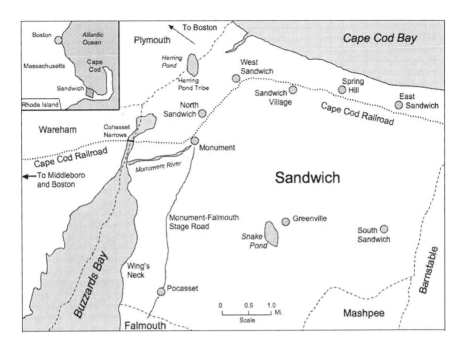

Map 1, Town of Sandwich Circa 1860

Chapter One: A Pre-War Town

Among the first European settlements of the North American continent were those of the 1620s at Plymouth and Boston of present-day Massachusetts. Colonization from those places soon spread southward and in 1637 reached the base of a long peninsula, some years earlier christened Cape Cod. The first settlement on the peninsula was Sandwich, named for a seaport in England. Further settlement followed so that by the time of the American Civil War in 1861 thirteen communities—or towns as they were called—dotted this strip of sand from Sandwich on the west to Provincetown on the east. The legal name given the peninsula was Barnstable County.

The Town of Sandwich at the time of the Civil War was home to 4,500 people, slightly fewer than Cape Cod's most populous town, Barnstable, with its 5,100 inhabitants. Sandwich, however, was largest in geographic size, large enough in fact to be the only Cape town to border both Cape Cod and Buzzard's Bays. Most of the town's people lived in or near the largest population center, Sandwich Village. Smaller population centers (with later names) were

Ox Cart in Jarvesville around 1870. Sandwich Historic Society/Sandwich Glass Museum (SHS/SGM)

Spring Hill and East Sandwich to the east, South Sandwich and Greenville (Forestdale) to the south, and West Sandwich (Sagamore), North Sandwich (Bournedale), Monument (Bourne), Pocasset and South Pocasset (Cataumet) to the west. Sandwich Village, Spring Hill, Monument, Pocasset, North, South, East and West Sandwich had post offices.

Sandwich entered the industrial age in 1825 when Boston manufacturer Deming Jarves established the Boston and Sandwich Glass Company along Sandwich Village's Cape Cod Bay shoreline. In October of that year he advertised wares produced at his "Flint Glass Manufactory in Sandwich." The factory employed seventy workers when it opened; ten years later its payroll numbered 321 men and boys. A company village known as Jarvesville grew up near the factory and by the early 1830s was home to some 371 workers and family members, a sizeable addition to Sandwich Village's small pre-glassworks population. [1]

Many of Jarvesville's residents were Irish immigrants who came from Boston and nearby Cambridge to work at the glass factory. Not only were they Cape Cod's first Catholics, they also built its first Catholic church, a simple wooden structure near the factory. Father Thomas R. McNulty was priest from 1846 to 1853 followed by Father William Moran.

One of the more skilled positions in the factory was that of glass blower. Such employees, called gaffers, earned $14 to $17 per week. At the low end of the pay scale were boys, who made $3 weekly. Management treated employees with some degree of benevolence. Boys received fifty cents every Fourth of July to buy fireworks while workers at Christmas got flour and coal. [2]

By 1855, the factory employed 500 men and boys. In 1856, a newspaperman toured its rooms and departments. Most impressive to him was the blowing room where he saw "so many men and boys performing such a variety of operations in blowing and pressing" that he gave up trying to describe the scene for his readers. Success bred duplication and in 1858 a second factory opened, the Cape Cod Glass Works, also in Jarvesville. The number of employees at both plants in 1860 totaled 530 males and 5 females. [3]

Growth of the glassworks called for more of glass production's prime needs, coal and sand, but the harbor at Sandwich Village was too shallow for their unloading and the conveyance of them by wagon from the better harbor at Monument was unsuitable. The solution to the problem was the railroad, a twenty-seven-mile stretch built east from Middleboro through Wareham, across the Cohasset Narrows of Buzzard's Bay to Monument, across the Monument River and on into Sandwich Village. A great day it was on the Cape when the locomotive and cars chugged into the Village May 26, 1848.

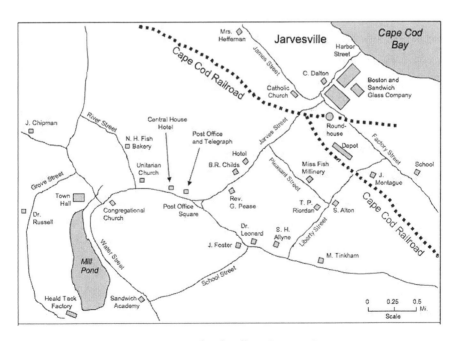

Map 2, Sandwich Village Circa 1860

Although built to haul freight, the Cape Cod Railroad (as it was called) quickly became popular for passenger service. Two trains daily traveled over the Sandwich-Boston-Sandwich route at $1.50 through-fare rate. Sandwich Methodist minister James D. Butler marveled that a passenger could stay in the same car from Boston to Sandwich and travel "away down to Cape Cod...in three hours." Another passenger delighted in the pastoral aspects of Sandwich, seeing from the car windows in mid-June apple trees in bloom and "twenty-seven cows in on one field, up to their eyes in good feed." Still another admired the Cohasset Narrows bridge, calling it a romantic and picturesque entry into Sandwich. Passenger stations from west to east were at Monument, North Sandwich, West Sandwich and Sandwich Village. Another, at East Sandwich, was added when the railroad was extended in 1855 to Barnstable. The first depot master at Monument was Ellis M. Swift, soon succeeded by Erastus O. Parker, while first at North and West Sandwich were Charles Bourne and Isaac Keith respectively. George Atkins and his son Thomas F. were first to perform such duties at Sandwich Village. Parker, Bourne and Keith served as both depot and postmasters. [4]

The railroad sliced through Sandwich Village in such a way that its older, upper, Puritan part lay on one side of the track and the newer, lower, Irish part (Jarvesville) lay on the other. As historian Harriet Barbour wrote, the two parts were "above and below the crossing." In essence, that which existed before the railroad's arrival, an arbitrary division of the village, became a well-defined one after. [5]

The glassworks produced high-quality decorative pressed and blown glass. To protect it during shipment to showrooms at Boston and elsewhere, workers packed it in marsh hay in barrels. Several water-powered mills in Sandwich made heads and staves for the barrels. One was along the Herring River in North Sandwich and another was at Spring Hill. At the latter, three men could produce 2000 staves and their heads in a day. [6]

Critical to the production of pressed glass were iron molds. As with barrels, outlying facilities made them. One was a foundry in North Sandwich, established by Deming Jarves. Mold makers were specialized craftsmen. The Sandwich census takers of 1860 denoted such men as machinists and listed around twenty for the town.

Sandwich's industrial output in the pre-war period went beyond glass. Perry G. Macomber's grist mill in Pocasset produced four barrels of flour per hour. Ground by an "experienced miller," it was said to be of excellent quality. The Pocasset Iron Foundry turned out pots, kettles and other hollow ware, employed thirty-five men and paid them wages of $35 per month. Francis D.

Handy's edge tool factory there hammered out axes and knives of all kinds. His employees earned $30 monthly. [7]

Several other manufacturing establishments color in the rest of the Sandwich pre-war industrial picture. Isaac Keith's works near the depot at West Sandwich employed four men and utilized steam and water power to produce wagons, carts, wheel barrows and iron carriage axles. William C. and Isaac K. Chipman's marble lamp base shop, operating out of the Sandwich Town Hall, employed six men who turned out 300 lamp feet daily. The Sandwich Tack Factory, near Grove Street and Upper Mill Pond in Sandwich Village, employed fifteen men and thirteen women to produce a variety of nails and tacks. The business was on an uneven financial footing until 1859 when Hiram H. Heald acquired it. [8]

Augmenting Sandwich's land-based economy was its sea-based one. Several men of the town were whaling ship captains, viz., Joshua T. Chadwick, Nathaniel Hamblin and Henry G. Smith of South Sandwich, Isaac H. Wing and Zenas W. Wright of East Sandwich, and John A. Beckerman and Ebenezer F. Nye of Pocasset. Influential in whaling at the nearby whaling center of New Bedford was Monument native Jonathan Bourne 2nd. When John B. Dillingham of Sandwich requested Bourne's help in securing a whaling crewman position for nineteen-year-old Charles W. Tobey, also of Sandwich, Bourne got it for him. [9]

Coastal shipping was also important in Sandwich's sea-based economy. Such vessels arrived at and cleared from Monument and Pocasset. Two captains who sailed in and out of those places were Josiah Godfrey Jr. and John Bourne. The latter traded between Monument and New Bedford in the sloop *Greenport*. Shipright Heman S. Hinds had a seasonal shipyard in Pocasset in the 1850s. Assisting him as a ship's carpenter was Ward F. Swift. To assist mariners, the federal government erected a lighthouse at Wings Neck off Pocasset in 1849. Sailing in deeper waters were Monument ship captains Seth S. Burgess, Thomas C. Perry and Abram Phinney who engaged in the coffee trade between Brazil and Baltimore in the bark *Mondamin,* schooner *Forest King* and brig *Clarence*. Phinney's wife Lucinda Burgess Phinney was too frail to

Jonathan Bourne 2nd. New Bedford Whaling Museum

Sportsman's Retreat. SHS/SGM

sail with her husband but strong enough to travel to Baltimore when he was in port. [10]

Travelers to Sandwich could find lodging at a hotel kept by William Fessenden and later Sabin Smith. After Smith died in 1841, Elisha and Sarah Pope assumed the hotel's management and named it Mansion House although it was often called Pope's Hotel. Sewell Fessenden leased it in 1854 and noted in advertising it was a few minutes walk from the railroad depot. Just before the war, glassmaker David Thompson ran the hotel under the name Central House. [11]

Travelers preferring a boarding house could take a room at Sportsman's Retreat, opened in 1848 by English glassworker William Teasdale and his wife Harriet. Even closer to the depot than Central House, it had an attached stable where horses received "the best care." After Harriet Teasdale died in 1851, glasscutter William H. Marston and his wife Louise Tobey Marston ran the establishment. An unmarried female lodger there in 1855 found that for an unprotected female such as herself it was superior to "a regular tavern." Marston noted in late 1855 that he had added gas lighting and that his table fare was "the best our market affords." [12]

Still another place of lodging was Washington House on Jarves Street, run by harness maker Braddock R. Childs. Glasscutter John M. L. Badger assumed its management in 1860. Around the same time William H. Harper ran Harper's Hotel, said to be a boarding house for glass factory operatives. [13]

Along with lodging, Sandwich had eating places. In 1855 George N. Chamberlain took over an oyster saloon from French immigrant Anthony Chapouil. Chamberlain advertised that he had oysters in and out of the shell and chowders every Friday and Saturday night. He closed his ad with a jingle popular at the time:

Tis oysters that alone have power,
To make a man feel easy,
When fried with spirit at the hour,
All looking fat and greasy. [14]

Just seven years after the United States' first daguerreotype photography began in Boston in 1840, Sandwich glassworkers Joseph and Samuel Blackwell advertised "daguerrian miniatures" prepared at their house near the post office. In 1853 daguerreotypist Francis Hacker of Providence leased the hall over William Loring's store opposite Pope's Hotel and in 1855 operated it as "Hacker's Sunbeam Gallery." That year he put his equipment in a glass-topped carriage and went on the road as an itinerant photographer, taking his mobile "daguerreotype saloon" to other parts of the Cape. In 1858 photographer John D. Heywood advertised likenesses of sick or deceased persons done for twenty-five cents. He made several important Civil War era photographs and because of it is Sandwich's best known photographer of the period. [15]

John D. Heywood New Bern, NC Civil War Era Photograph. Library of Congress

The town's first newspaper, the *Sandwich Observer*, made its debut in 1845 and published until 1851. The *Sandwich Mechanic* published a few issues in 1851 and was followed in 1852 by the *Cape Cod Advocate* and *Nautical Intelligencer* which printed the next twelve years. Its editors, Matthew Pinkham and Benjamin Bowman, purchased the library collection of postmaster-druggist Charles B. Hall in 1857 and announced that the library, consisting mostly of works by Dickens and heretofore kept by Hall at the post office-drug store, would remain there for public use. Near Hall's post office-drug store-library was the telegraph office, manned in the late 1850s by young operator Augustus Sears. The railroad, newspapers, library and telegraph all increased Sandwich's contact with the outside world. [16]

In the healing arts, seven physicians served the Sandwich communities. The dean of them was Jonathan Leonard who began a practice in Sandwich Village in 1827 and continued it almost to his January 29, 1882 death. Englishman John Harpur came to Sandwich around 1830 and practiced almost thirty-five years. Another Englishman, Joseph O. Parkinson, practiced in West Sandwich where he marketed his own Dr. Parkinson's Cordial, "an infallible remedy for...summer complaints of children." Henry Russell arrived around 1845 and advertised his patent medicines in the *Barnstable Patriot*. Homeopathic physician Isaac N. Swasey practiced in Sandwich in the 1860-1863 period. He and his wife Lucy were close associates of abolitionist William Lloyd Garrison. [17]

Dartmouth Medical College graduate John B. Bachelder filled Monument's physician needs. He came there around 1844, married Martha Keene in 1846 and in the early 1850s served as secretary of the Sandwich school committee. He and his family moved to Plymouth around 1856. Succeeding him was New Hampshire native Andrew Jackson Runnells, who married local woman Susan E. Perry. [18]

In the entertainment field, Sandwich had a band as early as 1849. Its members played at a variety of functions as cornet and cotillion ensembles and in 1851 they acquired new instruments, several of which were a violin, clarionet, post horn and bass. Four Sandwich families, the Balls, Daltons, Marstons and McLaughlins, had excellent musical abilities and furnished band members. Christopher B. and William B. Dalton, brothers of 1850's band leader James Henry Dalton, were listed as musicians when they enlisted in the army in 1861. [19]

Educating Sandwich children ages five to twenty-one was a network of twenty-four district (public) schools. The two-room one at Jarvesville in 1848 had 177 pupils, ninety-two younger ones in one room and eighty-five older ones in the other. The school committee despaired over this school because attendance was poor and parents frequently kept their children out to work or run errands. Parents also resented discipline for bad behavior. According to

Sandwich Band around 1880. SHS/SGM

historian R. A. Lovell Jr., they had a low opinion of education. [20]

The school hadn't improved much by 1860, despite the hard work of teachers Rosanna Duffy and Sarah T. McLaughlin. The school committee regarded it as backward, in part because some students were always tardy while others had to devote more time to nearby factories than their studies. [21]

Sandwich had several private schools. The Reverend Jonathan Burr established the Sandwich Academy in 1804. Its building, at Water and School Streets in Sandwich Village, was surmounted by a belfry. In 1859 the school had twenty-five boarders. In 1840 Eliza Gould Wing opened Apple Grove, an East Sandwich girl's school that stressed botany and natural sciences, and which in 1859 had six boarders. Nearby was Spring Hill School with forty-five boarders. Henry Russell, when not concocting medicines, operated the Sandwich Female Seminary which he and his wife Mary opened in 1846. Board and tuition, washing and lights included, was $30 per term. [22]

In 1845 the Reverend Frederick Freeman opened the Sandwich Collegiate Institute, "a boarding school for boys and misses." Advertising of 1849 stated that the school was in a "large and commodious building." Freeman also compiled census and mortality data for Sandwich. When sixteen-year-old Sarah Fisher died in an 1859 fire started by her light, Freeman commented that "an interesting young lady [was] sacrificed to the practice of reading in bed at night..." 23

Women operated retail businesses in Sandwich as early as 1849. Misses L. F. and A. A. Chapman advertised bonnet and millinery rooms that year and noted that they carried the latest fashions from Boston. In 1851 Miss Lauretta W. Wing offered bonnets and ribbons, and emphasized that she had mourning goods and grave clothes constantly on hand. In 1858, Elizabeth M. Fish advertised millinery and straw goods available from her widowed mother's house on Pleasant Street. 24

Attending the spiritual well being of Sandwich's Protestant population were a number of ministers. Their exact number for the 1840 to 1860 period is hard to ascertain because of high turnover rate, especially in Methodists, whose annual spring conferences often re-assigned pastors to new pulpits. For

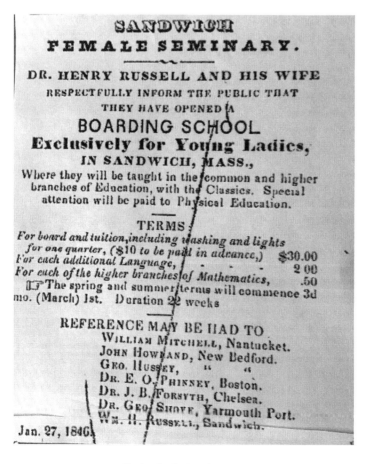

Dr. Henry Russell school ad of 1846. Barnstable Patriot

example, George H. Winchester came to West Sandwich's Methodist Church in April of 1850 and left on re-assignment in early 1852. [25]

Pastor Winchester and family lived in half a house in West Sandwich. In the other half dwelt Captain Freeman Cahoon and family. Winchester was not impressed with the piety of his new congregation, finding many "backslidden" and "callous" about religion. This notwithstanding, he brought much comfort. On September 23, 1850 he visited Benjamin Norris who was close to death from consumption. "I found him ready to go at the biding of God," wrote the Reverend. Norris died four days later. On September 24th he went to the North Sandwich house of Thomas Fletcher of the Herring Pond Wampanaog Native American tribe. Fletcher's wife Maria had summoned the minister to baptize her sick daughter. On December 22, 1851 he consoled the family of young Joseph Nightingale who went out on frozen Herring Pond with his gun, broke through and drowned. [26]

Winchester also lent comfort at the West Sandwich home of Samuel B. Gurney, who had left New Bedford with his brother-in-law Ebenezer Skiff in March 1849 on the schooner *Horace* for the California gold rush. Cholera broke out in San Francisco in the fall of 1850 and Gurney succumbed to it November 17th. When word of his death reached the family January 8, 1851, Winchester went to the home of the widow Deborah Gurney and found the family all together. "I have never seen a family so afflicted…" he wrote. Adding to the tragedy, Ebenezer Skiff died December 9, 1850 on a voyage home from San Francisco. [27]

Another minister who stayed just two years in Sandwich was Jacob G. Forman. He was installed at the Unitarian church in 1854 and left in 1856 for an Illinois pastorate near St. Louis. The Reverend John Orrell succeeded him. [28]

Thomas and Maria Fletcher's North Sandwich Native-American tribe had around fifty members just before the war. The men worked mostly as farmers and mariners. Methodist and Methodist-Episcopal clergymen Abel Allton, Moses Brown, George Pierson and Joseph K. Wallen served as tribal missionaries. [29]

Regarding nineteenth-century America's predominant issue, slavery, five Sandwich men formed an anti-slavery society in 1834. The group grew and in 1837 numbered eighty-one. Early members included sea captain-farmer Charles Nye and store owners William Loring and William H. Russell. When a state anti-slavery agent visited Sandwich in 1844, Nye, Loring and Russell welcomed him. The latter's brother Henry was not only a doctor and director of the female seminary but also antislavery. He was also a member of Sandwich's Society of Friends. [30]

The Reverend Giles Pease accepted a call to Sandwich's Congregational Church in 1842. A year later he delivered an anti-slavery address at the town hall. Sandwich abolitionist, itinerant preacher and glassworker Joseph Marsh attended and accused the local Methodist minister of sabotaging attendance at the address by holding a prayer meeting the same evening. [31]

In late 1849, abolition and women's rights advocate Lucy Stone lectured to a Sandwich audience, within which was the *Sandwich Observer* editor. He came away with the opinion that a woman addressing men in public was unseemly and that her hard-edged antislavery expressions were better suited coming from the mouth of a man. In November 1850, Thomas Swift of West Sandwich picked up the Reverend Winchester and the twosome went by wagon to Sandwich Village where they attended a Free Soil meeting. The Free Soilers were a political faction that opposed extension of slavery into new territories of the country. [32]

The already mentioned Methodist minister James D. Butler, who served a Sandwich Village church from 1849 to 1850, was a strong anti-slavery supporter. Others sympathetic to the cause included Sandwich Village Congregationalist minister Henry Kimball, itinerant preacher Benjamin Haines, educator Paul Wing 2nd, furniture maker Samuel H. Allyne, glassworks gaffer Francis Kern and the previously mentioned Dr. Swasey and Reverend Winchester. A man of modest means and background who supported the movement was Josiah F. Clarke. Born in Plymouth in 1808, he came to Sandwich around 1833 and a year later was a founding member of the town's anti-slavery society. In 1847 he married Mary H. Allyne (not related to Samuel), who also supported the cause. African-american William Cooper Nell spent time at the Clarke's house in 1852 and described the family as "thoroughly anti-slavery." The Clarkes moved to New York State in 1854. [33]

*Lucy Stone.
Library of Congress*

In early July 1852 Samuel H. Allyne, Francis Kern, Paul Wing, and the Reverends Joseph Marsh and Giles Pease, all members of Sandwich's antislavery society, met at the town hall to discuss a social cause of perhaps more local relevance than slavery—temperance, or the lack thereof. What specifically brought them together was a state law slated to go into effect July 22nd restricting possession and sale of liquor, a law for which they wanted to be ready. [34]

And ready they were. On August 4th Kern came before a justice of the peace to complain that Theodore Fisher of Sandwich was selling liquor illegally from his house. A search of the premises found four barrels of gin, rum and cherry brandy in the house and under a pile of oats in the barn. The barrels were seized and on August 5th their contents dumped into the creek beside the Town Hall "in the presence of a large assembly of men and boys." [35]

Violations of the new law continued, especially with certain citizens. One of them, thirty-year-old Irish glass blower Thomas Ball, was indicted several times in 1854. A year later Sandwich's selectmen appealed to Barnstable court authorities not to press indictments against him as he "positively asserts before us that he will not transgress the law again by selling liquors...." Furthermore, noted the selectmen, "Mr. Ball has abstained from the selling of liquors for the past six months." His record, however, did not remain clean. He was indicted for more illegal sales in 1856. Keeping busy as town liquor agent during this turbulent period was Jonathan Chipman. [36]

Samuel H. Allyne.
Stanford University Historical
Photograph Collection

As the 1860s arrived, Sandwich was enjoying prosperity. Evidence of this could be seen in the smoke billowing from the glassworks' chimneys and heard in the din of hammer mills in factories and foundries. It could also be measured in the steady population growth, in increments of 400 or so for every decade since the 1820s.

Not only had Sandwich become prosperous, it had become cosmopolitan. The large Irish immigrant population drawn by the promise of employment and upward mobility had woven itself into Sandwich Village's social and cultural fabric. Lesser numbers of English, French, German and Canadian immigrants also lived and worked in Sandwich's communities. The diverse makeup of the population, the daily arrivals and departures of the trains, the clattering of stagecoaches over the streets, the blaring of steam whistles at the glassworks, the movements of schooners and sloops up and down Buzzards Bay, the arrival of packet boats from Boston, the oratory over all the important matters of the day made Sandwich a vibrant and lively place. This was the tapestry out of which would come the town's Civil War soldiers, sailors and sons.

Chapter Two:
A Pre-War Heritage

An impressive tally of 294 men of Sandwich volunteered for Civil War army or navy service. Around 200 of them were descendants of the town's early Puritan families while sixty-seven were native born or first generation Irish. Fourteen more were of recent English extraction. The remainder were Dutch, German, Canadian, Native-American and African-American. Who were these men? What made them volunteer? The answer to the second question is unanswerable since the men who did the volunteering are long dead; however, looking at who they were and the circumstances in their lives as the war years of 1861 to 1865 arrived provides some insight into why they took the course they did. [1]

Looking first at the Irish, one of the first Sandwich Irishmen to petition for American citizenship was Daniel Fogarty. Born in County Waterford, Ireland in 1809, he and his mother Ann emigrated to Canada in 1823 and three years later reached Sandwich. He may have apprenticed at the glass works because in 1836 he became a glass blower. In his 1837 petition at Barnstable County Courthouse, he renounced the King of England and Ireland and pledged to support the constitution of the United States. [2]

Another early petitioner was County Tyrone native Patrick McGirr. In his 1840 petition, glass blower McGirr said he was born in 1817, came to Boston in 1822 and to Sandwich in 1833. He became a Sandwich constable around 1852 and as such was one of the first town Irishmen to hold public office. [3]

In 1842 Daniel Fogarty returned to the courthouse as a U.S. citizen to support the application of a Sandwich cohort. That same year Patrick McGirr and Thomas McDermott as U. S. citizens vouched for the application of Christopher Dalton while Edward Ball (brother of Thomas) vouched for Samuel Alton. Dalton was born in County Westmeath in 1806, came to Boston in 1826 and resided thereafter at Boston and Sandwich. Alton, born in County Limerick in 1806, arrived in Boston in 1833 and soon came to Sandwich. [4]

Also applying in 1842 was John Montague. Born in County Armagh in 1808, he came to Sandwich in 1831. He worked at the glassworks and ran a boarding house for glass factory workers with his wife Sarah. Edward Heffernan also applied that year. He was born in County Tipperary in 1795, came to Boston in 1823 and to Sandwich in 1826. Edward Ball vouched for his character. [5]

An 1844 applicant was Titus P. Riordan. He was born in 1809 in Cork, Ireland, arrived in America around 1835 and Sandwich around 1840. It appears he did not work at the glassworks but instead ran a dry goods store along busy Dock Street in Jarvesville. He was prosperous enough to own a house, across the tracks from Jarvesville. He died in 1857. [6]

It took courage for Ann Fogarty and the others to leave the familiarity of the Emerald Isle for the unknown of America. What seems to have driven them was a vague sense that life could be better in that land across the seas. Once they reached Sandwich and established themselves in their new community they sought to demonstrate that they were no longer subjects of a monarch but loyal members of that freer society called Americans. The way to do that was to stand before an official at the Barnstable Courthouse and swear to their new allegiance. It was a proud moment, one reinforced when they returned to vouch for a colleague doing the same.

The native born Irish of Sandwich undoubtedly imparted their pride in becoming American citizens to the next generation. This may explain why they, sons and nephews of many Sandwich Irish who received citizenship in the 1840s, volunteered for Civil War service in the 1860s. To their way of thinking, secession by the South violated the constitution their fathers or uncles had sworn to uphold. Sons of Patrick McGirr, Thomas McDermott, Samuel Alton, Christopher Dalton, Edward Heffernan, John Montague and Titus P. Riordan all volunteered as did a nephew of Edward Ball. A son of Daniel Fogarty might also have volunteered except he was accidentally shot and killed in Sandwich on Christmas of 1857. [7]

Edward Heffernan did not long enjoy the citizenship he received in 1842. He died of consumption in 1848, leaving a widow Abigail and seven children. Second oldest child Edward, doing what he could, went to work at the glassworks and contributed his monthly earnings of $32 to his family's support. Around 1857 the family began living in a small house they purchased on Church Street in Jarvesville. Edward enlisted in the Union Army in 1862. [8]

Peter Fagan and Patrick Collins either never applied for citizenship or the record thereof is lost. Fagan came to America around 1840 with his family. After his death in 1846, second-oldest son John worked at the glassworks to support his mother Alice and siblings. Collins arrived in Sandwich in the 1830s and ran a store near the railroad depot. He also owned two wagons.

When he died in 1855 he left debts requiring sale of his real estate. His oldest son John T., age twelve at the time of the November 1856 sale (at the Sandwich post office), worked at the glassworks the next few years before enlisting in 1861 with John Fagan, William McDermott (son of Thomas) and Christopher B. Dalton (son of Christopher). [9]

Native born Irishman James Gaffney might have had difficulty finding someone to vouch for his character had he applied for citizenship. He and Bridget Dolan were married in Boston in 1849 and came to Sandwich around 1856. A year later he was convicted of illegal liquor sales and sentenced to 100 days in jail. One of his sales was to eighteen-year-old glassworker Owen McManus. Bridget, described as "notorious," was brought before authorities in 1859 for a fourth time on complaint of liquor selling and received a $20 fine and forty-five-day stay in the House of Correction. Gaffney enlisted in the army in 1862. [10]

Widowed Irish woman Delia Woods lived in 1855 in the household of Spring Hill farmer Lemuel Nye, possibly as a domestic, with her son James H. In March 1860 he and John Chadbourne stole fifty copper coins valued at $2.00 from the store of Sandwich stove dealer William H. F. Burbank. The two were convicted of larceny and sentenced to nine months in Barnstable County jail. Since this was Woods's first offense and he had never been an "artful, deceitful or ill-disposed boy," residents of Spring Hill as well as B and S Glassworks superintendent Theodore Kern and gaffers William E. Kern and Edward Haines appealed to the court for leniency. The appeal reached the office of Governor John Andrew and in March 1861 his secretary ordered the court to suspend the remaining three months of Woods's sentence. Upon release, he enlisted in the army. Apparently without friends to intercede, Chadbourne served the entire nine months. He too enlisted after gaining freedom. [11]

Three last Irishmen who enlisted merit mention. Edward Brady was born in County Fermanagh and arrived in Sandwich in 1848, following family members who came in the 1830s. He boarded with John and Sarah Montague in 1850 and in 1852 married Sarah Bowes of New Brunswick. At the glassworks he and Joseph Marsh worked together, Brady pressing glass and Marsh finishing it. Between 1858 and 1861 Brady worked at Cape Cod Glassworks under Superintendent C.C.P. Waterman who called him "one of my most active and energetic hands." [12]

Thomas Hackett and his wife Mary Ann lived in a Jarvesville house outside of which their cow grazed. Described as broad shouldered and full chested, the burly Hackett did the hardest and heaviest work at the glass factory. Englishman and factory color expert James D. Lloyd described Hackett before he enlisted in 1862 as "an ambitious, thrifty young Irishman." John McAlaney came to Sandwich around 1847 and was married that year by Father McNulty to Sarah Doran with Thomas Hackett a witness. McAlaney worked at the factory from 1849 to 1861 and, according to fellow Irishman Cornelius Donovan who worked alongside him, excelled at pressing goblets and tumblers. McAlaney enlisted in 1861. [13]

Turning next to the English, Hereford England native Samuel Lloyd worked in glassmaking in Birmingham before coming to Sandwich to work in the factory the year it opened in 1825. He was married in Sandwich in 1826 and fathered James D. Lloyd, the color chemist. Another son, George T. Lloyd, who enlisted in 1862, was said to be a natural musician who could easily learn to play any musical instrument. [14]

Another Englishman who began working at the factory in 1825 was Edward Haines's brother Benjamin, the itinerant Methodist preacher with abolition sympathies. When Benjamin petitioned for citizenship in 1840, Jonathan Chipman vouched for him. His son George F. W. and nephew James G. B. enlisted in 1861. Another nephew, George L. Haines, volunteered in 1862. [15]

Birmingham natives James Cox, Benjamin Davis, Thomas Hollis and Joseph Turner all emigrated to the United States and worked at the glassworks before volunteering in 1861. Cox, son of glasscutter Robert Cox, came to Sandwich around 1858 and began working at the factory in his father's trade. In May 1860 he married Emma Haviland whose mother was also from Birmingham and father Jacob also a glasscutter. [16]

Joseph Turner came from Birmingham to New York in 1850 with fellow Englishman James Howard. Turner's first wife, name unknown, came to New York a year later but was sick on arrival and soon died. Around 1852 Joseph married Mary Connor in New York. She was from Ireland, widowed and had a son Justin. Turner, his wife Mary and stepson Justin Connor came to Sandwich in 1853, where Turner and James Howard worked as glasscutters. [17]

Two Sandwich volunteers were sons of immigrants from continental Europe. Henry Knippe was born in Boston to Dutch parents. When Henry's father, "a man of intemperate habits," died of an alcoholic "fit" in 1854, his widow Isabella was left without means of caring for Henry and his two younger brothers. The latter went to Boston's almshouse and industrial school for boys on Deer Island, Boston Harbor, while ten-year-old Henry went to the family of Charles Dillingham in Sandwich where he worked on Dillingham's farm in exchange for board, clothes and four months schooling per year. Henry faithfully sent his mother his meager earnings, three to five dollars per week depending on the season. Dillingham described the young man as "respectful, obedient and industrious… a favorite in my family." Henry volunteered in 1862. [18]

Francis C. Geisler was born in Sandwich in 1843. His father, also named Francis, was born in the German part of Loraine, France around 1810, came to New York in 1832, married Elizabeth Heineman of Germany in Baltimore in 1835 and came to Sandwich around 1840. He applied for citizenship at Barnstable Courthouse in 1842 and worked at the glassworks until around 1850 when he and his wife moved to Boston. Francis C., whose mother had a limited knowledge of English, enlisted in Sandwich when the war began. [19]

Four African-Americans from Sandwich served. All were born in Massachusetts, evidently as free blacks. George H. Clark, born in Boston in 1823, was in the famous all-black Fifty-fourth Massachusetts Regiment. Anthony Johnson, born in Sandwich in 1835, enlisted in the navy. Little is known of either man.

Brothers James and Henry Boyer were born in New Bedford. While quite young their father, also named Henry, went to Portsmouth, Virginia in 1844 as captain's steward of a merchant ship, was caught assisting a slave to escape and sentenced to four years in a Virginia prison. Meanwhile, his wife Ophelia heard nothing from her husband as she and her children grew destitute. Shortly before he gained his release in 1849 she married Wampanoag Native American Spencer Edwards of Monument. In 1853 her eleven-year-old son James left Monument as a crewman of the whaling ship *Robert Edwards*. Four years later, he went out on the whaling ship *Rebecca Simms*. That ship returned from a four-year cruise in April 1861, just as the war was beginning. Three months later he enlisted in the navy. Six months afterward his brother Henry enlisted. [20]

Turning to the Puritan or old stock volunteers, Charles Chipman was born in 1829, attended the Sandwich Academy and in 1850 was working as a machinist. On December 26th of that year he enlisted at Boston for five years in the army. He did not complete his enlistment, resigning as a corporal while at New Columbus Harbor, New York in 1853. Assisting him in obtaining his discharge were President Millard Fillmore and the Reverend George W. Hosmer, both of Chipman's Unitarian faith. Also assisting was Sandwich selectman C. B. H. Fessenden. Though brief, Chipman's enlistment gained him something that set him apart from his Sandwich contemporaries—army experience. [21]

In 1854, Chipman married Elizabeth F. Gibbs in a ceremony conducted by

Unitarian minister Jacob Forman. They lived at the house of her mother in West Sandwich and he continued his work as a machinist. He and his father Jonathan, the Sandwich liquor agent, were staunch Democrats. Jonathan participated in a Democratic Party meeting in Sandwich in 1858 while in 1859 the party chose Charles to be a delegate to a state convention. [22]

Around June of 1860 a militia unit called the Sandwich Guards formed at Sandwich commanded by "Captain" Charles Chipman. Members of the Guards included James Atherton, Charles Brady and Horace Lovell. Atherton was age nineteen and a printer by trade. Brady was born in Ireland in 1823, came to Sandwich around 1850, worked at the glassworks and in 1860 had a wife and five children. Lovell, age twenty-one, was a son of a Sandwich Village harness maker. [23]

One of the Guards's first public appearances was at Sandwich's 1860 Independence Day celebration. Later that day they took the "cars" (railroad) to Barnstable Village where they marched in a political rally for Democratic presidential candidate John Breckenridge. In September, Chipman and his brother George served as delegates to the state Breckenridge convention in Boston. [24]

Chipman's Democrats won presidential elections in 1852 and 1856 but partway through that run of success a new party, the Republicans, emerged to challenge them. Bringing together factions of moderate Democrats, abolitionists, Free Soilers and anti-Catholic, anti-foreigner Know Nothings, the Republicans had as a principal tenet opposition to extension of slavery into new territories of the nation. Interest in the new party was strong enough in Sandwich that in 1855, just a year after the its birth, Cambridge attorney and Sandwich native George A. W. Chamberlain came to town to explain its principles. [25]

As a member of the more conservative Democratic Party, Chipman believed foremost in preservation of the Union, even if it required abiding slavery. The Irish, including those of Sandwich, were also pro-Union and tepid about abolition. They were fearful that freed slaves would compete for their jobs and that Republicans might impose anti-Catholic repression. Therefore, for somewhat different reasons, Chipman's politics and those of Sandwich's Irish were in concert.

A name established as long as Chipman in Sandwich was that of Gibbs. Charles I. Gibbs, born there in 1835, was christened with his two sisters in 1843 at Sandwich's Unitarian Church and went to sea in 1850. When his sister Elizabeth married Charles Chipman in 1854, the two Charles's became brothers-in-law. In 1856, Gibbs left Boston as a ship's officer under Captain

Gorham F. Bassett in the East India ship *Ceylon*. The *Ceylon* reached Honolulu in 123 days after passing through heavy snow off Cape Horn that reached a depth of three feet on the deck. Home from that voyage in 1857, Gibbs's sister Elizabeth helped him pack for the next in which the *Ceylon* cleared Boston August 15, 1857 and reached Penang, Malaya November 28th. [26]

The well-traveled Gibbs was next an officer of the bark *Valetta* that traded between Boston and Capetown, South Africa. The bark arrived at Boston May 9, 1860 and cleared for Capetown July 24th, giving Gibbs a between-voyage opportunity May 31st to marry Louisa Hunt of Sandwich. He entered the navy in 1861. [27]

Engaging in West African rather than South African trade was Bradford Gibbs of West Sandwich, captain of the brig *Caroline*. No relation to Charles Gibbs, Captain Gibbs left Boston April 4, 1858 for the Gambia, West Africa, a risky place for maritime commerce because British warships patrolled its waters for slave ships. Sure enough, the British warship *Alecto* stopped and boarded the *Caroline* off Sierra Leone on May 8th. Although British naval officers found "the strongest suspicion" of the *Caroline* being in the slave trade, viz., slave beams and planks, no definitive proof could be found. The detention, however, cost the *Caroline* the opportunity to take on a valuable cargo of African hides, a $20,000 loss to her Boston shipping firm. Although the firm sought compensation through the American State Department and British Foreign Office, none was realized. Seaman Gibbs, oddly enough, enlisted in the army. [28]

Another long established ancestral line of Sandwich was that of Hoxie. Four men bearing that name volunteered. From Sandwich Village was Nathaniel C. Hoxie while from East Sandwich came Charles H. Hoxie, one of eleven children of Charles A. and Rebecca Hoxie. They lived beside the Quaker Meetinghouse. From South Sandwich were brothers David and Zenas Hoxie. In 1858, seventeen-year-old Zenas moved into the home of Loring Crocker in Barnstable Village. Hoxie and Crocker's son Alexander worked at the elder Crocker's salt manufacturing operation that produced 4000 bushels of salt yearly. [29]

Like Edward Heffernan and John Fagan, Benjamin Fuller went to work when his father died. After Nathaniel Fuller's death in 1852, thirteen-year-old Benjamin worked at the glassworks for $20 per month, on a ship at sea for $15 per month and as a shoemaker to support his widowed mother Dorcas Myrick Fuller, a native of the Orleans part of the Cape. In 1860 he, his mother, shoemaker Levi Fisher and glassworkers Thomas Cahill, Lucy Dunham and Josephine Bryant all boarded with Cordelia Fuller, widowed sister-in-law of Benjamin. Fuller volunteered in 1861. [30]

Furniture maker and abolition sympathizer Samuel H. Allyne came to Sandwich from the Brewster part of Cape Cod around 1842 after the death of his wife. Coming with him were his five children Joseph W., Helen, Sophronia, Samuel H. Jr. and John W., ages fourteen to one respectively in 1842. Samuel married Nancy Nye shortly after moving to Sandwich.

In January 1849 Allyne's eldest son Joseph W. wrote his father from Boston that he had gotten the gold fever and had to go to [sic] Kalifornia. In April 1852 fourteen-year-old Samuel Jr. wrote a sister that he had been taking the horse and wagon to Paul Wing's school where he was studying drawing and natural philosophy. Also in 1852, his seventeen-year-old sister Sophronia was attending a normal school for teachers. Late that year Samuel H., Helen and Samuel Jr. left Boston for San Francisco on the clipper ship *Golden Eagle*. In March 1854, Joseph W. died of consumption on board a ship in San Francisco harbor. His father was with him when he died. In November 1854 Sophronia was appointed to a teaching position in San Francisco. [31]

Sophronia Allyne died at sea in May 1856 while en route to New York from San Francisco in the steamer *Illinois*. Helen Allyne married Josiah Stanford, brother of California Governor Leland Stanford in 1861. When the Civil War broke out that year, Samuel H. and his wife Nancy were living in Sandwich while Samuel H.'s surviving children of his first marriage, Helen, Samuel Jr. and John W., were living in San Francisco. Samuel Jr. enlisted in California that year. [32]

Like Charles Chipman, Benjamin Ewer of East Sandwich served a three-year pre-war enlistment, except in the navy. In July 1847 he joined the Navy's fastest ship, the *Jamestown*, at Boston. Carrying twenty-two guns, she became the flagship of the African Squadron and like her British naval counterparts, patrolled West African waters for slave ships. Life in the American navy in the 1840s was harsh. Forty-eight floggings occurred on the *Jamestown's* decks in 1848 alone. Ewer's enlistment ended in 1850 when his ship anchored at Norfolk. He enlisted in the army in 1861. [33]

South Atlantic waters were the cruising ground of several 1850s Sandwich whaling vessels. In 1854 the brig *Amelia* under Captain Nathaniel Hamblin began a two-year cruise there. Serving under him were several of his South Sandwich neighbors, including twenty-two-year-old boat steerer Ansel C. Fifield. He moved to the Charlestown part of Boston around 1856 and in 1858 was convicted of larceny and sentenced to one year and ten months incarceration at the state prison. Soon after release in 1860 he married Sarah Smith Linnell, whose family was from Orleans. Fifield enlisted in the army in 1862. [34]

The whaling bark *Ocean* under Captain Henry G. Smith of South Sandwich departed in July 1856 with a crew that included first mate/log keeper Nathan B. Fisher and greenhands John M. D. Badger, George F. W. Haines and James L. Lapham. While the *Ocean* lay at anchor off St. Helena Island in May 1857 for painting and coaling, the crew refused to do duty until the brig underwent a seaworthiness survey.

The survey revealed eaten away timbers that condemned the ship. Despite this, Captain Smith insisted on continuing the cruise. In the end, he had no choice but to consent to the crew's wish to take the *Ocean* home. Since a premature ending of a cruise was irregular, Fisher had to appear before the American consul at St. Helena and swear that his log was true and faithful. Although the crew's action to protest an unsafe workplace was technically a mutiny, the modern day terms of strike or work stoppage seem more applicable. Haines enlisted in the navy in 1861, Fisher in the army in 1862. [35]

Whaling ate away more than ship timbers. In August 1851 chief mate Nathaniel P. Howes of the whaling schooner *Belle Isle* fastened onto a whale but "failed to turn him up." So eaten up with despondency was Howes, he threw himself into the Atlantic and drowned, leaving a widow and three children in Spring Hill. Two of those children, Charles A. and Alvin C. Howes, served in the army. [36]

Ship *Scargo* notice. Boston Daily Advertiser *January 31, 1861*

William H. Childs, son of harness maker-hotel keeper Braddock Childs, went to sea at Boston in March 1861, bound for Melbourne, Australia in the ship *Scargo*. When the war began a month later, the *Scargo's* owner wrote her captain, Daniel W. Howes of Dennis, advising him for safety's sake to keep the ship on the Asian side of the world, far from the war. Although leaking badly, the *Scargo* made it to Melbourne. From there, she sailed to Java where she took on a load of sugar and rattan for Amsterdam. On March 12, 1862, she encountered a hurricane in the Indian Ocean while Childs was at the wheel. The wheel ropes broke and the spokes of the wildly revolving wheel injured Childs in the side. The ship took on water and began to come apart. Fortunately, another ship came into sight and the crew of the sinking *Scargo* transferred to it. Childs made it home later in 1862 and a year later entered the Union navy, perhaps thinking it safer to be near the war than distant from it. [37]

Sailor John H. Bourne was born in Monument in 1835, the eldest child of Joshua T. and Mary Cady Bourne. Sea captain Joshua T. was a brother of Jonathan Bourne 2nd, the New Bedford whaling merchant. Mary Cady Bourne was of Irish ancestry. When eighteen-year-old John H. ran away from home on August 20, 1853, his father posted notice of it in the *Barnstable Patriot* and forbid masters of vessels or others from employing him without fatherly consent. [38]

Two more Bourne children left home six months later when debt-ridden Joshua T. died. Joshua W. moved into the household of his uncle, attorney Charles F. Cady in St. Louis, where the young man worked as a notary public before enlisting. His brother Jerome went to Peoria, Illinois to live with another uncle, Melatiah T. Bourne, who had taken up a land grant claim there in the 1830s. [39]

Meanwhile, runaway son John H. went to Brooklyn, enlisted in the navy in December 1856 and was with the sloop of war *Falmouth* that watched over tense U.S.-Paraguayan relations in the Rio Plata River in 1858 and 1859. He left the *Falmouth* at New York in May 1859 and was next attached to the steamer *Harriet Lane*. He apparently was in the navy when the war began.

Davis Magoon of Monument was a twelve-year-old when his mother died in 1846. A few years later Russell Harris of that place took the young man into his family. To earn his keep, Magoon chopped wood, often alongside boyhood companion Daniel S. Gifford. If put to it, Magoon could swing an axe to the tune of two cords of wood a day. He and companions Gifford and James Hathaway also shoveled coal out of the holds of schooners docked at Monument. In 1860 Magoon married Harris's daughter Freelove. Two years later he enlisted in the army. [40]

Melatiah Bourne House in Sandwich. SHS/SGM

Incipient consumption forced Gilbert Avery of Pocasset to leave his job at the iron foundry and take the less demanding and lower paying position of driving the "accommodation" stage between the Monument railroad station and Pocasset. Oldest son Watson D. compensated for the diminished family income by doing farm work, earning $3.00 per week when he began working as a thirteen-year-old in 1854 and twice that amount just before the war. Gilbert Avery died of his disease in 1860. Two years later Watson D. and his brother Rodman volunteered. [41]

Cousins Francis H. and William H. Swift of Pocasset, like Davis Magoon of Monument, spent a lot of time as youths chopping wood. They also spent fun-filled days swimming on the farm of Wayman Swift, father of William H. In the evenings, they took the cows by the tail and swam them across a creek. Wayman Swift farmed seventy-five acres at Pocasset and kept four milch cows, four oxen and nine head of other cattle. He also raised oats and Indian corn. Francis and William volunteered in 1862. [42]

Around 1850, shipwright Heman Hinds of Pocasset took his family, including six-year-old son Leonard, to Elizabeth City, North Carolina where Heman worked for three years in a shipyard. In 1853 he returned the family to Pocasset. In 1859, he and his son Leonard returned to Elizabeth City's shipyard. When the war broke out in 1861, seventeen-year-old Leonard was a shipbuilder living there. [43]

Shipmaster Josiah Godfrey Jr.'s brother John W. was born at Pocasset in 1818, married Louisa N. Barlow in 1839 and became captain of the schooner *Hume* around 1850. In the 1850 to 1854 fall and winter seasons he took the *Hume* up the coastal rivers of South Carolina to load freshly harvested rice and transport it to brokerages in Charleston. For instance, in December 1853 he transported 4,000 bushels of raw rice down South Carolina's New River and on to Charleston. In 1855 he took the helm of the schooner *L. N. Godfrey*. Launched that year and named for his wife, he continued to transport southern rice. Years in the trade gave him knowledge of southern coastal waterways that would prove useful when he volunteered for the navy. [44]

Two Sandwich volunteers were sons of ministers. In 1856 the Reverend Giles Pease moved to Boston, taking seventeen-year-old son Giles M. with him. More than a minister and abolitionist, Reverend Pease opened a practice of homeopathic medicine in Boston. In announcing the opening, he noted he had had sixteen years experience in that branch of medicine. Giles M. Pease began attending Harvard Medical School around 1859, his father serving as his preceptor. To defray school costs, Giles M. did some acting and at times was on the stage with John Wilkes Booth's brother Edwin. Pease entered the navy in 1861. [45]

Methodist-Episcopal pastor Thomas D. Blake arrived in North Sandwich in 1854 and four years later died leaving a widow and six children in desperate financial need. Oldest child David A. Blake, just sixteen, stepped into the breach and supported the family by gardening and teaching school for three- and four-month long winter terms, earning $35 per term. He was planning to teach the 1861-1862 term but the war intervened and he enlisted. [46]

These vignettes illustrate some of the circumstances in which Sandwich's young men found themselves with the outbreak of war in 1861. A variety of experiences awaited them.

Chapter Three:
To Virginia's Sacred Soil—
April to December 1861

"Civil War! The Fight Begun!" proclaimed the headline of the *Barnstable Patriot's* April 16, 1861 issue. A day before, President Lincoln, in response to the attack on Fort Sumter in South Carolina, had put the machinery of war into motion by calling for 75,000 militia to serve three months to suppress the rebellion and repossess government property. A day later, the day of the *Patriot* headline, Massachusetts received word that its quota of the 75,000 would be twenty militia infantry companies, six of them from the Third Massachusetts Regiment. One of the six was the New Bedford City Guard to which belonged George H. Freeman of Sandwich. He and his company arrived in Boston from New Bedford April 16th, sailed the 18th and reached Fortress Monroe, Virginia the 20th, making him the first Sandwich soldier to go to the war. [1]

At a war rally in Boston, also on April 16th, Thomas Cass and other leading Irishmen of the city urged Bostonians of Irish ancestry to unite in support of the Lincoln administration and the Union. "The place for Irishmen now is in the front of the battle," shouted one speaker, to which responded another, "They were never in the rear." A few days later Cass advertised for volunteers for an Irish Regiment he was forming. The Irish of Sandwich probably soon heard of the rally and regiment through the *Boston Pilot,* an important Irish newspaper. [2]

The excitement grew. On April 18th, flags flew all over Sandwich amidst great enthusiasm. A day later a mob fired into and killed Massachusetts militia soldiers passing through Baltimore en route to Washington. Telegraphed news of the massacre reached Massachusetts a day later, a Saturday. That evening a "large and enthusiastic" crowd met at Sandwich Town Hall to see about organizing a company of troops and providing financial aid to their families. Dr. Leonard presided, Dr. Swasey and Samuel Allyne made patriotic addresses and the band played martial music. Serving as secretary was Eben S. Whittemore, a recently established attorney in town. Over the next few days a

> **Faugh au Bealaugh!**
> **Massachusetts Irish American Brigs**
> WANTED IMMEDIATELY. 500 true active men, of vigorous constitutions, between the ages of 18 and 45 years, as volunteers to complete a Regiment of the above named Brigade, for the defence of our adopted country, its flag and its freedom.
> Applications to be made to the Head-Quarters of the Brigade, WARREN HALL, corner of South and Beach streets, Boston, or to any of the following committee:—
> Capt. Thomas Cass, corner Friend and Sudbury streets; Francis O'Dowd, do.; John F. Doherty, do.; Daniel Corcoran, do.; P. T. Hanley, do.; D. S. Tresnor, 12 Tremont st.; Christopher Plunkett, Head-Quarters; James E. Galligher, do; Peter T. Rooney, do.; James J. Flynn, Washington square; or Messrs. Mahan & Madigan, 141 North street.
> Per Order,   Capt. THOMAS CASS.
> Head-Quarters, April 19, 1861.
> CAUTION. The public are cautioned against giving subscription to irresponsible persons.   3t*   a20

Thomas Cass recruiting ad. Boston Herald *April 22, 1861*

committee from Sandwich petitioned Governor Andrew about the company while "Captain" Charles Chipman signed up volunteers for it.[3]

In the meantime, more militia troops went forth. Former Sandwich resident Sumner B. Fish left Boston with Company K of the Fifth Massachusetts Regiment for Washington while Josiah Foster Jr. left New York, also for Washington, with the Twelfth New York Regiment. Foster Jr. was the son of a Sandwich tinsmith. Howard Burgess, Charles Packard and brothers Sylvester and William W. Phinney of Monument sailed to Fortress Monroe and were mustered into George H. Freeman's Third Regiment April 30th.

Mobilizing as well were Confederates. Ship builder Leonard Hinds enlisted in the Elizabeth City, North Carolina Independent Grays April 23rd. A month later he and his unit proceeded to Hatteras Inlet of the Outer Banks where they assisted in construction of forts. Hinds had the good fortune to be on furlough in Elizabeth City in August when a Union expedition bombarded and seized Hatteras. Had he been on duty, he might well have suffered the fate of comrades defending the forts—capture and imprisonment in New York or Boston.[4]

In Massachusetts, Governor Andrew issued an order May 6th granting the petition of Chipman and sixty-three others of Sandwich to form an infantry company. The order attached it to the Third Regiment in Virginia, designated it as Company D (there being no such lettered company in the Third) and called for election of company officers. Town selectmen presided over the election in which Chipman was elected captain, Charles Brady first lieutenant and Henry A. Kern second lieutenant. [5]

On May 7th, the War Department notified Massachusetts and other northern states that it no longer would accept troops for three months, only for three years. Thinking their service would be three months like the other companies of the Third Regiment, the men of Company D left Sandwich May 8th to join the Third at Fortress Monroe. While laying over in Boston, liveryman William E. Boyden of Sandwich presented Chipman a sword, belt and scarf, while *Barnstable Patriot* editor Sylvanus Phinney treated the men to refreshments at the United States Hotel. Only as the company prepared to board the steamer *Pembroke* for Virginia May 9th did it learn of the War Department's new order. Unprepared for a three-years' absence from home and in some shock over the news, the men refused to enlist, laid down their arms and went home to Sandwich. The next day, May 10th, they assembled at a packed town hall where they heard an "eloquent" speech by Barnstable County Probate Judge Joseph M. Day. His message urging them to enlist for three years must have been compelling because at its completion, in a critical moment for survival of the company, Chipman called the roll and all but one signed up. Judge Day, who lauded the volunteers as "all right" for reconsidering, maintained that only Chipman's determination to keep the company viable and the respect of his men for him kept the company from disbanding. [6]

As important as were the judge's speech and Chipman's influence in persuading the men to sign on for three years, a factor perhaps equal in importance was that of town financial aid to dependents. With approval of it at the April town meeting, Chipman's men knew that when they left for the war, a social safety net fell into place for loved ones at home. As historian Richard Miller has pointed out, Massachusetts communities such as Sandwich recognized that the soldier's well-being was inseparable from that of his family's. [7]

With enlistment matter and affairs at home settled, the Company D volunteers reassembled at the Town Hall at 9 a.m. May 18th for send-off during which editor Phinney presented the company a blue silk flag. One side bore the inscriptions "The Right Arm of Old Massachusetts" and "God Speed the Right" while the other carried the words "Our Whole Country." Parting was hard for six-year-old Susan McAlaney. She cried when her father John left. The band and a party of well-wishers accompanied the volunteers to Boston where Sewell Fessenden, now agent of the Boston and Sandwich Glassworks, treated them to a fine lunch. At 6:30 p.m. they boarded the steamer *Cambridge* and sailed for Fortress Monroe. The departure happened quickly. As Chipman wrote from the steamer to his wife Elizabeth, "The band stopped in Boston to send us off, as also many friends, but after we marched aboard the steamer she cast off and I hadn't time to…bid them goodbye." [8]

In the same letter Chipman described food and accommodation differences between officers and men on the *Cambridge:* "We [the officers] live high, have first rate accommodation…The men of course do not fare so well, grumble some about having a dry piece of bread without butter for supper (and a little weak tea). About the same as I used to have when in the army which I always got along very well with." These lines reveal a key element of his idea of command, that he had not forgotten his 1850s army days and what was good enough then, i.e., "what's sauce for the goose etc," would be quite sufficient now.

The actions of one of Chipman's privates, Perez Eldridge, gave Chipman further opportunity to elaborate on his command philosophy. Eldridge committed an unknown offense in getting to the *Cambridge* May 18th and was placed under arrest. The situation was awkward for Chipman as he and Eldridge had been friends. Nevertheless, he recognized that friendship could not get in the way of a firm hand, or as he wrote his wife, "Men have to get used to discipline. And my men will never disobey the slightest order without being punished…they will thank me for it, and have more respect for me than though I overlooked such offences." [9]

After a two and one-half-day passage, the *Cambridge* reached Fortress Monroe May 21st and discharged Company D plus several other three-years companies for the Third Regiment. It was an odd arrangement, three-years and three-months companies in the same regiment. General Benjamin Butler arrived May 22nd to a twelve-gun salute and took command of Union troops in the area. One of his first orders was a health inspection of three-years men. It was a thorough one, the men having to strip "stark naked." Two Sandwich volunteers, Martin Monahan and Henry Parks, failed it and were sent home. Those who passed took the oath of allegiance and were mustered into service. [10]

Fifty-eight soldiers—three officers and fifty-five men—comprised those from Sandwich in the new company. Its ethnic make-up mirrored the melting pot town from which they came: twenty-three Puritan/Old New England, twenty-four Irish, six English, two German, one French, one Nova Scotian and one unknown (Table 1). Truly, Sandwich could be proud that it put a company in the field so early in the war and that it was one of the first to enlist for three years. While the company's existence was to some extent an

Table 1
Ethnicity of Men of Sandwich in Company D, "First Sandwich Company"

Name	Ethnicity	Name	Ethnicity
1. Atherton, James H.	American	30. Hoxie, Charles H.	American
2. Badger, George W.	American	31. Hoxie, David A.	American
3. Badger, Gustavus	American	32. Hoxie, Zenas	American
4. Ball, James	Irish	33. Hunt, Samuel W.	American
5. Brady, Charles	Irish	34. Jones, Charles E.	American
6. Brady, Edward	Irish	35. Kern, Henry A.	German
7. Breese, William	English	36. Kern, Martin L. Jr.	German
8. Bruce, George F.	American	37. Long, Patrick	Irish
9. Bumpus, Frank G.	American	38. McAlaney, John	Irish
10. Campbell, John	Irish	39. McDermott, Wm.	Irish
11. Cheval, Alfred	French	40. McElroy, Patrick	Irish
12. Chipman, Charles	American	41. McKenna, Michael	Irish
13. Clancy, Patrick C	Irish	42. McNulty, Peter	Irish
14. Collins, John T.	Irish	43. Phinney, Isaac	American
15. Cook, James	Irish	44. Robbins, Caleb T.	American
16. Cox, James	English	45. Russell, Peter	Irish
17. Dalton, Christopher	Irish	46. Russell, Phillip	Irish
18. Dean, Timothy	American	47. Smith, James Wm.	English
19. Dean, Warren P.	English	48. Swift, Francis C.	American
20. Donnelly, Edward	Irish	49. Turner, Joseph	English
21. Eaton, Joseph W.	English	50. Ward, James	Irish
22. Eldridge, Perez	American	51. Weeks, John	Nova Scotian
23. Fagan, John	Irish	52. Wood, William H.	American
24. Fuller, Benjamin	American	53. Woods, Francis	Irish
25. Guiney, James	Irish	54. Woods, James H.	Irish
26. Hamlen, Benjamin	American	55. Woods, John	Irish
27. Harkins, Charles	Unknown	56. Woodward, Wm.	American
28. Heald, James H.	American	57. Wright, Anderson	American
29. Heslin, Michael	Irish	58. Wright, Charles S.	American

outgrowth of the Sandwich Guards of 1860, most credit for it rested with the hard work in 1861 of Chipman and town citizens.

Runaway slaves began entering Union lines at Fortress Monroe around May 24th. When their masters came to claim them, General Butler, in a pivotal moment of the war, astutely pointed out that because Virginia had seceded, laws mandating the return of runaways no longer applied and they would become Union contraband of war. The phrase "contraband of war" was soon shortened and popularized to a term meaning self-emancipated slaves, "contrabands."

In a letter to his wife of May 28th, Chipman wrote that Butler's contraband policy was still just a rumor but if true, he couldn't see the advisability of it. In other words, he couldn't see how African Americans could assist the Union cause. Such thinking was not uncommon in northerners, many of whom were racially prejudiced. In a letter of June 2nd, Chipman chided his Uncle P. (perhaps Pelham Gibbs of West Sandwich) for being an abolitionist and said he "ought to be here to fight for his abolitionist principles." Not only was Chipman prejudiced against African Americans, he disliked abolitionists and believed their meddling in national affairs had caused the war. He also branded white Republicans of Sandwich as "black republicans," the commonly used racial slur applied to them at the time by Democrats. [11]

Company D's cook at Fortress Monroe was thirty-five-year-old glassmaker William H. Wood. He must have had some culinary talents because Chipman told his wife to send receipts (recipes) of dishes he liked and he'd have Wood prepare them. [12]

Anchored off Fortress Monroe in Hampton Roads in May and June was the naval steam frigate *Minnesota*. Sergeant of her marine guard was Franklin R. J. Clarke, born in Sandwich in 1841. His father John died around 1855 leaving the widowed England-born Ann Bradfield Clarke (often spelled Clerke) to rear the large family. In June 1861 Clarke presented himself for medical survey to the *Minnesota's* surgeon. He found evidence of epilepsy and sent him to the marine hospital in New York. Clarke, Sandwich's only marine of the war, later served in the army. [13]

Far to the west of Virginia was St. Louis resident Calvin G. Fisher. He had moved from South Sandwich to Illinois in 1855, heard the Lincoln-Douglass debates in 1858 and moved to St. Louis in 1859. On May 8, 1861 he enlisted as a private for three months in the largely German Third United States Reserve Corps of Infantry commanded by Colonel Franz Sigel. Two days later a detachment of his unit was part of several regiments sent to break up a Confederate encampment on the outskirts of the city. The confrontation turned deadly, twenty-eight men, women and children died and Missouri went from largely neutral to deeply divided in its Union-Confederate sympathies. On May 15th General William S. Harney, commanding the Union Army's Department of the West at St. Louis, had notary Joshua W. Bourne prepare an affidavit about the incident. Three weeks later Bourne enlisted as a private in Company E of the Irish Seventh Missouri Regiment. He may have enlisted in that regiment because of the Irish Cady side of his family.[14]

In Boston, Thomas Cass continued to recruit for his Irish regiment, now designated the Ninth Massachusetts. The first of three Sandwich men to enlist in it was James Kelley, born in Ireland and supporting a wife and children. The regiment camped and trained at Long Island in Boston harbor much of June 1861. When the Catholic bishop of Boston came there, he confirmed Kelley who thenceforward was James H. Kelley. He and Sandwich's two other volunteers in the regiment, James O'Neill and former constable Patrick McGirr, marched from Boston's Long Wharf to the Statehouse in a huge June 25th parade in which two color sergeants of the regiment proudly carried American and Irish flags. Adorning the green silk of the latter were Irish harp, shamrock and two wolf dogs with motto "Gentle when stroked, but fierce when provoked." Later that day the men sailed for Washington. Upon disembarking June 30th, President Lincoln and other dignitaries addressed them and welcomed them to the city. [15]

Also going off to war was Patrick McGirr's son Edward. He and the rest of his Fifth New York Regiment left their training ground along New York's East River, boarded steamboats and cruised downriver past cheering crowds at Throg's Neck and Riker's Island. After disembarking at lower Manhattan, they marched to City Hall where more cheering crowds marveled at their dapper Zouave uniform of red trousers, white leggings and white turban. Among the many onlookers might have been Edward's mother Margaret and sister Catherine. [16]

Three men of Monument, Joseph M. Perry, George E. Phinney and Jesse F. Phinney, enlisted in the navy at New Bedford May 21, 1861. They were assigned to the steam frigate *Colorado,* which sailed from Boston June 18th for duty in the Gulf of Mexico. Coasting sailor Jesse F. Phinney was a son of Jabez Phinney who in the late 1850s succeeded John W. Godfrey as captain of the coasting schooner *Hume.* Perry and the two Phinneys received discharges from the navy in June of 1862 when the *Colorado* returned north from her Gulf cruise. None of them did further war service. [17]

The *Colorado* blockaded in the Gulf of Mexico in company with another steam frigate, the *Powhatan.* On August 13th the

Typical Zouave uniform. Historic Data Systems (HDS)

Abby Bradford *telegram received by Captain Ezra Freeman.*
National Archives (NA)

latter captured the schooner *Abby Bradford,* which had been captured three weeks earlier by a Confederate privateer. On September 5th a telegram came into Sandwich informing *Abby B.* captain Ezra B. Freeman that his schooner had arrived in Philadelphia in the hands of a prize crew. He and *Abby B.* co-owner George G. Ryder of Boston went immediately to Philadelphia, bought their own ship in prize court for $1,250 and took her to New York where cargo accounts were settled. Sandwich co-owners of the *Abby B.* included William E. Boyden, Isaac K. Chipman and Henry and Paul Wing. [18]

The inactivity of the sizeable Union Army in and around Washington put pressure on its commanders to attack the Confederate Army massed at the important rail junction of Manassas, Virginia. "On to Richmond" was the phrase popularized by politicians and the press. Also increasing the pressure on Union commanders was the imminent expiration of terms of enlistments of three-months troops.

If the attack at Manassas was to be successful, a second Confederate Army in the Shenandoah Valley had to be kept from reinforcing the one at Manassas. Toward this end, Josiah Foster Jr. and his Twelfth New York Regiment boarded trains at Washington July 7th and journeyed to Baltimore and Harrisburg, where other regiments joined them. From Harrisburg south to the railroad terminus at Hagerstown, Maryland, the crush of soldiers filled the coaches and overflowed onto the roofs from which the men waved flags and handkerchief-tipped bayonets to throngs that lined the tracks. At Hagerstown on July 9th Foster began a twenty-three mile march keeping time to the tune "Jordan's a Hard Road to Travel" that took him and his regiment across the Potomac River onto the "sacred soil of Virginia" at Martinsburg. "One thing is certain," wrote Foster July 11th from his camp just five miles from the enemy army, "they will have to fight or run." The Confederate army at Martinsburg, however, did neither but rather outmaneuvered the Union force and headed for Manassas. [19]

In June, Sumner B. Fish's Fifth Massachusetts moved its camp from Washington to a section of Alexandria, Virginia near the slave pen made famous in the book *Twelve Years a Slave* by Solomon Northrup. President Lincoln visited the camp June 14th. The Fifth began marching to Manassas July 16th, passing along the way some three-months units that had discontinued the march and turned for home, their ninety-day enlistments having expired. During the battle of Manassas July 21st—the first major engagement of the war and a Union defeat—Fish was struck by a cannonball and killed. Sandwich's first fatality of the war, he has a marker at the town's Bayview Cemetery. [20]

At Fortress Monroe the three-months Massachusetts companies departed for home in mid-July, their enlistments completed. This left Sandwich's Company D and six other Massachusetts three-year's companies militarily unattached. Since they were three companies short of being a regiment, the seven companies were combined into what was designated the Massachusetts Battalion. General Butler ordered Captain Joseph H. Barnes, captain of the East Boston three-years company, to its command.

Enlisting continued steadily in Sandwich, where a number of glassmakers signed up. In the period May 23rd to July 26th twelve such workers joined the boys in blue. Adding that number to the thirty-three already mustered into Company D meant that by August 1861 forty-five glass workers had gone to the war.

Perez Eldridge continued to be a thorn in Chipman's side. When he ordered an intoxicated Eldridge to the guardhouse August 9th, the latter drew his bayonet, threatened to use it if approached and said "he would be d__d if he did not make him [Chipman] pay for this." Rumor of the incident soon reached Sandwich, prompting fifty-two-year-old widow Alice Fagan to write Chipman to see if the wrongdoer might have been her son John. Chipman told her to disregard rumors and only believe that which came to her through official channels. As for Eldridge, he was court martialed, convicted and ordered to serve five-month's hard labor at Rip Raps Island near Fortress Monroe with twenty-five-pound ball attached to his right leg by a three-foot chain. His sentence also included loss of pay but Chipman, feeling sorry for

Eldridge's family in Sandwich, had that part dropped. [21]

A week after the Eldridge incident, Lieutenant Brady had command of a guard detail near Fortress Monroe when a gun accidentally discharged and took off the upper joint of the right thumb of Private William McDermott. He was taken to the post hospital where he spent three weeks recovering. Bedmates with him from Company D were Benjamin Hamlen and John McAlaney. Corporal David Coleman of the company felt that the gun accident was due to carelessness. [22]

On August 18th the battalion moved several miles westward from Fortress Monroe to Camp Butler at Newport News Point, Virginia. The camp commanded the James River from a thirty-five-foot bluff upon which were mounted heavy guns on breastworks. Just off the camp's wharf lay naval support and blockade vessels, initially the frigate *Savannah* and later the sloop of war *Cumberland* and frigate *Congress*. A lengthy picket line protected the camp's wooded rear. Communication between Camp Butler and Fort Monroe was by the steamer *Express* and telegraph. General John Phelps, former Colonel of a Vermont Regiment, commanded the camp.

Across the continent at San Francisco, Samuel H. Allyne Jr. enlisted at the Presidio August 15th in Company E of the First California Cavalry. The first assignment of his company was protection of an army outpost in southern California on the San Francisco-Fort Yuma mail and stagecoach route. [23]

In October, six men of Sandwich enlisted in Company A of the Twenty-fourth Massachusetts Regiment. The "old man" of the six was sailor Jesse Allen, age forty-two. The others were John F. Fish, Benjamin Ewer, Phillip Riley and brothers Isaiah and Watson Adams. Fish had a busy October. He enlisted the 4th, was married the 13th to Hettie N. Chipman of Sandwich, underwent medical examination at Boylston Hall in Boston the 15th and was mustered into service the 16th. He was married by the Reverend Benjamin Haines who had lived with Fish in South Sandwich. [24]

Isaiah and Watson Adams came to Sandwich to enlist in the Twenty-fourth from East Bridgewater where they were working at a nail factory. When the regiment left Massachusetts in December, Isaiah's wife Elizabeth Briggs Adams began boarding in the house of her sister in East Boston. At Annapolis, Maryland, the regiment's first encampment in the south, the men learned they would be part of the Burnside Expedition to capture Roanoke Island, gateway to eastern North Carolina. Detailed to serve on the gunboat *Pioneer* in the expedition were Fish, Riley, Allen, Ewer and Watson Adams. The latter three were tentmates. The *Pioneer* was a former Hudson River towboat. [25]

Also in October, steps began to raise a second Irish Massachusetts regiment.

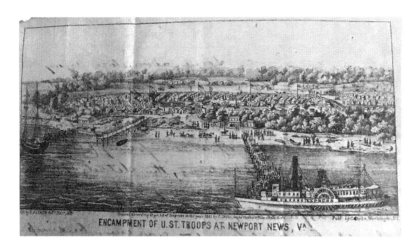

Camp Butler. Massachusetts Archives Executive Letters Vol. 34

Advertising exhorted Bay State Irishmen to enlist in what would become the Irish Twenty-eighth Massachusetts. William B. Dalton, brother of Christopher in the Sandwich Company, was authorized to recruit in Sandwich. Men of the town entering the new regiment were John Chadbourne (upon his House of Corrections release), Thomas Wheeler Jr., John McCabe and Bernard Woods (father of Francis Woods of the Sandwich Company). Dalton and Michael A. Ball were in the regiment's band. [26]

October brought the war close to home in Pocasset when Sandwich Company soldier John Weeks, oldest son of Eunice and fisherman Willard Weeks of that place, died from a fever the 20th. Captain Chipman had Weeks's body sent home, his friends in Pocasset received it October 25th and his largely attended funeral took place the 27th. [27]

Another Pocasset man who suffered the misfortunes of war service was coasting sailor Francis Little. After enlisting in the navy in September and reporting for duty in October on the bark *Kingfisher* at Boston, he contracted a case of measles so virulent it cost him much of his hearing. It also cost him duty on the *Kingfisher*, which sailed to her station in the Gulf of Mexico while he was recovering. In November he was assigned to another naval bark, the *Fernandina*, and was aboard when she went into blockade duty off North Carolina. [28]

Aboard a steamer that arrived at Fortress Monroe October 29th from Boston was Captain Chipman's twenty-one-year-old brother William N. ("Willie") Chipman. The captain was hopeful his wife Elizabeth could join Willie on the trip but as she was eight-months pregnant, it was too much for her. In

Second Massachusetts Irish Regiment ad. Boston Pilot *January 18, 1862*

a letter to her of November 7th, he expressed his hope she would "get along finely" through her "troubles." Captain Chipman helped Willie obtain a clerk position with the sutler store of Voorhees and Bell at Fortress Monroe. [29]

Willie brought news that a photograph of John Breckenridge (Captain Chipman's favorite in the 1860 presidential race) left hanging by the captain in the parlor of his house when he departed in May was still in place. Such news wouldn't have been of much consequence except that Kentuckian Breckenridge had just denounced the Unionist legislature in his home state and joined the Confederate Army. Chipman immediately wrote his wife and told her to take down the photograph. "He is a Traitor," he wrote. "If it were not for men such as he I should be home now although I consider them not more to blame than many abolitionists that we have got at home." Not only did he blame abolitionists for the war but also Union defectors such as Breck-

Charles Chipman as captain in 1861, in single-breasted line officer uniform. He holds a non-regulation model 1850 sword, possibly the one presented to him by William Boyden. U.S. Army Heritage and Education Center (USAHEC)

enridge. Since preservation of the Union was a central to Democrat Chipman's political beliefs and Breckenridge had gone back on his word on that support, he looked upon his former champion's defection as a betrayal. [30]

Chipman was often officer of the day at Camp Butler. In that capacity, he and an orderly made the rounds of the picket guard posts at Camp Butler on horseback. An orderly looked after an officer's needs, such as polishing his boots or caring for his horse, and by so doing was excused from a private's usual duty of standing guard. Chipman's orderly was his West Sandwich neighbor Francis C. Swift who may have become experienced with horses through his uncle, horse merchant Thomas Swift. [31]

October wedding bells rang out in Sandwich for nineteen-year-old James G. B. (Birney) Haines, nephew of minister Benjamin Haines, and seventeen-year-old Maria Hartford, daughter of glasscutter Joseph W. Harrford. As with John F. Fish, Reverend Haines performed the ceremony. On Sunday November 10th, a month after the wedding, Birney asked his father Edward Haines at the family residence at Spring Hill for a few dollars to take the train to Boston so he could volunteer for the army. When his father refused the request, he got the money from his older brother George L. even though, as the latter put it, it took "the clothes off my back to do it." Later in November, Birney reached Camp Butler where he was mustered into the Sandwich Company. [32]

Also in November, Sandwich's citizens mounted a soldier aid drive. Spearheading it was George L. Fessenden, paymaster at the Boston and Sandwich Glassworks and son of its Boston agent Sewell Fessenden. The younger Fessenden canvassed the town and obtained $52.00 in subscriptions used to purchase yarn which ladies of Sandwich stitched into seventy-two pairs of socks in a knitting club. Rebecca Kern, wife of superintendant Theodore Kern of the B. and S., went around town soliciting donations of blankets. When Chipman and his men received the socks and blankets at Camp Butler, he wrote that clothing and bedding were most welcome as November nights in a tent, even in Virginia, were chilly. [33]

Among the men of Sandwich who contributed to the drive were bandleader James H. Dalton and businessman Abel S. Heald, both of whom had brothers in Chipman's company. Donating two blankets were Rebecca Kern, Mary Fessenden (wife of George), Isabella Dillingham (wife of Charles), Mary Southack, Jane Scott, Charlotte Hoxie and Abby Pope. Lucy Swasey, wife of the abolitionist homeopathic physican, contributed a blanket to Sandwich's drive and a copy of Harper's Magazine to one held in West Sandwich. [34]

Sandwich Town Hall was a busy place. To it went dependents of soldiers to sign for and pick up town aid. Often a trusted family member went on this important errand. Fifteen-year-old Mary Collins, sister of soldier John T. Collins, picked up the money for their widowed mother while thirteen-year-old Margaret McNulty, sister of soldier Peter McNulty, did the same for their mother Ann. Mary could sign her name but Margaret could only leave her mark. Perez Eldridge's mother Nancy signed for two of his four motherless children while his mother-in-law Eleanor Ellis signed for the other two. [35]

On November 17th twenty officers of the Massachusetts Battalion gathered at the Camp Butler quarters of Captain Barnes to vote for recommendations for lieutenant colonel and major of a regiment to be formed out of the battalion, the recommendations to be sent to Governor Andrew in Massachusetts. Unanimously selected for the respective positions were Barnes and Captain Chipman. Judge Day wrote the governor in support of the Chipman recommendation and noted that Barnstable County had no field grade (major to colonel in rank) officers in the army. [36]

"That night the wind blew pretty hard, I felt kind of sick, sat down under the portico, and fell over before I knew it." That was the defense statement of Private Peter McNulty of the Sandwich Company, on trial for being asleep at 12:30 a.m. the night of November 30th at Camp Butler while standing guard. McNulty was in fact sleeping so soundly that officer of the guard Lieutenant Kern took McNulty's gun and walked forty feet away before he awoke and called out for it. As with Perez Eldridge, the hammer of military justice came down hard. Found guilty, he was sentenced to three month's hard labor at Rip Raps Island and forfeiture of pay. [37]

Judge Joseph M. Day. USAHEC

Getting off with a lighter sentence was Joshua W. Bourne, now a First Lieutenant in the Seventh Missouri Regiment. Convicted of remaining in his tent near Sedalia, Missouri on November 22nd when detailed for guard duty, he was sentenced to a reprimand by the regimental commander. Aiding his case were several of Bourne's co-officers, who testified favorably in his defense. At the St. Louis part of Missouri, Calvin Fisher applied for and obtained an officer commission which he used to recruit, organize and muster militia units to fight guerillas in the state. [38]

Reaching Sandwich around December 16th on a much-needed twelve-day furlough was Captain Chipman. Upon arrival he learned that the Massachusetts Battalion would be expanded to form the new Twenty-ninth Massachusetts Regiment. Unable to conceal his pride, he walked around with "29" in his hat. The "29" might not have attracted much attention on the streets of Sandwich but his large black uniform hat looped up at one side, embroidered with bugle and eagle and finished off with tassels and plumes would have turned a few heads. [39]

With recommendation for promotion approved, Chipman went to Boston December 20th to exchange his captain's bars for a major's oak leaves. By going on the 20th, he missed by one day seeing a one-time-only spectacle in the Hub City. On the 19th, around 980 horsemen of the First Massachusetts Cavalry Regiment paraded through the city. "Our people," wrote a newspaper reporter, "never have enjoyed the opportunity of seeing such a number of armed men on horseback before." The mounted column made up of horses and riders four abreast stretched over a third of a mile. Among the troopers were three men of Sandwich, George Hobson on a bay, Nathaniel Fish on a sorrel and William W. Phinney on a black. None of the three would seem to have had any pre-war equine proclivity, Hobson having been a glassworker, Fish a baker and Phinney a mariner. The latter had served a three-months enlistment earlier in 1861. [40]

Upon Major Chipman's return to Sandwich the 20th, he and town recruiting agent Charles B. Hall signed up a volunteer for Company D of the new Twenty-ninth, Joseph Madigan. Chipman returned to Camp Butler December 28th. His promotion to major of the regiment produced officer advancement opportunities in Company D. First Lieutenant Brady was promoted to captain and assumed company command while Second Lieutenant Kern moved up to First Lieutenant and second-in-command. [41]

When Alice Fagan wrote Chipman in August about the rumored incident in Company D, she might have done so in part because of intimate knowledge of her son John's habits. On the day after Christmas, he was arrested at Camp Butler for drunk and disorderly conduct, roaming about the camp after curfew and striking a sergeant of the police guard. His spree garnered him forfeiture of pay and six months of hard labor at Rip Raps. [42]

Celebrating Christmas in a more subdued way was Cambridge Private Thomas Darby of Company D. He received a Christmas box of edibles from Sandwich, presumably from his sister Susan Quinn. Her husband Charles was a gaffer at the glassworks. Unfortunately, the box arrived late with much of the contents spoiled. This notwithstanding, Darby and his messmates scraped the blue mold off the duck and chicken, declared them good enough for soldiers and consumed the lot with gusto. [43]

As 1861 closed, approximately 100 men of Sandwich found themselves in army camps from Virginia to Missouri to California. Another twenty-five or so were on naval vessels. Three had died in battle or of disease. The Sandwich economy at year's end was in a slight downturn because of closure of the Cape Cod Glassworks, reduced production at the Boston and Sandwich works and falling off of business at small iron factories along the Cape Cod Railroad line. [44]

Chapter Four:
Not Much of a Celebration—
January to July 1862

The war's second year, 1862, began with Company D garrisoned at Camp Butler, Newport News, and awaiting absorption into the Twenty-ninth Regiment. The boys of Sandwich hadn't laid eyes on many of the enemy and the few they had sighted hadn't impressed them: "I have not seen but one dead rebble since I left home and he was a hard-looking sort I tell you," wrote Anderson Wright of Pocasset in a letter to younger brother Noah. Noting what was important to him at home he told Noah, "Take good care of my guns and dog." [1]

Five days into the new year, whisperings of scandal (apparently an illegitimate pregnancy of a local girl) buzzed about Sandwich, murmurings too salacious for Elizabeth Chipman not to send along to her husband. The major, perhaps eyeing the revolver on his belt, responded indignantly, "About that Chamberlain Girl—Were I her Brother, Crocker would live just long enough for me to get within Pistol Shot of him, and I am not sure that I should not serve her the same." [2]

Of more immediacy for Chipman than mischief in Sandwich was the vacant second lieutenant position in Company D. He felt that Sergeant James Atherton, former officer of the 1860 Sandwich Guards, was most deserving but it went instead to outsider Augustus Ayling of Lowell. Since the men of the company wanted their own man Atherton for the position, Ayling was nervous as he stepped into his first command, especially since the company had, in his words, "some pretty tough specimens." Nevertheless, the men soon warmed to him. [3]

Chipman heard about but did not see the armada of transports and army gunboats making up the Burnside Expedition that arrived at Fortress Monroe from Annapolis January 10th. He guessed its destination was "up one of these rivers." One of the gunboats was the *Pioneer* with its five Sandwich soldier-crewmembers. Lieutenant Ayling, at the fort on the 10th, got to see this "city afloat" as it was often described. The assemblage was especially memo-

Deming Jarves Jr. SHS/SGM

rable by night, with vessels illuminated and bands aboard playing. Ayling called it "a scene never to be forgotten." [4]

Sailing with the expedition was Deming Jarves Jr., son of the founder of the B and S Glassworks. Bostonian Jarves Jr. had been a frequent pre-war visitor to Sandwich to fish, duck hunt and help his father and because of it was well-known in the town. When the war began, he was appointed a lieutenant in the Twenty-fourth Massachusetts and at Annapolis was detailed to serve in the Signal Corps. The vessel transporting its officers reached Fortress Monroe January 13th. On the 15th, Jarves Jr. went ashore and, as luck would have it, ran into Major Chipman and Captain Brady who happened to be there that day. The three of them had dinner (lunch) at a hotel at the fort and spent an enjoyable day together. [5]

Back at Camp Butler the next day, January 16th, Chipman made a morning visit to the bedside of gravely ill company cook William H. Wood. He and his wife Phebe Lloyd Wood were son and daughter of English-born glass blowers of Sandwich. William had worked his way up at the glassworks from boy to being himself a glass blower and was well thought of in Sandwich, as was Phebe.

As the sinking-fast Wood spoke to Chipman, he asked the major to write Phebe for him, which he did except he withheld from her the seriousness of her husband's illness, as he did not want to stress Phebe who he knew to be pregnant (she had actually already delivered). Wood died that afternoon. His body was placed in a coffin and sent to Sandwich at the expense of Company D comrades. The remains arrived January 23rd and for the funeral that day at the Methodist-Episcopal Church, Sandwich's citizens honored their fallen friend and factory mate with flags flown at half-staff. [6]

January 17th was notable for Company D as on that day it was formally incorporated into the Twenty-ninth Massachusetts Regiment. After eight months, it had a permanent organizational home in the Union Army. In command of the new regiment was Colonel Ebenezer Pierce of Freetown. Second-in-command was Lieutenant Colonel Joseph H. Barnes and third-in-command Major Chipman. Over the past three days, January 15th to 17th, Chipman had experienced the full range of emotional peaks and valleys of Civil War command.

Two men of Company D, Alfred Cheval and John McAlaney, missed the birth of the Twenty-ninth and death of Wood, as they were in Sandwich on furlough. Cheval was seeing his wife and twin children while McAlaney was with his wife and daughter. "Many more [of Company D] would like to go," wrote Private Darby. [7]

Meanwhile, Massachusetts's second Irish Regiment, the Twenty-eighth, headed south. William B. Dalton, his five Sandwich comrades of the Twenty-eighth and the rest of the regiment traveled by train from Boston to Norwich, Connecticut January 11th where they boarded a steamer for a nightmarish voyage to New York. The steamer got lost in the fog and the men had almost no water or provisions. While awaiting orders at New York, they quartered at bleak Castle Williams on Governor's Island and suffered terribly from cold, hunger and thirst. Governor Andrew came to New York to do what he could for them. "I think," wrote Private Darby of his friend Dalton, "the flame of Patriotism that once burned in his bosom is now extinguished." After a month's stay at New York, the regiment went on to South Carolina. [8]

Ethnically opposite to the Irish Twenty-eighth Regiment was the Puritan Eighteenth. With most of its soldiers from small towns south of Boston it was largely, according to one of its privates, "without the Irish elements." That made the regiment, according to the same private, without "desperate characters" and "determined to lose the citizen in the soldier." There may have been something to this because the Eighteenth won a competition for drill and discipline, receiving as prize highly coveted chasseur uniforms from French people of the United States. Serving in the Eighteenth were four men of Sandwich, Josiah Ellis, Persia Harmon, Charles Howes and former Sandwich Guard member Horace Lovell. [9]

While the Eighteenth drilled in Washington, the gunboat *Pioneer* cleared for action in North Carolina February 7th and in concert with other vessels of the Burnside Expedition bombarded a principal expedition target, Roanoke Island. Benjamin Ewer and Watson Adams fired 30-pounder shot at enemy gunboats and shore fortifications from the midships rifled Parrott gun. The Signal Corps assisted in directing fire. During the afternoon bombardment the Parrott gun crew became undermanned and Jesse Allen was summoned from the pilot-house to assist. As he approached the gun, the concussive force of a discharge sent him flying from the spar deck onto a spar and hatchway combings, injuring him severely. The *Pioneer* was in the hottest of the action at the battle, according to Marine Lieutenant Benjamin Baxter of Hyannis, aboard another gunboat. [10]

The Burnside Expedition captured Roanoke Island on February 8th, a significant victory for the Union. A day later the men at Camp Butler received a telegraphic dispatch from Fortress Monroe reporting another Union victory, that of General Ulysses S. Grant and his army at Fort Henry in Tennessee. The elation of that day turned to sorrow two days later when the large Sawyer gun at Camp Butler exploded, killing Private Charles E. Jones of Company D. He had worked as a glass gilder before the war. With his brain penetrated by a gun fragment, he muttered his last three words, "Oh, my God!" fell over and died. He was buried at Camp Butler a day later. [11]

Eight days after Jones's February 11th death, word began reaching northern communities of another victory for Grant's army in Tennessee, at Fort Donelson. Attorney Eben Whittemore recorded in his diary that on February 19th a salute was fired in Sandwich "in honor of our late victories of Forts Henry and Donelson." A soldier in the Henry and Donelson battles was blacksmith Thomas F. White of Pocasset. He had moved to Chicago around 1860 and in August 1861 enlisted in the Twelfth Illinois Regiment. When besieged Confederates attempted a breakout from Fort Donelson February 15th they overran White's Company A, deployed as skirmishers, and killed several of its men, one of them White. He is buried in a mass grave of unknown soldiers at the Fort Donelson National Cemetery. The sacrifice of White and other soldiers enabled the Donelson victory—the Union's most important to date—and put the star of General Grant on the ascent. [12]

Around the time of the Donelson battle, Major Chipman sent his orderly Francis C. Swift and Willie to a horse and mule depot at Perryville, Maryland to buy horses for him and Colonel Barnes since field grade officer status entitled them to be mounted. With Willie handling the money and Swift judging the horseflesh, they made an able team. They returned with 2 six-year-old bays, purchased for the modest price of $303.00, blankets included. Chipman's new mount reminded him of Jenny, his horse at home. [13]

Also saddling up were the men of the First Maine Cavalry Regiment. Their horses, purchased by Maine quartermaster officials, had never been ridden on the back so they kicked and bucked when mounted. A private in the regiment was North Sandwich schoolteacher David A. Blake. His career as a cavalryman was brief. His horse kicked him so severely that on February 13th he died at a private home in Augusta, Maine. When his body came home, minister Moses Brown of North Sandwich saw the wounds on Blake's corpse and attended his funeral. [14]

Far from Maine and Sandwich when the war began was John W. Godfrey, former schooner captain of Pocasset and South Carolina. In 1859, he and his wife Louisa had moved to Morrison, Illinois and begun farming with her father and brother, both named Solomon N. Barlow. The elder Barlow had taken up land there based on a claim made to the United States regarding the seizure of a brig by the French in 1798. [15]

After the war broke out Godfrey came east, received an officer position in the Union navy and went into duty in waters he knew well, those off the southeastern coast. When Admiral Samuel Du Pont of the South Atlantic Blockading Squadron saw Godfrey's familiarity with southeast waters, he made him a pilot. On February 18, 1862 he was aboard Du Pont's flagship *Wabash* at Port Royal, South Carolina, to suggest a route through Cumberland Sound at the Georgia-Florida border. A few weeks later an army-navy expedition approached Cumberland Sound and Godfrey left the *Wabash* to board the steam gunboat *Ottawa* and sound the dangerously shoaled waters. With his valuable navigation assistance, the expedition pushed through the sound and captured Fernandina, Florida, which became a vital supply and coaling station for the squadron. [16]

South Carolina and Georgia planters and businessmen were not unaware that the Godfrey guiding the Union navy through their backyard waters in 1862 was the same one they had worked with in the 1850s. Calling him a spy and traitor, a Charleston newspaper urged southerners to be cautious henceforward regarding those in whom they entrusted their interests. [17]

At Port Royal, a need arose for a large storeship. Meeting that need was the massive ship-of-the-line *Vermont*, in ordinary many years at Boston Navy Yard since her completion in 1818. To get her to Port Royal, the steamer *Kensington* took her in tow February 24th. That night, in a wintry gale off Cape Cod, the towline parted and the *Vermont* began to drift. Aboard the *Vermont* were two enlisted men from Monument, Samuel C. Bourne and Charles W. Nightingale.

In the teeth of the gale, Bourne was ordered aloft to secure the *Vermont's* foresail, exposing him to freezing gusts that tore at him for hours. Afterward he had to stand a watch. When finally relieved, he visited the ship's surgeon for a frost-bitten left testicle. Despite the swollen and painful gonad, he carried on with his duties as best he could as the ship was short of able seamen. Also victimized by the *Vermont* was seaman Nightingale. In heavy seas, the ship lurched and threw him down a hatchway, injuring him internally. The ship's rations of raw salt pork and wormy hard bread added internal illness to internal injuries. Both men must have felt a great deal of relief when the

Ship-of-the Line Vermont. *Naval Historical Center*

Vermont finally reached Port Royal. [18]

In Sandwich, flags waved and bells pealed February 22nd to celebrate Washington's Birthday. In the evening, citizens packed town hall for singing and speechmaking. Two speakers, physician Isaac Swasey and Congregationalist minister Henry Kimball, lit up the gathering with pro-abolition messages. Hearing of it, Major Chipman suggested that the best place for both was a jail cell at Boston harbor's Fort Warren, home to northern political prisoners. [19]

A day after Washington's Birthday the Twenty-eighth Massachusetts arrived at Hilton Head Island, South Carolina. Thomas Wheeler Jr. was surprised to see two Sandwich friends, Thomas Cahill and George Hobson, camped nearby in the First Massachusetts cavalry. Wheeler Jr. wanted to send letters to Sandwich female cousins Susan Blackwell, Lucy Bates and Lucy and Mary

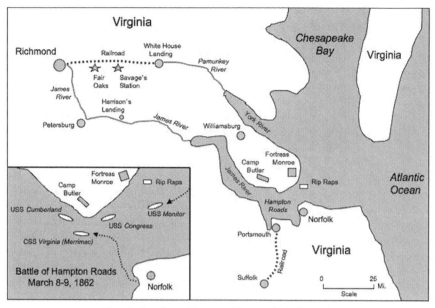

Map 3, Southeast Virginia May 1861-July 1862

Ann Heffernan but first he had to write his father and siblings. His March 25th letter to them, after the deaths of his mother Susan in January and uncle Thomas Blackwell March 5th, had the young man in a pensive mood: "Mother is dead and gone and sow Uncle Thomas is tow [too] and that is the way we all will gow sometime..." [20]

The quiet early afternoon of Saturday March 8th at Camp Butler erupted in chaos when the Confederate ironclad *Merrimac (CSS Virginia)* steamed into waters just off the wharf and attacked the two ships stationed there for months, the steam frigates *Congress* and *Cumberland*. First the *Congress,* then the *Cumberland* felt the fury of the *Merrimac*. Camp Butler sprang into action and returned fire from batteries and shore guns. After the *Cumberland* sank and the *Congress* struck her colors, the *Merrimac* lobbed a few shells into Camp Butler. The next day, the Union ironclad *Monitor* arrived and the men of Camp Butler had a front row seat to watch her and the *Merrimac* duel to a draw.

Marine Lieutenant Charles Heywood of the *Cumberland* distinguished himself for bravery on his sinking ship. He and Chipman knew each other before the war, apparently because Heywood visited Sandwich to see relatives Cynthia Heywood and Cynthia Blackwell Swift. In November 1861, four months before the ironclad attack, Chipman commented, "I see Lieut. Heywood often. He comes into my tent nearly every day." When Heywood came ashore at Camp Butler March 8th from the sunken *Cumberland,* he was soaking wet. "I gave him some whiskey and a dry suit of clothes," wrote the major, who expected Heywood would visit Sandwich while awaiting a new ship assignment. [21]

A sixty-pound shell from the *Merrimac* struck near Chipman and his friend Colonel Barnes but didn't explode. The major wrote his wife that he was going to send it home. He also sent her a sketch of it. A member of the gun crew firing at the *Merrimac* on March 8th was Alfred Cheval, just a month returned from furlough in Sandwich. The deafening cannon noise that day destroyed much of his hearing. [22]

Also firing at the *Merrimac* was Battery L of the Fourth United States Artillery, a member of which was Lieutenant Henry B. Beecher, son of the famous abolitionist and nephew of author Harriet Beecher Stowe. "He [the lieutenant] spent the evening with me last evening," wrote Chipman March 20th. "He is a son of H. Ward Beecher and I understand his views are very much like his father's. I liked him very much and as long as he don't force his views upon me, I can get along well enough." When circumstances were right, Chipman abided abolitionists. [23]

With Camp Butler rules forbidding intoxicating drink on the premises, St. Patrick's Day passed quietly for both Irish and non-Irish soldiers. "I did not see any drunken men throughout the whole day," wrote Private Darby. Further south at Hilton Head Island, the Irishmen of the Twenty-eighth Regiment celebrated the day with foot races and jumping matches. [24]

In Virginia, Union General George McClellan's army's began a spring offensive, a drive up a peninsula toward Richmond. The first step in this operation was the disembarkation of troops, thousands of them, at Fortress Monroe. Noticing all the activity, Surgeon George Cogswell of the Twenty-ninth Massachusetts commented on April 4th, "The army of the Potomac has been pouring in here over the last fortnight." Departing instead of arriving, however, was Sergeant Benjamin Hamlen of Company D who developed fever and ague at Camp Butler and on April 21st went to Sandwich on a month's furlough to regain his health. While there, Dr. Leonard treated him. Major Chipman described the nineteen-year-old as "a fine young fellow and good soldier." [25]

One of the Army of the Potomac soldiers disembarking at Fortress Monroe was glassmaker and liquor transgressor Thomas Ball, with the First Massachusetts Regiment. As the army advanced up the peninsula, his regiment as part of 3rd Army Corps attacked a Confederate rear guard May 5th at Williamsburg. In action that day, a piece of copper percussion cap from the discharge of a comrade's rifle penetrated Ball's left eye. George Dillaway of Sandwich and the same regiment removed the foreign body but friendly fire (not called that at the time) had permanently damaged Ball's eye. [26]

In Sandwich, Attorney Whittemore was busy. The parents of deceased soldier John Weeks of Pocasset engaged him to submit a claim to Washington for two months back pay of $26.00 due them for their son from 1861. In non-war related activities, he bought his wife Mary a parasol for $1.75, had a tooth filled by local dentist Dr. Fowler for the same price and planted six rows of Peach Blow potatoes and five rows of peas. Business in the town was on the upswing. The Cape Cod Glassworks was again in production while the Boston and Sandwich works was employing more workers full time. Business at the tack factory was also quickening. [27]

At Camp Butler, the military incompetence and boorish behavior of Colonel Pierce, commander of the Twenty-ninth, engendered enmity in officers serving under him. In a letter to his wife, Major Chipman went so far as to call Pierce an "ass," a word he used reluctantly out of deference to her but of necessity to best describe him. On May 2nd, Lieutenant Kern of Company D could no longer hold his tongue and cursed Pierce "in a most public manner." The next day, Pierce had Kern arrested and placed in close confinement. A court martial proceeding for Kern—with Chipman presiding—began May 8th but adjourned the next day because the Twenty-ninth received orders to leave Camp Butler and proceed to Norfolk. Later in May, Pierce offered to drop the charges if Kern would resign. Kern accepted the offer, resigned May 30th and was home in Sandwich June 20th. [28]

Kern's resignation created another Company D officer vacancy. A petition supporting Sergeant James Atherton of "D" for the position circulated through Sandwich and went to the governor but the position devolved to Alfred O. Brooks of Boston, who had been in Company F of the Twenty-ninth. Atherton continued waiting. Signers of the petition included Sarah McAlaney, wife of Private John McAlaney of Company D, and boarding house operators Cordelia Fuller and Sarah Montague. As of mid-June 1862, Company D's officers were Captain Charles Brady and Lieutenants Ayling and Brooks. [29]

Like Lieutenant Kern, Private "Birney" Haines came home in June but under different circumstances. He contracted typhoid fever in May at Camp Butler and arrived home on a medical disability June 21st, only to suffer a relapse the 22nd. For the next month, family and friends watched over him at his bedside at the family home in Spring Hill. Two of the more devoted watchers were his brother George L. and step-mother Sarah. Delirious from unrelenting fever, he had to be subdued with drugs. It was a terrible time in the household, exacerbated when George and Birnie's step-grandmother Sarah Goodspeed sprained her sound knee and became a second bed-ridden family member. Mercifully, Birnie died July 26th. He left as a widow eighteen-year-old Maria Hartford Haines. [30]

Meanwhile the war went on. Vital was the logistical support of vessels chartered by the army quartermaster. The chartered brig *Ellen Barnard* under Captain Thomas C. Perry of Monument brought a load of troops from Key West, Florida to Hilton Head, South Carolina in June. Shortly thereafter his neighbor Captain Reuben Collins Jr. transported a chartered cargo of ice from Boston to Hilton Head, also in the *Bernard*. The latter vessel was built and initially commanded by another Monument man, Henry A. Bourne, who spent much of the war as captain of the oft-chartered steamer *Tillie*. [31]

Three thousand miles to the west, Lieutenant Samuel H. Allyne Jr. and his company of California cavalry left their station in southern California and proceeded to Fort Stanford, north of Tucson, Arizona Territory. The numerous Apaches near the fort feared the large contingent of soldiers and would have liked a treaty but, as Allyne noted in a letter to his brother, "…the opinion is that their treaty would not amount to much and would only last until our backs were turned and they would be as bad as ever. They are a thieving race and would as lief kill a white man as eat their breakfast." [32]

The killing of white men on the Virginia peninsula ground on through May, culminating at month's end in the battle of Fair Oaks. Casualties on both sides were high, high enough on the Union side for General McClellan to summon reinforcements. Part of this call-up was the Twenty-ninth Massachusetts. After lengthy duty at the rear and flanks of the war, the regiment was going to the front, assigned to 2nd Army Corps. Private Anderson Wright would soon experience more than one dead "rebble."

The orders to move came on June 6th when the Twenty-ninth was camped near Suffolk, Virginia. The men climbed onto railroad flatcars and rode to Portsmouth where they boarded the steamer *Catskill* that transported them up the York and Pamunkey Rivers to the Army of the Potomac supply base at White House Landing. A private of the regiment, watching the passing countryside, wistfully contrasted it to Massachusetts: "We seldom see a hill, stone or woman." [33]

Arriving at White House at nightfall, the men bedded down in an open field or as another private expressively put it, "We encamped…in God's great tent, and under his starry blanket we passed the night." Over the next two days they marched west beside railroad tracks and on June 9th arrived at the front at Fair Oaks, center of the Union line about seven miles east of Richmond. Signs of recent battle abounded. The trunks of trees were filled with bullets and enemy dead lay unburied in the woods. Other dead lay in shallow graves over which vermin crawled after a rain. The stench of decomposing men and horses made the air almost unbreathable. "This place," wrote Private Darby, "bears the Stearn realities of War." [34]

Upon arrival at Fair Oaks, the Twenty-ninth was assigned to a brigade consisting of three Irish New York Regiments, the so-called "Irish Brigade," a unit with a reputation for fierce fighting. Describing the three regiments, Private Darby wrote, "They carry the Irish flag with the American. The rebels cannot Stand their charge of Bayonets when accompanied by their wild Native Shout. It is said the green flag is a terror to them." [35]

When the Twenty-ninth took its place in the Union line at Fair Oaks June 9th, Private James Heald of Company D was regimental mail carrier but his health soon failed and he had to be admitted to nearby Savage's Station field hospital. Replacing him as mail carrier was Samuel Hunt, also of "D" and a brother-in-law of Major Chipman. Serving near the Twenty-ninth was the Eleventh Massachusetts Regiment and with it Private George Riordan of Sandwich. Private Darby mentioned in a letter of June 25th that he had seen Riordon and that he was looking well. Riordan's Eleventh had seen hard duty since arrival on the peninsula and had participated in the Fair Oaks battle. [36]

Life on the Union lines at Fair Oaks in June was rigorous. As if the sickening odors of death were not enough, rain was incessant and shelter minimal in skimpy tents. Scurvy thrived. Sanitation was rudimentary and diarrhea prevalent. The opposing lines were so close that picket and artillery fire often broke out. The men were constantly on edge and frequently called into line of battle by false alarms. Sharpshooters perched in treetops presented a constant danger. To reduce that threat, six companies of the Twenty-ninth including Company D and commanded by Captain Brady went on a tree-cutting detail June 25th. One of the trees fell on the left leg of Private Patrick McElroy and injured his knee. [37]

When Elizabeth Chipman wrote her husband that people in Sandwich were complaining about the slowness of McClellan's advance on Richmond, the major countered that they should see the swampy and forested terrain through which it was proceeding, where roads and bridges had to be built, and not just any bridges but strong ones to support heavy artillery and wagon trains. "Those people [who complain] should come out here and do what we have to do both day and night. They would then realize the labor that has been performed before we can attack the enemy by general engagement." [38]

To inch closer to a piece of high ground from which Richmond could be besieged, elements of McClellan's army that included the First Massachusetts engaged the enemy in close combat June 25th. In that day's fighting George Dillaway, who had aided Thomas Ball of the First, was shot in the neck. Dillaway was sent to White House Landing where he was placed on a hospital boat that took him to Mount Pleasant Hospital in Washington. [39]

The battle of June 25th was the first of seven on successive days, known afterward as the Seven Days Battles. In the final six the Confederates, not waiting for McClellan to besiege Richmond or bring on the general engagement Chipman had anticipated, were on an offensive that drove the Union Army away from Richmond, forcing it to abandon its supply base at White House Landing and relocate it at Harrison's Landing on the James River.

In the third of these battles, called Gaines' Mill, the Ninth Massachusetts with its three Sandwich Irishmen James H. Kelley, Patrick McGirr and James O'Neill, took heavy casualties. Although the three of them came out of the fight safely, many of their wounded comrades were treated badly by the enemy. In revenge, the men of the Ninth took no quarter and brought in few prisoners when they might have had many. [40]

In the fifth battle, the Union had to leave behind to the enemy hospitalized men at Savage's Station, among them James Heald of Company D. In the sixth, a rear guard action at Glendale, the Irish Brigade played an important role in defending White Oak Bridge that had to be held at all cost. In this battle, First Sergeant Benjamin Hamlen, back from Sandwich with improved health, lay beside Lieutenant Ayling as artillery fire screeched over their heads. [41]

Battlefield reports coming into Sandwich from Virginia put Attorney Whittemore on an elation-despair roller coaster. "This morning," he wrote on June 30th, "rumor came that Richmond was taken. This evening report came looking rather dark appearing as though we had got the worst of it at Richmond." Three days later he penned, "News came this P.M. that McClellan had been driven 17 miles toward the James River and left all his siege guns on the field and all dead and wounded. This sounds like the death knell." A day later it was the Fourth of July. Recalling past festive Fourths in Sandwich and contrasting them with the present dismal one, clouded with unfavorable news that had figuratively rained on the day's parade, he wrote glumly, "Not much of a celebration in Sandwich this year."

Chapter Five:
Reinforcements Now Appearing—
July to December 1862

Although General McClellan termed the Army of the Potomac's withdrawal from Richmond to the banks of the James River as nothing more than a "change of base," President Lincoln, Attorney Whittemore and many northerners perceived it for what it really was, a defeat. The stress of dealing with McClellan exacted a toll on the president. When he visited with the army at Harrison's Landing July 8th, Lieutenant Ayling thought he looked "sad and care-worn." [1]

The army's new supply base at Harrison's Landing of the James River was some four miles long and one mile deep. Crowded into this narrow strip was the 90,000-man Army of the Potomac with all its wagons, supplies, horses and mules. The numbers of sick and wounded soldiers so overwhelmed the meager hospital facilities that when an ill Lieutenant Ayling tried to get admitted he found it full, with those who could not be accommodated lying outside in the rain and mud. [2]

Seeing the need for more troops, the president arranged for northern governors to call for 300,000 volunteers for three-years service. Massachusetts's quota in the July 7th call was 15,000 men, apportioned among all the towns and cities. Sandwich's quota was fifty-six men. Washington wanted to utilize a draft in the call but Governor Andrew rejected that idea for Massachusetts as he favored voluntary enlistment.

On July 10th, just three days after the call, Attorney Whittemore and boarding house operator William H. Harper went to the courthouse in Barnstable to present a petition requesting a town meeting in Sandwich regarding raising the town's quota. Five days later they presented it to a "large and spirited" gathering at Sandwich's Town Hall. Attendees included the Reverend Henry Kimball and physician Swasey. Town dignitaries spoke, the cornet band played and a chorus of young ladies sang. Whittemore announced that Willard Weeks Jr. of Pocasset was ready to enlist. To much applause, he stepped to the platform. [3]

Weeks Jr. was the second son of Willard and Eunice Weeks. They had buried their eldest son John just eight months earlier after he died of disease in Virginia. A third son Stephen was ill with measles with the Twentieth Massachusetts in Virginia at the time of the rally in Sandwich. [4]

Few came forward as readily as Weeks Jr.; as of July 22nd, just five had done so. Furniture maker Samuel H. Allyne feared the town would have to resort to a draft. Moreover, he found the direction of the war troubling. In a July 24th letter to his son he wrote, "Things look rather dark just now. The rebels appear to be defiant…the government has dealt too mildly with this rebellion." A town meeting of July 22nd authorized the Reverend Frederick Freeman to meet with the governor about formation of a Sandwich company. A week later, he reported the governor as amenable. By that time, nine more men had volunteered. [5]

Through the recruiting efforts of Harper, the drumbeat of rallies, financial inducement of $200 town-federal bounty plus $38 advance pay per volunteer and a promise from the governor that the men could elect their own officers, the pace of enlisting picked up and on August 16th a contingent of forty-two volunteers left Sandwich for Camp Stanton north of Boston. Known as the second Sandwich company, these men became the nucleus of Company I of the Fortieth Massachusetts Regiment (Table 2). An accident prevented one of them, glassworker Matthew Quinn, from reaching Camp Stanton. The cars transporting him and the others severed two of his toes. He returned to Sandwich and was never mustered into service. This notwithstanding, his wife Dianna collected $6.00 town aid in his name September 27th. [6]

Harper was elected captain of the company and received a sword, sash and revolver as a gift from the citizens of Sandwich in a ceremony at the town hall on September 4th. Hartwell Freeman, son of the reverend, was commissioned a company lieutenant and received a sabre and revolver but that presentation was less ceremonious than Harper's. Because the train transporting Freeman and his Fortieth Regiment from Camp Stanton to Washington departed sooner than expected, Sandwich citizens dispatched young William C. Spring to Boston where he intercepted it, made Freeman a hurried presentation and wished him Godspeed. [7]

Participating in a ceremony of a different sort was farmer Thomas Ellis of West Sandwich. The Reverend Moses Brown married him and seventeen-year-old Deborah Pierce of North Sandwich August 9th. A week later he went to Camp Stanton and on August 31st was mustered into service.

Sandwich's selectmen enlisted Cornelius Dean, Edward Heffernan, Thomas

Table 2
Data of "Second" Sandwich Company
(Company I, 40th Massachusetts Regiment)

Name	Lived At	Name	Lived At
1. Avery, Rodman	Pocasset	22. Little, Charles H.	Pocasset
2. Avery, Watson D.	Pocasset	23. Lloyd, George T.	Sandwich Village
3. Baker, Henry B.	Sandwich Village	24. Magoon, Davis	Monument
4. Ball, Thomas A.	Sandwich Village	25. Manimon, Barzillai	Monument
5. Burbank, Luke P.	Sandwich Village	26. Manimon, Seth T.	Monument
6. Chamberlain, Benj. F.	Sandwich Village	27. Manley, William	Monument
7. Ellis, Abner	West Sandwich	28. McMahon, Patrick	Sandwich Village
8. Ellis, Charles E.	West Sandwich	29. Perry, David Jr.	Pocasset
9. Ellis, Nathaniel S.	West Sandwich	30. Perry, Henry	Sandwich Village
10. Ellis, Thomas	West Sandwich	31. Perry, John M.	Pocasset
11. Freeman, Hartwell W.	Sandwich Village	32. Perry, Nathan C.	Sandwich Village
12. Hammond, Luther T.	Monument	33. Sampson, Samuel	Pocasset
13. Harlow, James	Sandwich Village	34. Swift, Charles E.	Pocasset
14. Harper, William H.	Sandwich Village	35. Swift, Clark	West Sandwich
15. Hathaway, James E.	Monument	36. Swift, Dean W.	West Sandwich
16. Healy, Abraham	Sandwich Village	37. Swift, Francis H.	Pocasset
17. Huddy, John T.	Pocasset	38. Swift, Thacher H.	Pocasset
18. Johnson, John F.	Sandwich Village	39. Swift, William H.	Pocasset
19. Kern, Daniel V.	Sandwich Village	40. Weeks, Willard Jr.	Pocasset
20. Lawrence, Edward J.	Pocasset	41. Wood, Samuel J.	North Sandwich
21. Lincoln, Ensign	Sandwich Village		

Mason, James McNulty and James McKowen on August 18th. Their entry into the Forty-first Massachusetts Regiment brought Sandwich close to filling its quota. Twenty-seven-year-old glass-blower McKowen, who had a wife and two children, entered the service from the wrong side of the law. On July 30th he assaulted thirty-eight-year-old Sarah Woods of Sandwich who was married and had eight children, one of them Private John Woods of the Twenty-ninth Regiment. McKowen appeared at Barnstable Superior Court August 1st, was convicted and sentenced to thirty days in the house of correction. He was mustered into the Forty-first on September 20th, having apparently done some or all of his time. [8]

Nineteen-year-old Hartwell Freeman's commissioning as a lieutenant was intrigue-filled. Despite the governor's promise, the enlisted men of the new Sandwich company (Company I) did not get to elect their preference for the lieutenant position, former glassworks operative Alfred E. Smith, living in Somerville in 1862. Rather, Freeman was selected for the position through an "open" meeting in Sandwich on August 15th in which prominent town citizens signed a petition recommending him. More skulduggery followed when the petition was "mutilated" during its delivery to the governor so that names on it were supposedly altered. Smith did not accept amicably what he perceived as an injustice in the selection of Freeman, showed up at Camp Stanton, tried to ingratiate himself to his friends from his glassworks days and did all he could to undermine Freeman, already unpopular with the men. [9]

A stratagem of a different sort kept eighteen-year-old George W. Perry of Monument out of military service. His father, Thomas C. Perry, did not want his son to enlist and made that wish clear in an August 8th letter to him. "George," he implored, "Don't you for a moment think about going to the war." Whether George or his brother William entertained thoughts of enlisting is not clear. Whatever the case, their recently retired ship captain father was taking no chances. He used what influence he had to secure them positions on merchant ships and keep them there, away from on-shore recruiting temptations. [10]

Even as Sandwich was filling quotas for three-years troops, Congress passed the Militia Act of 1862 calling for 300,000 more men, for nine-month enlistments. These men were to be drafted from the enrolled militia, i.e., lists of able-bodied male citizens ages eighteen to forty-five submitted by town assessors to the state adjutant general. Appointed to superintend the draft for Barnstable County was attorney Whittemore. In a hired horse and carriage, he and a clerk traveled to Barnstable County towns where they heard claims for exemption, allowed for men at sea and the medically unfit. The exemption for men at sea placed a heavy burden on land-based enrolled militia in those Barnstable County towns with large portions of their enrolled militia at sea. That burden was lighter in Sandwich, with more land-based enrolled militia. [11]

Barnstable County avoided the draft in the Militia Act because volunteers from the enrolled militia came forward in sufficient number to fill quotas. Sandwich's twenty-two volunteers ranged in age from eighteen-year-old farmer's apprentice Henry Knippe to forty-four-year-old Pocasset iron moulder Stillman Wright. A surprising volunteer was sea captain Watson Fifield, who qualified for the maritime exemption. George L. Haines volunteered but only after much soul-searching because his brother Birnie's death had left him as his father's only surviving son. Another consideration was the advisability of giving up his excellent clerk position at the glassworks. Dr. Leonard examined most of the volunteers August 23rd. Only one, blacksmith Henry Benson, acknowledged a habit of drinking. The men entered Company D of the Forty-fifth Massachusetts Regiment. [12]

*Massachusetts recruiting poster of summer 1862.
Historic New England*

While the Militia Act was in force, August 8th to September 8th, young men subject to it were liable to arrest if they left the state. Only with written permission could they do so. Using that provision, young Quaker Gideon Wing of Spring Hill requested permission to go to Montgomery County Indiana where he had relatives. [13]

While men of Sandwich were answering troop calls and filling out new regiments, their comrades in old (veteran) regiments in the war zone were suffering from poor diet. When scurvy appeared in 2nd Army Corps at Fair Oaks in June 1862, the medical director of the Army of the Potomac ordered regimental commanders to make certain their men received vegetables. This order was apparently not well followed because Private Peter McNulty of Company D of the Twenty-ninth—with sentence of three months hard labor behind him—came down with the disease and was hospitalized at Craney Island near Fortress Monroe. Hospital mates were Gustavus Badger and Patrick McElroy of "D" and Patrick McGirr of the Irish Ninth Massachusetts. Badger was a son of widowed glass cutter and boarding house keeper John M. D. Badger. Fortress Monroe was the departure point for 453 sick and wounded soldiers on the hospital steamer *Vanderbilt*. One of them was Sergeant William Breese of Company D, suffering from chronic diarrhea. [14]

Scurvy also bedeviled the crew of the naval bark *Midnight,* blockading along the Texas coast. One of her crew was Andrew Lane, brother-in-law of Twenty-fourth Regiment Private Jesse Allen. Scurvy and other disease so disabled the *Midnight's* crew that in early August 1862 squadron commander Admiral Farragut sent the bark to New York so that her men could regain their health. Apparently not too weakened by disease, Lane deserted once the *Midnight* arrived and a few weeks later enlisted in the Twentieth Massachusetts Regiment. [15]

Back at Harrison's Landing, General McClellan rested his Army of the Potomac through July. More active was another Union army, General John Pope's Army of Virginia, which threatened rail lines north of Richmond. In response, elements of the Confederate Army moved away from the Landing toward that sector. Pope called for reinforcements and in answer the War Department brought north from the Carolinas several 9th Army Corps divisions, the Twenty-eighth Massachusetts among them. After a series of marches, its men reached the vicinity of Culpeper, Virginia where on August 18th the regimental band was mustered out. Thus ended the military service of bandsmen Michael A. Ball and William B. Dalton.

Seeing the need to unite McClellan's army with Pope's to offset the strengthening Confederate army, the War Department ordered McClellan in early August to bring his army north. McClellan, however, failed to comply with alacrity. Only on August 16th did the Twenty-ninth, as part of the Irish Brigade, leave Harrison's Landing. River transports and marches brought the brigade on August 28th to McClellan's new headquarters of Alexandria, Virginia. The Twentieth Massachusetts, in the same army corps (2nd) as the Irish Brigade but different division, also arrived there the 28th.

Just as the War Department had feared, the Confederate Army struck

Pope's army before McClellan's could unite with it. The fight began August 28th near the 1861 Manassas battlefield site and raged for three days. While making a charge into a wooded area August 30th, the 28th Massachusetts drew fierce counter fire from Confederates dug in at a railroad cut. "It was a hard fight," wrote a private of the regiment. "The ground was covered with the Dead and wounded of both parties…" Mortally wounded was Thomas Wheeler Jr., the third of his family to be cut down by the grim reaper in 1862. He is probably buried in an unmarked grave near the railroad cut. Considering the carnage in the Twenty-eighth and the fact that band members had the dangerous duty of stretcher-bearer, musicians Ball and Dalton might have felt fortunate to have been discharged. "I tell you," wrote a bandsman of the Twentieth Regiment, "it does chafe the bands awfully…carrying the litters and doing that business." [16]

Another Sandwich soldier wounded at the August 30th battle was Edward McGirr of the Fifth New York Zouaves. He was captured while wounded, exchanged into Union hands September 2nd and taken to Emory Hospital in Washington where he failed to survive leg amputation surgery and died October 3rd. Like Thomas Wheeler Jr., his place of interment is unknown. [17]

On August 30th, the day of Wheeler Jr.'s death and McGirr's wounding, the Irish Brigade as part of 2nd Corps was ordered to "use their legs" and make a forced march west from Alexandria to join Pope's army. This hard march of some twenty miles brought the brigade within sound of the battle just as it was ending in Union defeat. Falling out were Privates John W. Campbell, James Cox and Warren P. Dean. Over the next few days Pope's army fell back toward Washington and as it did the Irish Brigade performed rear guard action, as it had done at White Oak Bridge two months earlier. The series of marches and countermarches the Irish Brigade made in the four-day August 30th to September 2nd period were hard. Making them even harder was a lack of tents or other shelter. [18]

The Confederates had the initiative after their victory at Second Manassas (Bull Run). While still uncertain as to whether they were headed east to Washington or north into Maryland, President Lincoln sacked Pope, combined his army with that of McClellan's as the Army of the Potomac and placed McClellan in its command. When it became clear September 3rd that the Confederate destination was Maryland, 2nd Corps crossed the Potomac and took a position north of Washington. As the enemy tracked north, the Army of the Potomac marched in parallel. South of Frederick, Maryland on September 11th, Captain Brady of Company D of the Twenty-ninth could no longer keep up. Lung disease contracted from nights sleeping with no shelter on the Second Manassas marches forced him to take an ambulance to the rear to a hospital in Washington. [19]

Refreshment Saloon in Philadelphia where 40th Massachusetts stopped en route to Washington. NA

Brady might have encountered some acquaintances at Washington. The Fortieth Massachusetts, with its forty-one men of Sandwich in Company I, arrived there September 10th and marched from the train station up Pennsylvania Avenue. Their march may not have presented a picture of military might. Carrying knapsacks heavier than they had ever borne, many men fell down from sheer exhaustion. Being green troops, they were not sent into the Maryland campaign but rather went into guard duty at Fort Ethan Allen on Washington's western outskirts. Quartermaster bungling was not limited to the knapsacks. For the next few weeks the men had no tents, only overcoats and blankets for shelter. When tents finally arrived, sixteen-year-old drummer Thomas A. Ball tented with Company I First Sergeant Josiah Elder of Boston. Elder developed rheumatism from exposure and Ball rubbed his sergeant's sore joints with liniment. He was a son of glassworker Thomas Ball. [20]

With Lieutenants Ayling and Brooks off duty sick, Captain Brady's September 11th departure left Company D without officers. Fortuitously, a lieutenant commission for Sergeant Atherton came through the 13th, the day Company D as part of 2nd Corps and the Irish Brigade marched through Frederick. Although officially still a sergeant, he assumed company command. Also in Frederick, Private Joseph Turner's heart gave out forcing him to fall out of the march. When Atherton and Company D marched westward

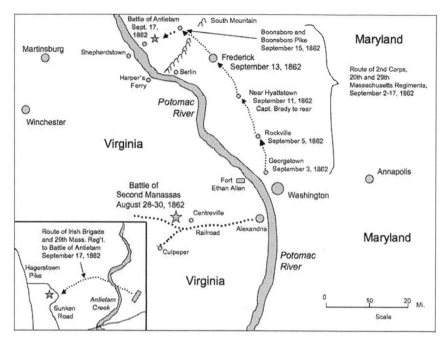

Map 4, Virginia and Maryland August and September 1862

September 14th, they left Turner behind in a hospital. His wife Mary Connor Turner came to Frederick from Sandwich to be his nurse. [21]

As the men of 2nd Corps rested alongside the Boonsboro Pike near Antietam Creek some twenty miles west of Frederick September 15th, they heard cheering arising from thousands of Union soldiers; General McClellan and his staff were riding along the lines. As he approached the Twentieth Massachusetts, color bearer Thomas Hollis held high his tattered Twentieth flag. McClellan reined his horse straight for Hollis, brought his mount alongside Hollis's shoulder, turned to his staff and remarked pointedly, "These men with the colors have seen service." For Hollis, one of Sandwich's most valiant Civil War soldiers, the incident was "the happiest moment of my life." [22]

A less happy moment for Hollis occurred two days later in the September 17th Battle of Antietam. In mid-morning action Hollis, already missing his left index finger from 1861 combat, sustained a severe gunshot wound to his right forearm that sent him to a long hospital stay. Shot through the lung in the same action was drummer Thomas Davis. Left for dead on the field, he managed to hold on for sixty hours until finally found by two comrades who carried him in for medical care. Not expected to live, he cheated death and after a four-month convalescence was discharged from the service. Damaged lungs, though, kept him from resuming his old trade of glassmaker. [23]

The hard marching that got the men of the Twenty-ninth and Company D to Antietam made Sergeant Edward Brady's left knee swell so much he had to slit his trousers. Despite this he lined up with Company D's men as they formed to advance toward the enemy September 17th. When Surgeon Cogswell saw Brady there, he ordered him out of the line under threat of arrest, explaining to him that he could bleed to death if wounded in the swollen knee. Dutifully, he went with Cogswell to the rear to the division field hospital where he held down wounded men while Cogswell performed amputations, that is, until ether fumes overcame the medically unsensitized Brady. [24]

Surgeon Cogswell's order pulling Sergeant Brady from the ranks was a wise one since reveille for 2nd Corps on September 17th sounded at 2 a.m. and the men stood in tightly packed ranks for hours awaiting orders to move to the front—a lot to ask of an able bodied man, much less one with a swollen knee. Once ordered forward, the Twenty-ninth under Colonel Barnes and Major Chipman (Colonel Pierce was on furlough) and Company D under Sergeant Atherton engaged the enemy at an old farm lane later called the sunken road. Heading rearward rather than forward was Company D Private John W. Campbell who deserted, taking his rifle with him. Ireland native Campbell was supporting a wife and four children when he enlisted in 1861. Replacing him was Private Caleb T. Robbins who had been hospitalized since July but was discharged just in time to get to Antietam and enter the fray. His brother, Verilo H., serving in the 104th New York Regiment, died in the battle September 17th. [25]

A bursting shell the day of the battle wounded Company D musician Christopher B. Dalton and put him in Cogswell's field hospital for ten days. After recovering he became acting chief bugler of the regiment. Also wounded was John Fagan. Comrades James Cook and Francis Woods saw him struck in the chest by a rifle ball. A surgeon extracted it. Sergeant Brady was "snake bitten." Already suffering from his swollen knee, Surgeon Cogswell sent him to a baker's wagon to get bread for the wounded but just as he put his foot on the wagon's tongue something startled the horses, they jerked their traces and threw Brady against the wagon tongue, severely injuring his wrist. [26]

An exploding shell at the sunken road also wounded General Israel B. Richardson, commander of the Twenty-ninth's division. Private Samuel Hunt of "D" helped place him in an ambulance. After the battle Hunt saw dead enemy soldiers three and four feet deep, plus other gruesome sights "which I shall never forget." [27]

The day of the Antietam battle, September 17th, the steamer *Haze* arrived in New York from North Carolina with Private Jesse H. Allen aboard. He was returning home after receiving a medical discharge a week earlier. At his stop in New York, Allen was too unwell to see to the forwarding of boxes and a red half-barrell containing his gear. When on September 26th they had not reached Sandwich, the worried Allen had his neighbor Francis A. Fisher write to New York about them. [28]

Three days after Antietam, the Eighteenth Massachusetts Regiment was part of a Union brigade that clashed with Confederates south of Antietam at the Potomac River town of Shepherdstown, Virginia. Captured there was Horace Lovell. Confederate guards marched him and fellow captives to Winchester, where they were confined in a compound near the courthouse. While there, infamous spy Belle Boyd looked in on the men and sent her regards to their Union Army superiors. One by one on September 28th, Lovell and the other prisoners entered the courthouse, placed their hands on a Bible and signed a parole, after which they were marched to Harpers Ferry and transferred to Union pickets, their eight-day captivity ended. [29]

A second captivity, however, awaited Lovell. From Harpers Ferry, he went by train to Washington and then on to the Camp for Paroled Prisoners at Annapolis, Maryland where some 10,000 heavily guarded Union paroled prisoners awaited exchange and return to their regiments. While they waited, they were formed into regiments by state. The camp population grew around October 12th when 300 men from "the filthy hole of Richmond" (the infamous Libby Prison) arrived. They were so bedraggled that at first glance they were mistaken for enemy soldiers. Lovell's exchange occurred around December 20th, at which time he finally returned to his regiment. [30]

Absent from the Antietam battle was Stephen Weeks. While his Twentieth Regiment was marching through Maryland September 6th, he was being admitted to the newly opened Portsmouth Grove Hospital in Rhode Island with measles, diarrhea and "southern fever." Stephen's older brother Willard Jr. of the Fortieth Regiment wrote his mother September 23rd that he was pleased Stephen had gotten to a hospital so close to home. Mindful of the purpose of his Fortieth Regiment as reinforcement for veteran regiments like Stephen's Twentieth, Willard Jr. closed his letter with several lines of an evangelistic hymn popular at the time: "Oh my comrades see the signal waving in the sky. Reinforcements now appearing, victory is nigh." [31]

Reinforcements were certainly justified, considering the number of losses from disease. Three soldiers from Sandwich alone died therefrom between August and October. Private Patrick Long of Company D died of typhoid fever in August at a hospital in Newport News. The government owed Long's family back pay for their deceased son but the precise amount was unclear because Company D's books were lost in the frenetic seven days battles of June. Nevertheless, Long's father Thomas engaged attorney Whittemore to submit a claim to Washington just as he had done the some months earlier for John Weeks. [32]

James H. Heald gravestone in Sumner, Maine. Find A Grave Internet Site

Company D private James H. Heald, captured at the Savage's Station hospital near Richmond in June and herded off to a Confederate prison, was paroled September 13th and three days later admitted to a hospital in Annapolis. Friends in Sandwich only heard of his hospitalization around October 6th. On receiving the news, his brother Abel went to visit James but he died and was buried just before Abel arrived. He had the body disinterred and transported to Sumner Hill Cemetery in Sumner, Maine for reburial.

James's gravestone inscription says something about him and his motivation for serving: "...an exemplary and promising young man...He went forth patriotically to sustain the Constitution and Flag of his Country, cherishing each as his own life; and he gave his life for them." [33]

The third death was in the Fortieth Regiment. After its men spent a few weeks at Fort Ethan Allen near Washington, they were moved several miles further west to the more forward outpost of Miner's Hill where a number of Union regiments had camps. It was there that Watson Avery died on October 27th of typhoid fever. Earning good wages as a farm worker in Pocasset when he enlisted, his death hit his widowed mother Reliance hard, through loss of both a much-loved son and important family breadwinner. His body was sent home and he has a marker in the Pocasset Cemetery. [34]

The end of October meant political campaigns were in full throttle. In Massachusetts, Governor Andrew was running for re-election. His party affiliation of Republican and slavery stance of abolitionist made him anathema to Major Chipman, a Democrat. In a letter to his wife he grumbled, "Everyone I write to, I end with 'don't vote for John A. Andrew and prevent your friends from doing so if possible.' I must confess I have the most utter contempt for that man." Despite Chipman's efforts, Andrew won. In Sandwich he received 208 votes to 106 for his Democratic opponent. [35]

In the same letter, Chipman doubted ever seeing the country re-united. Indeed, autumn of 1862 was a despairing time throughout the North about national re-union. Specifically, Chipman feared Britain would intervene on the side of the South, forcing the North to sue for peace. Blame for such a possibility he placed on what he felt were the maladroit international skills of President Lincoln. "He is no diplomatist," wrote Chipman. Expressing thoughts about his commander in chief to be kept between himself and his wife he wrote, "I perhaps should not write it to any one else but you. I have always fought against Lincoln's election and every one of his stamp...." [36]

Charles Chipman in Field Officer (Major) uniform, perhaps 1862.
USAHEC

Chipman also wrote his wife in October about John Campbell, the Company D private who had deserted at Antietam in September. Campbell's wife Catherine had written Chipman in mid-October that she had not heard from her husband. Chipman knew Campbell had deserted but knew nothing of his whereabouts and told the dismayed Catherine as much. [37]

Not a mystery as to whereabouts was the new Forty-fifth Regiment, with its twenty-two Sandwich soldiers. They were at a camp near Boston receiving training. To denote their quarters, tinsmith Josiah Foster of Sandwich made them a metal codfish which they mounted on a flagstaff in front of their barracks. When the Forty-fifth broke camp in early November, Foster's son John D. of the regiment took the codfish to his father for safekeeping. [38]

The Forty-Fifth took the cars from their camp to Boston, marched through the city and on November 5th boarded vessels for transport south. On board, the men were so crowded that four slept in a bunk not wide enough for two. This might have been bearable had the vessels sailed promptly. A storm, however, kept ships and men wallowing in Boston harbor. Cooped up like swine in lower decks that lacked ventilation and illumination, where vomit of seasick men covered floors that could not be cleaned for lack of mops and buckets, the men languished in unspeakably foul conditions for five days after which they were finally transferred to clean ships and sailed for their destination of New Bern, North Carolina. [39]

While the men of the Forty-fifth were arriving at New Bern in mid-November and setting up camp and quarters, the men of Company D of the Twenty-ninth were making a hard march between the Virginia towns of Warrenton and Falmouth. During the march, Private John Woods (whose mother had been assaulted in August) gave out and lay down beside the road. A comrade, James Cook, was sent to the rear to check on him and found him pallid and complaining of pain in his side. A few days later, Woods and Company D mate Warren P. Dean were admitted to a hospital near Falmouth. [40]

Late November brought Thanksgiving, a day of bounteous food in Massachusetts but thin pickings in war ravaged Virginia. Hard tack and salt beef were the bill of fare for the men of the Twenty-ninth. Dining more lavishly was William W. Phinney, now in South Carolina with the Third Battalion of the First Massachusetts Cavalry. His spread included oyster soup and oyster pie. He had had fever and ague which worried his mother Betsy in Monument. She wanted him to get a furlough and come home to regain his health but he told her it was hard to get one. Besides, he was now "entirely recovered." He did wish he could be home for the winter so he could attend school. [41]

Further south in Lousiana, Private Robert H. Chadbourne (brother of John) of the Thirtieth Massachusetts Regiment was promoted in early December to a lieutenant in the black Third Louisiana Native Guards Regiment. This made him one of the first men of the war who commanded black troops, and the first of four Sandwich soldiers who did so.

December brought an organizational change for the Twenty-ninth. After a six-month attachment to 2nd Corps and the Irish Brigade, Corps commander Edwin Sumner transferred it to 9th Corps and Colonel Benjamin Christ's brigade, replacing it in the Irish Brigade with the Irish Twenty-eighth Massachusetts. In a farewell message to the Twenty-ninth, Colonel Meagher of the Irish Brigade called Major Chipman "a soldier of first rate order." Unfortunately, Chipman was too ill to appreciate the accolade. Suffering from severe intestinal disease, he received a twenty-day furlough and went to Sandwich to recover, arriving around December 10th. [42]

Also coming north to Massachusetts was the flag of the Irish Massachusetts Ninth Regiment. After eighteen months of campaigns, the regiment's distinctive green silk banner had become so tattered that it was being replaced with a new one. The colonel of the Ninth asked Governor Andrew to display the flag in the state house to demonstrate the loyalty of Massachusetts's Irishmen and counter past bigotry against them. [43]

While Chipman and the Ninth's flag were coming north, the Twenty-ninth and rest of the Army of the Potomac congregated at Falmouth opposite the enemy held town of Fredericksburg. General Burnside, who took over in November for McClellan as commander of the Army of the Potomac, planned to send his army across the Rappahannock River on pontoon bridges, capture Fredericksburg and move from there toward Richmond. Unfortunately, delay in the arrival of the pontoons gave the Confederates time to fortify the city.

Engineers began constructing the bridges December 11th. Despite covering fire from the telescope-mounted rifles of Private Nathan B. Ellis Jr. and his company of Massachusetts Sharpshooters, a brigade of Mississippi sharpshooters on the opposite river shore halted the work. Eager to silence them, men of the Twentieth Massachusetts voluntarily rowed themselves across the river in pontoons. Once ashore they engaged the Mississippians in urban combat heretofore unseen in the war. [44]

Sandwich glassworker Ezekiel Woodward of the Twentieth was grievously wounded in the December 11th house-to-house fighting and died a day later. He left a twenty-two-year-old widow Emeline Raymond Woodward and two young children. A second Sandwich casualty at Fredericksburg was glassworker Francis C. Geisler, also of the Twentieth. Gunfire on the battle's third day, December 13th, shattered his left arm necessitating amputation at the elbow.

The Twenty-ninth crossed the Rappahannock on one of the pontoon bridges in company with its new brigade, Colonel Christ's, on December 12th. In the next few days its men moved left and right in support of other units and waited for an order to advance into the battle, an order that never came. Lieutenant Ayling found the waiting and expecting any moment to be ordered forward as unnerving as being immersed in the battle. [45]

Burnside withdrew his army from Fredericksburg December 15th in what was another stunning Union defeat. On December 16th, Twenty-ninth commander Colonel Barnes ordered his men to stack arms, attended to in Company D by Orderly Sergeant Benjamin Hamlen. As he watched and took roll, he discovered that Private James William (William J.) Smith had failed to cross the river with the company to participate in the Fredericksburg battle December 12th to 15th. For the serious offense of absenting himself in the face of the enemy he was court-martialed, convicted and sentenced to six months hard labor at the Washington Military Penitentiary. [46]

War produces many twists of fate. A striking example is the transfer of the Twenty-ninth Massachusetts out of the Irish Brigade just two weeks before the battle of Fredericksburg. That transfer put it in a brigade at Fredericksburg that saw little action and received almost no casualties. On the other hand its replacement in the Irish Brigade, the Twenty-eighth Massachusetts, was at the heart of the combat and had a huge casualty count, almost forty per cent of its men.

Simultaneous with the attack on Fredericksburg by the Army of the Potomac was a Union expedition from New Bern, North Carolina into the state's interior to destroy a railroad transporting supplies to the Confederate army in Virginia. The expedition left New Bern December 11th with around 10,000 men, among them the twenty or so men of Sandwich in the Forty-fifth Regiment, and a few others in the Twenty-Fourth, which had been at New Bern several months.

The expedition encountered and defeated an inferior Confederate force at the battle of Kinston, North Carolina on December 14th. During the battle, blacksmith and occasional tippler Henry Benson of the Forty-fifth was badly wounded, with means of how it happened recounted by comrade Private George L. Haines: "He [Benson] fought like a tiger, and after his gun was useless, he turned to get one from a fallen man and a ball struck him in the spine." Benson, who was married and the father of three, died December 28th at New Bern and was buried there. [47]

Private Haines and strapping glassworks laborer Thomas Hackett were near each other during the Kinston battle. When roll call afterward revealed Hackett was missing, Haines went looking for him and found him crawling on his hands and right leg, with left leg useless and gun strapped across his back. Haines and comrade John D. Foster helped him get off the field and back to New Bern with the rest of the regiment. He had been shot in such a way that the ball struck his haversack, was deflected away from vital organs and entered instead his left leg. And how was it that his haversack had redirected the flight of the ball? It was full of hardtack or hard bread. Hackett's hardtack was so hard it saved his life! Several days after the battle his nine- and six-year-old girls heard at school in Sandwich of their father's wounding. [48]

A day after the December 15th Kinston battle, South Sandwich seaman Solomon H. Jones enlisted in the navy at Boston and was assigned to the ironclad ship *Nahant*, built in Boston in 1862 and the first ironclad warship constructed in New England. With vessel completed and ready for boarding December 29th, Jones and the rest of the seventy-five- man *Nahant* crew assembled aft on the receiving ship *Ohio* for roll call, collected their bags and hammocks and stood ready to disembark. From the *Ohio*, they were ferried to Boston Navy Yard, marched down the yard and on reaching their new ship, filed on board. [49]

Happening upon a means of doing some Union service at sea but out of uniform and in less restricted quarters than an ironclad was Warren P. Keene of Monument. In November of 1862 the young seaman went to the New York sailor's home to obtain a position on a merchant vessel and found one on the U. S. coastal survey steamer *Vixen*, under Captain Edward Cordell. The *Vixen* steamed to the coast of southeast Florida and at the site of present day Miami, Cordell stationed Keene as a tide observer. For the next four months he recorded his observations, which contributed to making nearby waters safer for Union merchant and naval vessels. [50]

As Keene watched the last tide of 1862 recede from his Florida beach, the 185 Sandwich soldiers and sailors in Union service at the time may also have pondered the ebbing year from campfire stool, hospital bed, stockade cell or watch station at sea. A lot had happened in the year's span. As they looked ahead to the new year, all shared Attorney Eben Whittemore's final diary entry for the old: "I hope…and pray that the great rebellion may be crushed."

Chapter Six:
Hard Tack and Mule Beef—
January to May 1863

The war's third year, 1863, opened with the greatest numbers of Sandwich soldiers in three companies of three Massachusetts regiments, forty-two in Company D of the Twenty-ninth, forty in Company I of the Fortieth and twenty-one in Company D of the Forty-fifth. All three regiments were in winter quarters, the Twenty-ninth at Falmouth, Virginia, the Fortieth at Washington and the Forty-fifth in shed-like barracks at New Bern, North Carolina. Attrition had nibbled away the ranks of the fifty-eight men who had mustered into Company D of the Twenty-ninth in May of 1861. Thirteen were off company rolls because of death, desertion, disability discharge or resignation while three others were gone through promotion or transfer.

Attrition had also hit Company D's regiment, the Twenty-ninth. Thomas Darby, now a sergeant, reported that the many discharges and hospitalizations of ailing men had left it with a fit for duty strength of not much more than 300 men. For those hardy enough to hold off illness and remain in camp, January at Falmouth had its pleasantries. For New Year's Day dinner, Company D enjoyed boiled steak and duff, the latter prepared with apples in the absence of raisins. With fighting at a lull and opposing pickets separated by but a hundred yards of river, fraternization sprang up. A soldier of the Twenty-ninth made a boat of a piece of wood, rigged a sail on it, loaded it with coffee and sent it across to the enemy side. Before long, the "boat" returned freighted with Virginia tobacco. [1]

Music, alternately doleful and sprightly, added another diversion for the men of Company D at their Falmouth camp. "There is now a funeral passing," wrote Sergeant Darby. "I hear the melancholy strains of fife and drum and I see the slow tread of the soldiers following their comrade to his last home, but in a few minutes they will return playing Rory-O-More or some such lively tune." [2]

Spending January at a camp outside Washington was George F. W. Haines, cousin of Birney and George L. Haines. After a few months service in the navy, former whaleman Haines had enlisted in the Ninth Massachusetts Battery of Light Artillery. His duty at the battery's camp was the care and feeding of two of its many horses. When the horses developed sores, he had to dress them and in so doing he himself developed the sores. The horses probably had glanders, a serious equine disease that could be occasionally transmitted to humans. The disease also infected eighteen horses of the Fifth Massachusetts Battery at Falmouth and condemned them to be shot. Three men of Sandwich were in the Fifth, Ephraim Nye and brothers John and Joseph Alton. [3]

Nahant, *upper right,* bombarding Fort McAllister.
Harper's Weekly *January-June 1863*

January's cold weather kept army activities in Virginia in abeyance but warmer conditions in Georgia were conducive to Navy operations. The serpentine Ogeechee River near Savannah afforded a watery approach to vital railroads and roads of the Confederacy but standing in the way was earthen-constructed Fort McAllister. Pilot John W. Godfrey guided a fleet of vessels up the river to a point at which they bombarded the fort but it withstood the attack and the fleet retired. A second attack came a few weeks later, led by four ironclads. One of them was ordinary seaman Solomon H. Jones's *Nahant*. That attack also failed. [4]

Naval ships bombarding forts were but one aspect of the war afloat. Another was attacks on Union merchant shipping by Confederate raiders. One of the most infamous, the *Alabama,* plundered Union shipping in the eastern Atlantic in September 1862. In response, the Union naval frigate *Sabine* stood out to sea from New London, Connecticut. Aboard were South Sandwich officer John Ewer, Pocasset ordinary seaman Charles L. Howard and captain of marines Charles Heywood. Heywood, it will be remembered, was aboard the *Cumberland,* sunk by the ironclad *Merrimac* at Hampton Roads in 1862.

After an unsuccessful three months search, the *Sabine* came into New York. Howard went to a receiving ship to await a new assignment, contracted pneumonia and died in New York Naval Hospital in April. [5]

CSS Florida *destroys* Jacob Bell. Harper's Weekly *January-June 1863*

Sixteen-year-old Benjamin C. Fessenden of Sandwich obtained a merchant ship position in 1859 through the assistance of his uncle, Captain Ezra Nye. Six months later young Fessenden shipped on the clipper *Jacob Bell* for a far-east voyage of eighteen months that ended in New York in September 1861. He came to Sandwich, visited his family, got some new clothes and returned to New York for a second *Bell* sailing that began in November. Fifteen months later, on February 12, 1863, the Confederate raider *Florida* captured and burned the *Bell* in the South Atlantic. Fessenden and the rest of the crew were put on board the Danish bark *Morning Star* that called at the Virgin Islands and Cuba before coming into New York May 6, 1863. [6]

Also in the spring of 1863, the navy steamer *Sunflower* left Boston for duty in Florida waters with Patrick McGirr a crew member. After receiving an army disability discharge in Virginia on March 26th, he had enlisted in the navy at New Bedford April 18th. After the *Sunflower* came into Key West in late summer of 1863, McGirr was ordered confined in double irons for drunkenness. This was ironic since it was McGirr as constable who enforced Sandwich's liquor law in the 1850s. [7]

Far from the war at sea was the Reverend Jacob Forman, who had preached at Sandwich in the 1850s before leaving for Illinois. Now chaplain of a Missouri regiment in Arkansas, he observed mistreatment of contrabands by Union soldiers and wrote his commanding general about it. Forman's reform-mindedness caught the attention of army nurse superintendent Dorothea Dix in Washington and in February she wrote President Lincoln asking him to appoint Forman as chaplain for St. Louis's military hospitals. He eventually became secretary of the Western Sanitary Commission. [8]

Soldiers needed hospitals for many reasons. In early January Private Davis Magoon of Monument, doing night sentry duty at his Fortieth Regiment's camp near Washington, stumbled over a pile of lumber and injured his back. With body "bent over like a bow" he was admitted to the Harewood Hospital north of Washington in February. Also admitted there that month was Private John T. Collins of the Twenty-ninth, afflicted with rheumatism. [9]

Harewood Hospital's 600 beds in nine wards were getting full when Magoon and Collins arrived. To reduce patient load and disperse patients to hospitals nearer home, orders came March 17th for Harewood's Massachusetts men to prepare to depart. The next day ambulances collected Magoon, Collins and the hospital's forty other Bay State patients and jounced them along Washington's streets to Alexandria where they went aboard the hospital steamer *Daniel Webster*. Joining Magoon and Collins on board was Warren P. Dean of the Twenty-ninth, ill with chronic diarrhea. He came from Washington's Lincoln Hospital. [10]

Magoon, Collins and Dean had as company on the *Daniel Webster* 272 other sick and wounded New England men. The steamer departed March 19th with destination of Portsmouth Grove Hospital in Rhode Island, where several Sandwich men had already been patients. "There are some very sick men aboard this ship," wrote Private Oliver Ricker of Lowell, Massachusetts three days into the voyage, "and it is a very bad place for anyone between decks in the forward part of the ship. The air is very bad…." After a five-day voyage, the steamer reached Portsmouth Grove March 24th. [11]

After a stay of around three months at Portsmouth Grove, Collins returned to his regiment. Magoon had a visitor at the hospital, his wife Freelove, who came over from Monument. He never rejoined his regiment but rather performed light duty the rest of the war. Dean received a disability discharge in April. Receiving a similar discharge in April was long-term patient Stephen Weeks. He was discharged with "mental imbecility" caused by typhoid fever. [12]

Private Dean was not the only Sandwich soldier of Company D of the Twenty-ninth to receive a disability discharge in the first part of 1863. Others were John Woods, Alfred Cheval, Joseph Turner and Gustavus A. Badger. Their departures meant that of the fifty-eight Sandwich men who had mustered into Company D nearly two years earlier, just thirty-seven remained on its rolls. Three others from the Twenty-ninth, Major Chipman, Lieutenant Atherton and Private Anderson Wright, came to Sandwich in March to recuperate from illness. Atherton also came for business reasons. Prior to enlistment, he had worked for and held a financial interest in Sandwich's newspaper but recent mismanagement of it required his attention. While home some good news came his way, promotion to First Lieutenant. As of the end of March, the officers commanding Company D were Captain Brooks and Lieutenants Atherton and Darby, the latter just promoted from sergeant. [13]

Atherton might have also learned while in Sandwich that Company D and the rest of its Twenty-ninth Regiment and 9th Corps was on the move, from Virginia to Kentucky. To get there, the Twenty-ninth passed through Cincinnati March 26th. This was the first Massachusetts regiment the people there had seen and they found its men and their white Massachusetts colors flag of much interest. A large crowd cheered for the Bay State and Union in what Lieutenant Ayling called a "right royal welcome." From the Queen City, the men of 9th Corps crossed the Ohio River to Kentucky to garrison small towns and patrol for Confederate raiding parties. [14]

Despite health annoyances and a relocating army corps, Sandwich officers Atherton and Chipman remained with their Twenty-ninth Regiment. The same cannot be said for the town's officers of the Fortieth Regiment, Lieutenant Freeman and Captain Harper. Freeman's nemesis, Alfred E. Smith, followed the Fortieth to Washington, became a "hanger-on" at its camp and continued to subvert Freeman at every turn. Freeman's personality hampered him as well. A student in Boston before commissioning, he was a bookish young man who lacked the common touch needed by a commander in dealing with men under him. When he informed Fortieth Regiment commander Colonel Burr Porter that he wished to resign his commission, Porter did not oppose the idea as he felt such a move was in Freeman's best interest. [15]

Freeman soon landed on his feet. Taking advantage of familial roots with the state of Maine, that state's governor granted him a new lieutenant commission and on February 25, 1863 he was mustered in at New York into the Fourth Regiment of General Daniel Ullman's Brigade which sailed to New Orleans April 9th to recruit black troops, making him the second of four Sandwich officers who commanded African-American soldiers in the war. As for Captain Harper, he suffered from poor health while commanding Company I of the Fortieth Regiment, returned to Sandwich in March, resigned his commission and did no further service. [16]

Forty-fifth Massachusetts soldiers in front of their housing in New Bern, NC winter 1863. Historic New England

Poor health also affected the service of Private Isaiah Adams of the Twenty-fourth Massachusetts. Taken sick at New Bern, North Carolina in late 1862, he was admitted to Portsmouth Hospital, situated on a remote island in that state's Outer Banks chain. After his health improved, Adams remained at Portsmouth as a nurse. As part of his duty, he supervised contrabands unloading wood from vessels. Discharged from the hospital in June of 1863, he was one of its last patients because it closed a month later. [17]

Also at New Bern, the Forty-fifth Massachusetts made a housing upgrade. In late January its men moved out of barracks into three-story gas-lit houses that New Bern's residents had vacated in 1862 when Union forces captured the town. Quartered one company of soldiers to a house, the Forty-fifth policed New Bern as provost marshal keeping order and quelling fast horse riding and other carousing. Unfortunately, new quarters did not prevent old diseases. Private James T. Jones of East Sandwich and the Forty-fifth contracted "the black measles" leaving him so sick he had to be carried to the regimental hospital. Likewise, new quarters offered no protection from Mother Nature.

Lightning struck and prostrated former glassworker Ezra Hamblin while he was doing guard duty in front of the provost marshal's office. [18]

The arrival of the mail boat at New Bern April 14th brought great excitement for the men of the Forty-fifth. The regiment had not been paid for five months and on board was the long overdue pay. That night, young Henry Knippe was one of four men who guarded it at the paymaster's office. Knippe had plans for the $65 due him—dining on something besides hard tack and mule beef. [19]

North of New Bern in Virginia the Union Army grew more active as the weather warmed. On March 16th the First Massachusetts Cavalry, with George Hobson and Nathaniel Fish, left its camp at Falmouth as part of a 3,100-man troop that clashed indecisively a day later with a Confederate force at Kelly's Ford near Culpeper,

George Hobson wearing forage cap, shell jacket, high collar, shoulder scales and carbine sling typical of Union cavalryman of Civil War.
From Crowninshield History of First Massachusetts Cavalry

Virginia. In this action, Hobson sustained a saber wound to his head. Nine days later he, his saddle, pistol, equipment and black horse were captured near Falmouth. He was confined at Richmond, paroled March 31st and, like Horace Lovell, held at the Annapolis parole camp awaiting exchange. Hobson had to re-imburse the government $180 for the loss of his horse and equipment. [20]

Across the river from Falmouth at Fredericksburg, the Confederate Army also stirred with the advance of spring. Desperately short of food, General Lee dispatched elements of his army to southern Virginia with dual objectives of foraging for commissary stores and capturing the large Union garrison of Suffolk, Virginia. Arriving there April 18th, the Confederates put the garrison under siege.

Besieged Suffolk needed reinforcements and in answer the War Department pulled regiments away from the defenses of Washington and sent them to the embattled garrison. One regiment sent was the Fortieth Massachusetts with its forty Sandwich men of Company I, the so-called "second Sandwich company." After six months of defending Washington, the Fortieth headed to its first offensive action. In an odd coincidence, the "second Sandwich company" rode by rail into Suffolk, its first war zone, and the "first Sandwich company" left there by the same means to travel to its first active war in 1862. The Fortieth's white colors flag attracted attention at Suffolk, just as it had for the Twenty-ninth Massachusetts a month earlier at Cincinnati. [21]

Another unit that came to the defense of Suffolk was the Eleventh Rhode Island Regiment, and with it Corporal Charles M. Packard of Monument. After three-months service in 1861 at Fortress Monroe, he had re-enlisted in 1862 in the Eleventh. Also serving at Suffolk was Battery L of the Fourth United States Artillery and with it Private Isaac H. Phinney. He had transferred to the artillery from the Twenty-ninth Massachusetts the previous November.

Closer to home, concern arose in Massachusetts in the spring of 1863 over the vulnerability of the state's harbors. In response, Governor Andrew authorized formation of heavy artillery companies to garrison coastal forts. Recruiting around the state yielded eight companies to serve in them, one of which was at New Bedford. Recruiting advertising emphasized that men who enlisted would serve only in Massachusetts. Three men of Sandwich enlisted in the New Bedford company and were assigned to its fort. Since the three were minors, a parent had to sign a consent form for them. Signing for glassworker Frederick Norris of West Sandwich was his father, sea captain Benjamin Norris. Doing the same for farmer Seth F. Gibbs was his father Freeman B. Gibbs. The third, tack worker George F. Gibbs, had been an orphan since 1850 so Sandwich Selectman Mason White signed for him. [22]

Spring at New Bern brought an end to the Forty-fifth Massachusetts's provost duty and and on April 25th the men moved out of their houses into a tented camp outside town. The eight-feet square tents held four men. In a letter to his sister, George L. Haines chuckled that his new accommodations so accustomed him to tight living that when he returned to Sandwich he could live in his family's pigeon box. [23]

Scarcely had the men of the Forty-fifth pigeonholed themselves into their new life in tents when orders came for an expedition with object of preventing Confederate troops in North Carolina from reinforcing those laying siege at Suffolk. Taking the advance in the expedition, the men of the Forty-fifth boarded a train at New Bern and from flatcars watched for the enemy as a locomotive at the rear pushed them into "the interior of Dixie." Stationed on the leading flat car were the colonel of the Forty-fifth and the train conductor, scanning the tracks ahead with field glasses. Methodical searching from the train and from outlying skirmishers revealed the enemy in entrenched works lying athwart the tracks. A sharp engagement ensued which climaxed with the Forty-fifth making a bayonet charge, overrunning the enemy and planting the colors atop the captured works. "The Forty-fifth won the field," exclaimed Haines. While this minor action didn't leave much mark on history it does stand out for one particular, that of the victors being literally pushed into battle. [24]

After their successful expedition, the men of the Forty-fifth returned to New Bern May 1st and resumed camp life. Just three days later the Confederates broke off the Suffolk siege and returned to their main army, which had just defeated the Union at the battle of Chancellorsville, Virginia. With siege lifted and emergency over, the Fortieth Regiment left Suffolk as part of General George Gordon's division and took transports up the York River to a lodgement thirty miles east of Richmond at West Point where its men dug in and waited to see in which direction the Confederate Army would move after Chancellorsville. [25]

While General Lee contemplated his next move in Virginia, General U. S. Grant's Union Army of the Tennessee maneuvered in Mississippi. After a string of hard-fought battles from Port Gibson to Raymond to Champion Hill, Grant's army backed the Confederates into the Mississippi River stronghold of Vicksburg. Lieutenant Joshua Bourne of the Seventh Missouri Regiment participated in all that action.

John D. Heywood photo of locomotive and cars North Carolina.
Library of Congress

On May 22nd, Grant ordered an all-out assault on Vicksburg. In the face of strong opposition the Seventh Missouri advanced with scaling ladders and with the rest of the federals scrambled uphill against a well-entrenched enemy who from rugged bluffs poured down a fearful fire onto the attackers. Six color bearers of the Seventh were shot down while attempting to plant the regiment's Irish style flag on a parapet. Bourne seized the flag, held it in position and bore it from the field when the order to fall back was given. For bravery under fire he received promotion to captain and praise from his division commander. A second Sandwich combatant in the Vicksburg assault was sailor John W. Tinkham on the ironclad river gunboat *Benton,* which bombarded the city from the Mississippi River. Enemy return fire struck the *Benton* thirteen times. The land and water assault of May 22nd failed to capture Vicksburg and forced Union forces to lay siege to the city. [26]

Communication within an army on the move, like Grant's before it reached Vicksburg, was exceedingly important but couriers were unreliable. An improvement came from the Signal Corps which developed an innovation called a signal train. Consisting of a substantial wagon carrying telegraph set, telegraph poles and reels of wire, the signal train made telegraphing portable, i.e., kept an army in communication as it advanced its lines.

One of the first Signal Corps officers to work with signal trains was Deming Jarves Jr., who had remained with the Corps after being detailed to it in 1861. After completing Signal Corps instruction at Washington and assisting with a signal station at Point of Rocks, Maryland in 1862, he received orders in March 1863 to proceed from Washington to Philadelphia to deliver signal trains from there to the Union Army of the Cumberland in Tennessee. As that army advanced from a base south of Nashville to Chattanooga in the summer of 1863, Jarves helped set up its signal trains. [27]

Another Civil War innovation was the ironclad warship. Most were of design similar to the *Nahant,* turreted and low to the water, but one was different, the massive high-sided iron-plated frigate *New Ironsides.* On April 7, 1863 a battle line of nine ironclads, among them the *Nahant* and *New Ironsides,* entered Charleston, South Carolina harbor to attack the city's principal waterside defense, Fort Sumter. Low rate of fire of the turreted ironclads and poor maneuverability of the *New Ironsides* in the tricky currents of the harbor undid the attack and turned it back in failure. The *New Ironsides* took fifty hits from enemy guns, the *Nahant* thirty-six.

Three men of Sandwich witnessed and were part of this spectacle of iron steaming into Charleston harbor and blasting away at the fort. Standing beside flag officer Du Pont in the pilothouse of the flagship *New Ironsides* was pilot John W. Godfrey, providing the admiral important information about tides, water depths and channel markings. An enlisted man on board the *New Ironsides* was twenty-two-year old John Nickerson. On the *Nahant* was Solomon Jones.

Forays such as the one into Charleston harbor were brief departures for the Union sailor from his customary duty, the southern coast blockade, an endeavor that required a lot of ships and a lot of sailors to man them. Responding to the manpower need, sixteen-year-old Daniel F. Fisher enlisted at Boston May 6, 1863. One of Sandwich's younger navy men, Fisher left the receiving ship *Ohio* at Boston March 23rd and departed with 149 other sailors for Philadelphia on the commercial steamer *Saxon*. Close quarters on either the *Ohio* or *Saxon* infected him with "black spotted fever" which broke out when he reached Philadelphia. Taken to the naval hospital delirious with fever, he recovered but was left with fever-related sequelae of partial loss of vision and hearing. [28]

The day Fisher enlisted, May 6th, the Confederate raider *Florida,* made another capture, this time the brig *Clarence*. At her helm was Monument ship captain Abram Phinney, running northward from Rio de Janeiro for Baltimore with a load of coffee. His losses in the capture included a spyglass, marine opera glass, valuable gold watch and Bowditch navigator. Also, he lost his monthly wages of $75 for the three months it took him to get home and resume his employment. Serving as his cook, cooper and steward on the *Clarence* was his Monument neighbor Elijah F. Perry. He was put in irons on the *Florida* and lost his trunk and clothes bag. Five weeks later the *Tacony,* tender of the *Florida,* captured and burned the brig *Umpire,* co-owned by Henry Wing of Sandwich. His losses were $416.00. [29]

In Kentucky, the Twenty-ninth Regiment spent much of April garrisoning the Bourbon County community of Paris. Late that month they marched south to garrison another small Kentucky town, Somerset. After Paris, Somerset was a decided fall-off. "This place is not so pleasant…as Paris," wrote Sergeant Darby. "Soldiers do not get as much whiskey as when in Bourbon County. There are but few women here and they are not handsome." [30]

The few unhandsome women of Somerset were at least enterprising. They peddled pies, bread, eggs, chickens and butter. Unfortunately, the men of the regiment couldn't purchase any of the offerings because they had been paid only up to the first of March and were "nearly all broke." Major Chipman, who rejoined the regiment at Somerset after several months convalescence in Sandwich, was also short of money. This worried him because when he had none, his family also had none, he being sole monetary support of his wife, children and mother-in-law. He suggested they get food on credit from North Sandwich country store proprietor Charles Bourne and money from Sandwich Village druggist Charles B. Hall, with admonishment to repay Hall "as soon as I send you money." [31]

Worse than lack of food or money was the heartbreak of incurable disease. In Monument, Doctors Leonard and Parkinson pronounced forty-three-year-old Hannah Bourne's medical condition as hopeless. Despite switching to a doctor in far-off Barnstable, she died of cancer leaving her ship captain husband John Bourne a widower in the care of two children. [32]

May was happier for the men of the Forty-fifth Regiment in North Carolina. Their nine-month enlistment term was almost up and they would soon be headed home. The Fortieth Regiment spent the month in Virginia while the Twenty-ninth remained at Somerset. Two Company D men of the latter regiment, Patrick Clancy and James William Smith, deserted. Smith was just released from military prison. Their desertions meant that of the fifty-eight men who had made up the "first Sandwich company" in 1861, just thirty-five remained. With desertions, deaths and discharges mounting in Union army ranks, something was needed to bolster manpower. That something was about to be implemented.

Chapter Seven:
Only Son of a Widow—
The Draft of Summer 1863

With the arrival of June 1863, the war had been underway more than two years. Seventeen Union Army soldiers of Sandwich had died of disease or in battle, thirty had received disability discharges, five had deserted and two had resigned. Few men of the town had enlisted in the army since September 1862 when the twenty-two nine-month's men mustered in—and their enlistments were about to expire. That which was the case for Sandwich, manpower losses not offset by replacements, was repeated in community after community across the north. Volunteerism was at a low point.

Seeing this worrisome picture, Congress passed a conscription law in March 1863. The law took recruiting out of the hands of local officials and nationalized it, placing it in the hands of a provost marshal, one per congressional district. The conscription law and its workings were well known to the men in the ranks. In a letter of May 11, 1863 written from Kentucky to his wife, Major Chipman asked who had been appointed provost marshal for the district.

The district to which Chipman referred was Massachusetts Congressional District Number One, which stretched westward from Provincetown through Sandwich and on to the Rhode Island border. Administering it was the Provost Marshal's office in New Bedford headed by Provost Marshal Albert D. Hatch of that place, appointed around May 1st. Assisting him were Nathaniel Hinckley of Marston's Mills (Barnstable County) as commissioner and Foster Hooper of Fall River as surgeon. [1]

Provost Marshal Albert D. Hatch.
USAHEC

Hatch's first step in carrying out the law was the enrolling of all able-bodied male citizens of military age in the district. To do this, he hired enrolling officers to canvas door to door and house to house listing Class One and Class Two men. Class One were married or unmarried men ages twenty to thirty-five, Class Two married men ages thirty-six to forty-five. Men would only be drafted from Class Two when the Class One list had been exhausted. Enrolling officers collected name, residence, age on July 1, 1863, occupation, race, marital status and miscellaneous other data from men they enrolled.

The enrolling officer hired by Hatch to canvass Sandwich and neighboring Falmouth was thirty-five-year-old Sandwich furniture maker and dealer John W. Pope. Other hats he wore were inspector of the Port of Sandwich, assistant assessor of revenue, charter member of Sandwich's Masonic Lodge and secretary for town war meetings. He carried out his enrolling in June, receiving $3.00 per day for his services, then sent his list of draft liable men to Provost Marshall Hatch, whose office would draw from it the names of the lucky ones to be drafted. [2]

Pope enrolled 340 men of Sandwich. A sampling of them follow, beginning with immigrants John Colclough, John Parry and brothers Peter and Andrew Neiter. China decorator Colclough came to New York from England in 1854 and to Sandwich from Somerville around 1862. Fellow Englishman Parry arrived at Sandwich around 1856 and was naturalized at Barnstable Superior Court in 1861. The Neiters, from Alsace, France, reached New York in 1859 and Sandwich, by way of Cambridge, around 1862. All four worked as cutters and decorators at the glassworks. [3]

Enrollee Abram Schuster moved to Sandwich from Dennis in 1859 when he married Sarah Rogers, daughter of Sandwich cordwainer John H. B. Rogers. Former sailor Schuster worked at the glassworks until 1864 when he enlisted in the army. Another enrollee who came to Sandwich after an 1859 marriage to a Sandwich woman was Andrew F. Sherman. He ran a dry goods store and in 1862 was superintendent of the Methodist Church's Sunday school. His older brother Daniel P. was killed in action in Virginia in June 1863, just when Andrew was being enrolled. [4]

Another enrolled Sandwich merchant was Frank H. Burgess. He purchased a grocery store there in 1861 and was managing it in 1863. Eleven years later was born a nephew Thornton W. Burgess, who would become a renowned children's book author. [5]

Also enrolled was Sandwich bandleader James H. Dalton. He arrived from Cambridge with parents and siblings around 1840. Described as a man of "rare musical talents," he opened a class for "plain and fancy" dancing at Sandwich in 1863. Playing with Dalton in the band was glasscutter Jonathan B. Marston (brother of former Sandwich boarding house keeper William H.). Jonathan's oldest son Eugene, age twenty-one, was also enrolled but might have had trouble reporting if drafted since in 1863 he was on a four-year-long cruise in the whaling ship *Alfred Gibbs* in the Pacific Ocean. Young Eugene was lost at sea in 1865. [6]

Similar in situation was Charles W. Tobey. After obtaining a position on the whaling ship *Stephania* in July 1860, he went to New Bedford August 15th, signed shipping articles and the next day was aboard as a boatsteerer for a four-year cruise to the Indian Ocean. Despite being on the cruise in 1863, he was enrolled as were his brothers Thomas and Watson, who were home and farming near Sandwich Village at the time. [7]

Another whaler enrolled was James L. Lapham, who had been on the condemned whaling bark *Ocean* in 1857. In 1858 he married Mary A. E. Badger, sister of one of the *Ocean's* crewmen. Like Eugene Marston and Charles Tobey, he was on a whaling cruise when the enrollment was done.

Three more enrolled whalemen, all from Monument, were Cyrenius Eldridge, Charles W. Parker and Cranston W. Nickerson. Eldridge was on the bark *Sea Breeze* that left New Bedford for a three-year cruise to the Pacific in October 1861. Parker was captain of the ship *Draper* that was in the midst of a three-year Indian Ocean cruise during the 1863 enrollment. Serving under him was Pliny B. Handy of Pocasset. Nickerson left New Bedford in 1859 on the bark *Golconda* for a long Pacific cruise.

A final enrollee in this sampling, businessman Noble P. Swift, ran a prosperous livestock and meat enterprise in West Sandwich. In the spring of 1862 he donated land for a parsonage house there. That fall his wife died. Three weeks later Mary Harrison, who lived in Sandwich Village, asked thirty-two-year old Swift to take her eighteen-year-old daughter Emily for his wife. At first, romance blossomed. Swift took Emily to dancing school (perhaps Mr. Dalton's), advanced her money for a piano and reportedly declared he "didn't feel more than nineteen." A neighbor noticed that Swift's carriage sat in front of the Harrison house for two to three hours at a time. The affair cooled though. Arabella Blackwell, who was Emily's age, saw that Emily no longer cared for Swift. He never remarried while she, perhaps without the meddling of her mother, found herself a husband in 1868. [8]

The draft for Sandwich's Congressional District began July 13, 1863 at New Bedford. Enrolled men's names, on ballots, were placed in a circular drum rotated by a crank. While one official turned the crank, another who was blindfolded drew out the names. For Sandwich, ninety-seven names from the 340 enrolled men were drawn. Over the next ten days, enrollment officer Pope served draft notices to the ninety-seven, either at a man's usual residence or directly into his hands. Drafted men had to report to New Bedford in the next ten days. Three failed to report. Pocasset brothers John G. and Francis B. White were on a whaling cruise while James Cook was in the army and therefore had been incorrectly enrolled.

The ninety-four men of Sandwich who did report first underwent a medical examination. It exempted thirty-five for reasons ranging from varicose veins to consumption. Consumptive men were not difficult for the surgeon to recognize. Frederick A. Blackwell of Monument was exempted for that disease and two years later was dead of it. Benjamin A. Norris, exempted for epilepsy, couldn't just tell the surgeon he had that disorder but rather had to have an affidavit from a physician who had attended him while convulsing. Glassblower James Davis was exempted because of loss of his right eye, presumably the one used to sight down a gun barrel. Loss of his left eye would not have disqualified him. [9]

The fifty-nine men who passed the medical examination appeared before provost officials to see if they qualified for non-medical exemptions. Ten were exempted for being the only son of a widow. Two of these cases are of interest. Temperance Crocker of South Sandwich had three sons. In 1853 the middle one, Asa Jr., went to California, married and stayed. In 1858 her husband Asa Sr. abandoned his family and went there as well. In 1862, her youngest son Horace died of disease while in the army. Thus when oldest son Heman claimed exemption as the "only son" of a "widow," the claim was technically false but nonetheless reasonable. [10]

Sarah S. Swift of West Sandwich became a widow in 1852 when her husband Clark died of consumption. That left her with sons Francis C. and Shadrach F., and daughter Mary. Mary lost her hearing around 1840 as a baby and in 1850, through generosity of friends, was admitted to a school for the deaf in Hartford, Connecticut, where she spent five years. Her brother Shadrach also had hearing loss. Francis moved to Sandwich Village around 1860 and in 1863 was orderly for Major Chipman in the Twenty-ninth Regiment. These were the circumstances under which Shadrach claimed exemption as only son of a widow in 1863. [11]

Eight of Sandwich's drafted men were exempted for being aliens. One was Irish immigrant Patrick Fagan, whose brother John had gone off to war with the first Sandwich company in 1861. Patrick, who worked at the glassworks, was naturalized in 1870. [12]

Joseph S. Hewins had an interesting route to an exemption. He drove the mail stage between Monument and Falmouth. In November 1861 he was convicted of robbing the mail and sentenced to five years incarceration at the jail in Dedham, Massachusetts. Convinced of his innocence, 700 citizens of

Barnstable County signed petitions requesting clemency for him. In February 1863, President Lincoln granted the request and he was immediately released. Despite this, the weight of a criminal record hung so heavily over him that when he was drafted five months later, he was exempted for being a felon. [13]

Ultimately, fifteen of Sandwich's drafted men failed to qualify for an exemption and became draft liable. One of them was bandleader Dalton's brother, glassblower John W. Dalton. Regarding the latter, Twenty-ninth Regiment Sergeant Darby wrote, "I learn that my friend Dalton is one of the drafted ones and will have a chance to Wreathe His brow with Laurels Won on the Battle field." Dalton, however, never made it to any battlefield. Instead he and thirteen others of the fifteen found liable for military service sidestepped it by hiring substitutes or paying a $300 commutation fee. Substitutes were not hard to find. Brokers located near the provost marshal's office advertised "good and reliable" ones. The going price for one in New Bedford at the end of July was around $400.00. [14]

The many exemptions, failures to report, substitutes and commutations resulted in but one of Sandwich's ninety-seven drafted men, Quaker and conscientious objector Edward W. Holway of Spring Hill, being held for service. Although the conscription law permitted conscientious objectors such as Holway to avoid service by hiring a substitute or paying commutation, he declined both, seeing either as contributors to fighting and bloodshed.

Since the conscription law didn't provide Provost Marshall Hatch much guidance in dealing with a case such as Holway's, i.e., a man refusing service but liable for it, he forwarded Holway and other conscripts on September 2, 1863 to Boston Harbor's Long Island where they awaited transport south. Conscripts there were to be in uniform but Holway saw putting one on as a violation of his beliefs. The only way he would do it so as not to compromise his beliefs was if he were forced. It was under this circumstance that he exchanged his Quaker garb for a uniform on September 2nd, the day he arrived at Long Island. [15]

Since the authorities at Long Island were as perplexed as those at New Bedford as to what to do with Holway, on September 5th he was part of a detachment of 200 recruits that sailed on the steamer *Forest City* for Alexandria, Virginia for duty in the Twenty-second Massachusetts Regiment, camped near Culpeper, Virginia. Since Holway and several other Quakers refused to serve once in camp, Secretary of Agriculture Isaac Newton took their cases to President Lincoln. On November 6th the President asked Secretary of War Stanton to send Holway and the others home, thus allowing the government to move on from the thorny and unresolved matter of conscientious objectors and the draft. [16]

Chapter Eight:
Do You See the Beginning of the End?—
June to December 1863

Miles from the enrollment and draft in Massachusetts was 9th Army Corps and with it the Twenty-ninth Massachusetts Regiment, occupying Kentucky. As June began, the regiment was still at Somerset, its men looking for the paymaster and speculating as to where they might next be ordered. Some felt it would be Knoxville, Tennessee, but Major Chipman thought not. Of concern to him was Vicksburg, Mississippi, put under siege by Grant's army in May. "We are very much afraid of Grant's being driven away but I hope not," he wrote his wife the evening of June 3rd. [1]

Hours after Chipman finished his letter and bedded down, an aide rode up to his tent with orders for the Twenty-ninth to be ready to move at a moment's notice. At 3:30 a.m. of June 4th, the men began marching, not south toward Knoxville but north toward Cincinnati. After arriving there by road and rail June 9th, they promptly boarded westbound cars and were soon passing through Indiana and Illinois. At Sandoval, Illinois on June 10th they switched to a southbound train. They then knew their destination, Vicksburg, as part of a 10,000-man 9th Corps reinforcement for Grant's army. At Cairo, Illinois, the Twenty-ninth's men boarded a steamer bound down the Mississippi River and on June 17th, two weeks after leaving Somerset, disembarked and took up positions in the northern end of the looping Union line enveloping besieged Vicksburg.

While marching through a remote part of Kentucky on their way to Vicksburg, the men of the Twenty-ninth ran into the paymaster. Glad as Chipman was to get his pay, he got it miles from a place from which he could send any home. Knowing the desperate need of his family for money, he asked a stranger to take $50 to the nearest express office for mailing. He would have sent more but $50 was the most with which he could trust the stranger. He also sent money from the railroad station at Sandoval. Attending to both family at home and family of soldiers in a regiment on the move kept him occupied. [2]

Serving at Vicksburg when the Twenty-ninth arrived was Calvin G. Fisher, now a captain in one of the war's more unusual units, an amphibious strike force called the Mississippi Marine Brigade. In late June he and his brigade constructed a gun emplacement across the river from Vicksburg at Young's Point, Louisiana. From there they fired into a Vicksburg foundry that produced artillery. The enemy didn't take kindly to this and returned fire, one round of which sent a piece of exploding shell into Fisher's lower left leg. Despite his wound, he pressed on with his company commander duties. [3]

Calvin G. Fisher. From Crandall History of the Ram Fleet

Below Vicksburg on the steamer *Benton,* navy seaman John W. Tinkham developed a severe painful diarrhea June 16th. Little improved after receiving daily doses of opium, he was transferred on the 25th to the hospital steamer *Red Rover* and in July received a medical discharge when she put in to Memphis. Vicksburg was one of two enemy impediments in June 1863 to opening the Mississippi River. The other was the downriver stronghold of Port Hudson, Louisiana. Lieutenant Hartwell Freeman was there in June as an officer of the Ninth Regiment of the Corps D'Afrique, a unit of former slaves he helped recruit and train in May in the parishes west of New Orleans. His men dug trenches and performed other fatigue duties at Port Hudson, also under siege. [4]

June also marked the expiration of term of service of Sandwich's nine-months men in the Forty-fifth Regiment in North Carolina and their return north. Of the twenty-two who left Massachusetts the previous November, twenty returned. Thomas Simpson had come home early on disability and Henry Benson, dead of battle wounds, lay buried in the Tar Heel State. The regiment arrived at Boston June 30th and marched with an escort to the statehouse where it received a welcome from Governor Andrew. A day later its twenty men of Sandwich arrived home. [5]

Also coming north was General Lee and his Confederate Army. Following up on his Chancellorsville victory in May, he ordered his army to proceed toward Pennsylvania and by mid-June advance elements began entering that state. He was gambling that by invading the North he could draw the Union Army into a final monumental battle in which he would be victorious and win the war for the Confederacy. News of Lee's incursion traveled fast so that on June 24th Chipman wrote from far off Mississippi, "We all hear that Lee is in Pennsylvania...." [6]

In response, columns of Union Army soldiers departed their camps at Falmouth, Virginia and marched north, shadowing Lee's army. Infantryman Andrew Lane left Falmouth June 15th with his Twentieth Massachusetts, 2nd Army Corps, and over the next fifteen days marched 190 miles to the outskirts of the farming town of Gettysburg where the two armies were converging. The afternoon of July 1st brought him within sight and sound of the just-begun battle. Apparently not caring for what he saw and heard he deserted, the second time in eleven months. To his credit, his desertions were even-handed, one in the army and one in the navy. [7]

The first Sandwich soldiers to arrive on the actual battlefield were Henry Fish, William Kelley and James Chipman, brother of the major. The three were members of the Thirty-third Massachusetts Regiment of 11th Army Corps. Carrying a besmirched reputation because of poor battlefield performance at Chancellorsville, the largely German 11th was eager to redeem itself. During the first day's fighting at Gettysburg, July 1st, the Thirty-third and its brigade held Cemetery Hill, a piece of high ground at a crook in the northern portion of the Union line. When Union commander George Meade saw the ground and perceived its value, he deemed Gettysburg a favorable place to meet the enemy and ordered other army corps to concentrate there.

The next Sandwich soldier to arrive was Samuel T. Alton of the Second Massachusetts and 12th Corps. That unit was aligned to the right of 11th Corps on Culp's Hill at the northeast extremity of the Union line. First generation Irishman Alton was born in Sandwich in 1841 and like his father worked as a furniture maker. He moved to Salem around 1859, married there in 1860 and enlisted in 1861. He was captured at Winchester, Virginia in May 1862, spent the summer as a prisoner of war, was paroled and returned to duty October 25th. [8]

Arriving through the night of July 1st-July 2nd was the Eleventh Massachusetts, 3rd Corps, with Sandwich soldiers Colin Shaw and George Riordan. Third Corps's position was in the center of the Union line. Shaw emigrated from Prince Edward Island to Sandwich in 1850, engaged in furniture making and in 1851 married Samuel T. Alton's half sister. Shaw and family moved to Salem around 1854. His brother Neil, who lived in West Sandwich before the war, was also at Gettysburg but in a unit that saw little action. George Riordan, son of Sandwich merchant Titus P. Riordan, enlisted in the Eleventh in 1861 as a private and had been promoted to corporal by 1863. [9]

Second Corps, former home of Major Chipman and the Twenty-ninth, marched into Gettysburg at first light on July 2nd and went into position near 3rd Corps. The only Sandwich soldier left in that corps at Gettysburg (after the desertion of Andrew Lane) was John Chadbourne in the Twenty-eighth Massachusetts. It was attached to the Irish Brigade at Gettysburg, making Chadbourne its only Sandwich member there. As the brigade's men rested the morning of July 2nd, its chaplain gathered them together and administered absolution.

Fifth Corps arrived at Gettysburg with five Sandwich soldiers, James O'Neill in the Ninth Massachusetts, Charles Howes and Horace Lovell with the Eighteenth, Ansel Fifield with the Thirty-second and James Shevlin with the Seventh U. S. Infantry. Fifth Corps was situated to the rear of 3rd Corps, in reserve status. Five other Sandwich soldiers at Gettysburg were Nathaniel Fish with the First Massachusetts Cavalry and Ephraim Nye, John and Joseph Alton (brothers of Samuel T.) and George Haines in the Fifth and Ninth artillery batteries. Bartholomew Regan, formerly of North Sandwich, was at Gettysburg as a 1st Corps ambulance driver. As July 2nd began, Sandwich's nineteen soldiers at this small Pennsylvania town readied their weapons and steadied their nerves for the coming tumult.

A Confederate flanking attack of July 2nd overran 3rd Corps and the Eleventh Massachusetts, badly wounding Colin Shaw. Unable to move, he lay unattended in a no man's land between lines for two days. On July 4th, a day after the battle ended, he was found and taken to a hospital where his brother Neil visited him. Colin died August 2nd. His funeral was in Salem August 8th, after which his body was forwarded to Sandwich for burial. The Eleventh suffered many casualties in the July 2nd attack; George Riordon was lucky not to be one of them. [10]

As 3rd Corps fell back in disarray, 5th Corps came forward in relief. Its Eighteenth and Thirty-second Massachusetts Regiments, and Seventh U. S. Infantry engaged in fierce fighting near a wheat field where James Shevlin was slightly wounded. The Eighteenth, facing a brigade of South Carolinians, had to make a ninety degree turn to face the Gamecocks properly. This maneuver cost the Eighteenth dearly, as nearly thirty of its men were captured, among them Charles Howes of Spring Hill. Also in combat in this sector was John Chadbourne of the Irish Brigade, 2nd Corps. James O'Neill and his Ninth Massachusetts would have been in the wheat field action but his unit was dispatched to the left end of the Union line at Big Round Top where it fended off several assaults. [11]

Late in the afternoon, the Fifth and Ninth Batteries came to the defense of 3rd Corps. The two batteries worked their field pieces side-by-side, firing double canister into the enemy until return fire from sharpshooters and infantry forced them to retire. As they left the field, what horses they had left pulled the pieces backward so that gunners could continue to fire, a seldom used battlefield practice. The artillerymen of these two batteries fought bravely and managed to hold off the enemy at crucial points. One field piece of the Fifth emerged from the fight with shrapnel embedded in a wheel, seven of the wheel's fourteen spokes knocked out and gun barrel dented by hundreds of rounds of ricocheting fire, all of which made it an object of much interest after the battle. The mangled wheel would have been a memento worthy of display in the Massachusetts statehouse but unfortunately it was lost. [12]

Late on July 2nd, fighting broke out on the slopes of Cemetery Hill where 11th Corps and the Thirty-third Massachusetts had spent the day. Darkness as much as anything pushed back the attacking Confederates but nonetheless 11th Corps's men fought credibly enough to begin rehabilitating their reputation. In this action, three men of Captain James Chipman's company were killed. One of them, Corporal Jules Allen of Reading, Massachusetts, was "instantly killed…by a minie ball through the heart" as reported by Chipman. [13]

Early on July 3rd, the last day of the battle, action shifted to Culp's Hill where 12th Corps and the Second Massachusetts were ordered to charge a strongly defended enemy position. The charge was a disaster at every step. Forty-five men of the Second were killed and ninety wounded. Among the latter was Samuel T. Alton, shot in the thigh. He was taken to 12th Corps Hospital at the George Bushman farm, had his leg amputated around July 12th, died July 17th and was buried on the farm. He and Colin Shaw, Cape Cod's only fatalities at Gettysburg, have adjoining gravestones at Sandwich's Mount Hope Cemetery. [14]

Unable to dislodge the Union from its positions at Gettysburg, Lee began pulling back his army July 4th. He had lost his gamble that he could deliver a knockout blow to the Union Army. The war would go on. That same day, July 4th, the starving defenders of besieged Vicksburg surrendered giving Grant and his army a major victory. Sandwich celebrated the fall of that city July 8th with ringing of bells and firing of cannon at sunrise. [15]

Sandwich had further reason for celebration in July 1863. Business was bustling. The local newspaper found the high level of activity all the more

Colin Shaw and Samuel T. Alton Graves at Mount Hope Cemetery Sandwich. Photos by Author

remarkable since it was happening in time of war. The two glass companies together employed around 800 workers and wanted more. Their output of kerosene lamps, tumblers and table goods was almost endless in variety. Also doing a brisk business were the tack company and the Chipman marble works. The latter employed eleven men. [16]

While Sandwich was celebrating the Vicksburg surrender, the Twenty-ninth as part of a force under General William T. Sherman was marching into interior Mississippi in pursuit of a Confederate army under General Joseph Johnston. The march through war-ravaged country stripped of food and with almost no potable water was arduous. "Terrible march through cornfields, water scarce and what we had not fit to drink, very short of provisions," wrote Surgeon Robert Jameson of the Twenty-ninth. In the face of this, resourceful Sergeant Martin L. Kern Jr. and Lieutenant Ayling's black servant boy went foraging July 9th and brought in bacon and flour from which they prepared a bacon-flapjack supper for themselves and the lieutenant. [17]

After a brief siege at Mississippi's capital of Jackson, the city fell into Union hands and Johnston's army retreated southward. In a twist of fate, a general

Private Samuel W. Hunt. The sleeve of his frock coat has the blue piping of an infantryman.
USAHEC

across the lines from Chipman at Jackson was John Breckinridge, the presidential candidate he had supported in 1860. The day Jackson fell, July 17th, Chipman wrote his wife venturing to say, "Do you see the beginning of the end of the war yet? We think we do…" His pessimistic assessment of the progress of the war expressed in the fall of 1862 had changed. He and his brother officers had experienced skilled generalship by Grant at Vicksburg and Sherman at Jackson and because of it now anticipated eventual Union victory. [18]

With work at Vicksburg and Jackson completed, the regiments of 9th Corps began returning to Kentucky. While the Twenty-ninth awaited transport, Calvin Fisher paid a visit with Major Chipman. The Major found Fisher likeable, intelligent and a fast talker. When a transport steamer arrived for the Twenty-ninth, a sickly Private Samuel Hunt had to be helped aboard. Campaigning in Mississippi's heat had laid low the regiment's mail carrier with fever and ague, as it had a number of other men of the regiment. [19]

A victim of July's heat in Virginia was Private Charles E. Swift of Pocasset, with the Fortieth Massachusetts. During its July 10th march from Williamsburg to Yorktown as part of General Gordon's 5,000-man Division, he was sun struck. With the help of comrades, he made it north with men of the Fortieth on a steamer from Yorktown to Washington and on arrival was sent to a convalescent camp at Alexandria, Virginia where he remained several months. While there, his Pocasset neighbor David D. Nye visited him. Nye and his brother William F. were sutlers to the Fifth Massachusetts Battery and kept a storeroom in Washington. Their brother Ephraim was quartermaster sergeant of the Fifth Battery. [20]

The Fortieth, minus Swift, marched through Washington—for the second time in ten months—and just after midnight of July 12th boarded a Frederick, Maryland-bound troop train, one of two headed there that night. The lead train made a water stop near Frederick but the flagman, who had been drinking, failed to signal the trailing train and it smashed into the first. Many soldiers were injured but none from the Fortieth. The upshot was that two trainloads of fresh troops that could have been pursuing General Lee's retreating army waited hour after precious hour for tracks to be cleared while the enemy escaped into Virginia. [21]

When the Fortieth finally reached Frederick, sick Privates George Scobie and Charles H. Little had to be left in hospitals. Over the next few days the rest of the regiment, with its division, crisscrossed Maryland pursuing false leads as to the whereabouts of Lee's army. On July 16th and 17th the Fortieth assisted the Fiftieth New York Regiment, an engineer unit, in constructing a pontoon bridge across the Potomac River at Berlin, Maryland. The Fortieth's assistance consisted of moving pontoons from the nearby C and O Canal to the river. While doing this, a pontoon fell and severely injured the ankle of Private Henry Perry of Monument. On July 19th the regiment marched across the bridge and re-entered Virginia. [22]

On August 1st near Warrenton, Virginia, the Fortieth and rest of its division formed a three-sided hollow square. Into the open fourth side shuffled New York soldier Bradford Butler. Convicted of desertion, he stood with arms tied and eyes blindfolded. Then came the ringing volley and he rolled over dead beside his coffin and grave. Chances are good the Sandwich soldiers who witnessed this execution never forgot it. [23]

Five more executions occurred August 27th, near Culpeper, Virginia. Witnessing these were the 20,000 men of Fifth Corps, including James O'Neill, Horace Lovell, Ansel Fifield, James Shevlin, George Haines, Ephraim Nye and the two surviving Alton brothers. From fifteen yards the order to fire was given, forty guns went off in a single report and five deserters fell dead over their coffins. "We…got a good view of everything," wrote a sergeant of Nye's and the Alton's Fifth Battery. The executed were recent immigrants from Europe who barely spoke English and had been hired in Philadelphia as substitutes. Their convictions may have been a miscarriage of justice as they understood little of American military practices. [24]

A better method than substitutes for adding to the army's ranks in 1863 was enlisting blacks, as Hartwell Freeman had done in Louisiana. The first black regiment formed in the north was the Fifty-fourth Massachusetts in spring 1863. In July, Giles M. Pease, son of the former Sandwich abolitionist minister, finished his medical training at Harvard, received an officer commission from the governor and was assigned to the Fifty-fourth as surgeon. [25]

Pease joined the Fifty-fourth at Morris Island, South Carolina, a barri-

*Giles M. Pease, Surgeon of Fifty-fourth Massachusetts Regiment.
Massachusetts Historical Society*

er beach south of Charleston. The campaign to capture that city, begun in April with the navy's ironclad attack on Fort Sumter, had continued into the summer as a joint army-navy operation. To reinforce the campaign, the War Department ordered Gordon's Division to proceed there from Virginia. On August 12th it landed at and set up camp on Folly Island, a sandbar just south of Morris Island.

The Folly Island sandbar, bounded by ocean to the east and marsh to the west, was just a half-mile wide. Packed into this space was Gordon's Division of several thousand men. One company of forty or so soldiers, such as Sandwich's Company I of the Fortieth, lived in fifteen tents. On this spit, where sand found its way into every morsel of food, where drinking water was often brackish and sanitation no better than crude, intestinal disease flourished.

Little wonder the men of the Fortieth often heard the strains of the death march as a comrade was piped to a sandy grave. [26]

From Folly, the men of the Fortieth crossed periodically to Morris Island to assist siege operations against several forts. A steady pounding of them from Union land- and sea-based artillery forced enemy evacuation in early September. Two ironclads that participated in the bombardment were the *Lehigh* with John Ewer, transferred from the *Sabine,* and *Nahant* with Solomon Jones. A shipmate of Jones was Charleston-born African-american Clement Jackson, a twenty-two-year-old coal heaver. His occupation prior to enlistment in July, according to the ship's rolls, was "slave." [27]

Just before the Fortieth came to Folly Island, young drummer Thomas A. Ball of Sandwich's Company I suffered a sunstroke that rendered him unfit for marching. Even so, he remained valuable enough that when the Fortieth arrived at Folly its brigade commander, General Adelbert Ames, appointed Ball to be his mounted orderly. Apparently he and Sandwich's other Civil War orderly, Francis C. Swift of the Twenty-ninth Regiment, embodied qualities that commanding officers looked for in making such appointments. [28]

Swift and the rest of the Twenty-ninth returned to Kentucky from Mississippi in late August and began marching southeastward with their brigade and the rest of 9th Corps for Knoxville. With Colonel Pierce commanding the brigade and Colonel Barnes off duty sick, command of the Twenty-ninth devolved to Major Chipman. Lieutenant Atherton commanded Company D. Driving a brigade ambulance was Private William McDermott, who had lost part of his thumb in an 1861 gun accident. Riding in his ambulance was a comrade he had known since boyhood days in Sandwich, Private Francis Woods. When McDermott passed by Camp Nelson, Kentucky hospital on September 3rd he left the unwell Woods for hospitalization and continued toward Knoxville. [29]

Chipman's task of leading the Twenty-ninth across Kentucky was formidable. Wagons broke down every mile on the hilly, windy, rock-strewn roads. Rivers had to be forded. Supply trains lagged miles behind so that the men often had no food at day's end when they pitched camp. Horses had almost no forage. Amidst all this, Chipman had to supervise from afar repairs to his house in Sandwich. Finding a carpenter there, at least one up to his standards, was a challenge. Dismissive of the half-dozen ones "who call themselves masters of their trade," he advised his wife and mother-in-law to get "a good, modern, trusty and quick carpenter although I don't know of any in Sandwich unless there is someone to stand right over them and tell them what to do." [30]

Further diverting Chipman's focus was the deteriorating health of sixty-year-old Sandwich glassmaker Henry Hunt, father of Louisa Hunt Gibbs (Chipman's sister-in-law) and Company D Private Samuel Hunt. Several times Chipman's wife asked her husband to secure Samuel a furlough. Unfortunately, the only ones available were for twenty days, scarcely enough time to get to Sandwich and back. Overstaying the time, a strong possibility, carried the risk of a desertion charge. Henry Hunt died October 19, 1863 without his son reaching his bedside. [31]

A soldier of Company D who did get to Massachusetts was Sergeant Martin L. Kern Jr. He, Lieutenant Darby and five others of the Twenty-ninth constituted a detail that left September 15th and reached Boston the 21st for duty bringing conscripts to the regiment. Upon arrival, the seven received immediate furloughs and went to their homes. Sergeant Kern, doing double duty as a courier, carried $250 from Chipman and around the 22nd delivered it to his wife. [32]

Less diligent than Kern about his duty was Private Francis McKowen. He enlisted in the Second Massachusetts Cavalry in Boston on August 14th but a month later deserted. A $30 reward posted for his capture was collected in November when he was captured in Pennsylvania. Thereafter he served time at the Forrest Hall Military Prison in Washington. A prisoner of a different sort was Charles Howes of the Eighteenth Regiment. After capture at Gettysburg on July 2nd, he was sent to Belle Isle Prison in Richmond. The day after his September 29th exchange at City Point, Virginia he enjoyed something he had not had in ninety days, "a good cup of coffee." [33]

Around the time Howes was savoring his long awaited coffee, twenty-five-year-old Martha Fisher was working at the Mystic, Connecticut telegraph office when to her surprise a telegram came from her brother Calvin. After a six-year absence, he was coming home to Sandwich! This would not be the usual sort of visit, though. His leg wounded by shellfire at Vicksburg the previous June was inflamed and in desperate need of care.

Martha boarded her brother's train at Mystic and rode with him to Providence where they had to change cars for Boston. To manage it, Fisher had to use two crutches and enlist the assistance of two gentlemen. The train reached Boston late in the day, requiring that Fisher and his sister spend the night at the United States Hotel. To get there, he had to be carried; to get through the night he had to take multiple doses of morphine. Meanwhile, Martha telegraphed younger brother Francis in Sandwich.

Acting on Martha's wired instructions, Francis put a feather bed, pillows and wraps on a covered carriage and had it waiting at the station for his sister and brother's train. When it arrived, Francis entered his brother's car and found him lying across two seats on pillows. With the assistance of two men Francis took him out, placed him on the bed on the carriage and drove him and Martha the six miles to the family home near the Snake Pond part of Sandwich. Through the tireless care of Francis, Martha and older sister Lucinda, and applications of lotions and linseed poultices, the black and blue leg improved enough that in December Fisher was able to return to his regiment in Mississippi. [34]

Soldiers such as Fisher were being tested in 1863. Following the Emancipation Proclamation of early that year the war's opponents, known as Copperheads, tried to shake soldier commitment to it by questioning why they as white men were fighting and dying for blacks. The soldiers never succumbed to this ploy because they hated Copperheads for impeding enlistments.

Copperheads or Peace Democrats opposed both Lincoln and the war whereas War Democrats such as Major Chipman opposed Lincoln but supported the war. As strict constructionists, Copperheads argued that the constitution did not forbid the slave-holding states from seceding. Regarding the war, they believed that a negotiated peace rather than military victory was the best means of reunifying the country. They also opposed the draft and were intensely racist.

Copperhead talk cropped up in Sandwich, apparently in September. This would seem a logical time for it, after the edgy summer of 1863 with its draft, black enlistments and continuing bloodshed and war. Chipman first mentioned it in a September 12th letter to his wife. It can therefore be inferred that she mentioned it in a letter to him of sometime just before that date. Responding to her apparent mention of such murmurings, he retorted in his September 12th letter, "Tell Capt. Sears, Aunt Lucy, Uncle Watson, Charlotte and all my Copperhead friends not to talk too much but 'Wait for the Wagon.' "

Barzillai Sears became a ship captain as a young man around 1827, married Chipman's Aunt Lucy Smith Gibbs in 1852 and around 1856 took command of the ship *William F. Schmidt* that freighted coal and hay between New York, Europe and southern ports. He may have developed Copperhead leanings because of war-produced decline in freight income. His wife Lucy sailed with him and may have wanted the war brought to an end for the same reason. [35]

Watson Freeman Sr., who had an ancestral home in West Sandwich, was born in Boston in 1798 and was a deputy sheriff there in the 1840s. In 1853 Democratic President Franklin Pierce appointed Democrat Freeman as U. S.

Marshall of Massachusetts. At the time he was described as a member of the Codfish Aristocracy and a Hunker Democrat. The latter favored minimizing the slavery issue. Democratic President James Buchanan re-appointed Freeman to his U.S. Marshall position in 1857 but he lost it in 1861 when Republican Abraham Lincoln became president. Thereafter Freeman Sr. lived and farmed in West Sandwich. His daughter Charlotte was age thirty-two and unmarried in 1863. In the September 12th letter, Chipman twitted her that when he got home he and she could fight out their political differences over a bottle of scotch ale. [36]

Shocked about the anti-war position of Watson Freeman Sr. and hopeful he might renounce it, Chipman wrote his wife on October 4th, "Is Uncle Watson as Copperheadish as ever? I should think he would see the error of his ways and mend them." Freeman Sr.'s son Watson Freeman Jr. was apparently as "copperheadish" as his father and sister. He received a navy officer commission in 1862 and served on the ironclad *Sangamon* until he resigned in September 1863. Commenting on the resignation, Chipman wrote, "…if his sympathies are with the other side, he should have resigned long ago, in fact should never have accepted the situation." [37]

Around October 15th Elizabeth Chipman wrote her husband about still more Copperhead talk in Sandwich. In reply, he told her not to argue with those holding such views, specifically with Charles B. Hall, who had been making disloyal statements. Hall's talk rankled Chipman. The way he saw it, it was acceptable for a soldier such as he, exposed to the war's dangers, to criticize the government but reprehensible for civilian Hall, sitting safely at home, to do it. In Democrat Hall's defense, he had reason for displeasure with the Lincoln administration. In 1861 it had removed him for political reasons from his Sandwich postmaster position. [38]

Hall's grumblings were likely not much assuaged by the War Department's call on October 17th for another 300,000 men. The Massachusetts quota was 15,000 men and Sandwich's forty-eight. If quotas were not filled by January 5, 1864, deficiencies would be made up by conscription. In reaction to the call, the conservative and Democratic *Barnstable Patriot* urged local men of Copperhead inclination, and others, to support the government and troops in the field by volunteering. Sandwich held no war rallies or meetings to recruit its quota but rather, like a number of Bay State towns, used commutation money as bounty to entice enlistment. When insufficient number of local volunteers came forward, town selectmen used agents in Boston to hire non-local men ("aliens") to count against the quota, a practice widely used in Massachusetts in this stage of the war. [39]

Meanwhile, war continued to fell soldiers. Near Warrenton, Virginia Private John Chadbourne could not keep up in a march of his Twenty-eighth Massachusetts, straggled, was knocked down by a cavalryman, put in an ambulance, taken to an Alexandria, Virginia hospital, arrested and returned to his regiment under guard. He was court martialed for absenting himself without leave, convicted and sentenced to forfeiture of pay. Intestinal disease brought down Assistant Surgeon Giles M. Pease, camped with his Fifty-fourth Massachusetts at Morris Island, South Carolina, and forced him home to Boston in September. After two months of treatment by his father, a recovered Pease returned to South Carolina, delivering to his regiment twenty-four recruits from the conscript camp in Boston. [40]

Leaving Morris Island for Florida in October was the Twenty-fourth Massachusetts with Sandwich soldiers Watson Adams, James Dalton, Benjamin Ewer, Phineas Gibbs and Phillip Riley. Although they didn't know it, the men of this regiment were one of Florida's first flocks of "snowbirds." They spent the winter of 1863-64 at sunny St. Augustine commanding the post, regaining their health after unsalubrious South Carolina and doing theatrical productions. The men performed many plays at what they called the Olympic Theater. Enlisted men played the male roles, drummer boys the female ones. [41]

There was no acting about illness in the Fortieth Regiment at Folly Island. Three men of Company I, Edward J. Lawrence, Luther T. Hammond and Nathan C. Perry, came down with intestinal disease and in mid-November were patients at Hospital Number Seven in Beaufort, South Carolina. Lawrence died there on Thanksgiving Day. Apparently family or friends brought his body home as he has a marker at the Cataumet Cemetery and none at the Beaufort National Cemetery. His father Edward D. served as first keeper at Wings Neck Lighthouse from 1849 until his removal for political reasons in 1854.

Doing what she could for the sick of the Fortieth was young Helen Gilson of

Helen Gilson. Library of Congress

Boston's Chelsea neighborhood, who arrived at Folly November 9th. In addition to attending the sick, she operated a cookhouse to improve the men's diet and brought a woman's touch to table decorations on Thanksgiving. Although she was gone when Christmas arrived, the men enjoyed the day with a fine dinner and greased pig contest. [42]

Thanksgiving in Sandwich was pleasurable for twenty-two-year-old George L. Haines. Discharged from the army and freed of soldierly restraints, he was enjoying civilian life. On Thanksgiving evening he attended the wedding of William H. H. Weston and Sophia Quinnell. "It is the fashion here in S.," he wrote his sister, "to get married nowadays." Later he went to a ball at Carleton Hall with Mary Harper, daughter of ex-Captain William H. Harper, danced ten dances, stayed out until three in the morning, slept with his breeches on and still made it to work at the the glassworks at the usual 7 a.m. starting time. [43]

With the arrival of December, Sandwich selectmen Charles B. Hall (apparently putting political feelings aside) and Mason White made a little headway with the town quota imposed by the October troop call, enlisting for the First Massachusetts Cavalry Joseph A. Baker and Henry Knippe. Baker was born in Yarmouth and lived at Hyannis until 1862 when he moved to Pocasset to do farm work. In 1863 he worked as a packer at the glassworks. Though his connection to Sandwich was weak, he nevertheless counted against its quota. Knippe, who had already served a nine-month enlistment, had agreed in summer 1863 to work a year for farmer Charles Dillingham for board and $100 but when the October call came, he enlisted. Selectmen Hall and White also enlisted John W. Tinkham who went into the army after two years service in the navy. [44]

The selectmen also enlisted Sandwich African-american laborer George H. Clark, who entered the Fifty-fourth Massachusetts. He went to the conscript camp in Boston which by the end of 1863 held over 100 recruits for Massachusetts's two black regiments, the Fifty-fourth and Fifty-fifth. These recruits, almost totally volunteers, were known while at Boston as the "colored detachment." On special duty with it was African-american recruit James Boyer of Monument. A soldier commanding it was Sergeant Martin L. Kern Jr., still on conscript detail from the Twenty-ninth Regiment. [45]

The Twenty-ninth, minus Kern, ended the year in a woeful state at bleak Blaine's Crossroads, Tennessee outside Knoxville. Rations were short, tents inadequate against wintry winds and uniforms ragged, patched and lice infested. One means of combating the rigors of "Valley Forge," as the camp was called, was with alcohol. Three days before Christmas, Lieutenant Atherton procured some whiskey and with it he and his tent mates "warmed up." [46]

Meanwhile, at Beaufort, South Carolina Hospital Number Seven, Private Luther T. Hammond clung to life. Too weak to write home, a kind ward mate sent a letter for him to his family in Monument. Hammond died on Christmas Day and the next day an escort of soldiers followed his flag-draped coffin to his grave. His death was a severe blow to his widowed mother Zilpha as he had lived with her and since 1857 supported her with his daily wages of around $2.50 earned as a moulder at an iron foundry. He has a marker at Beaufort National Cemetery. [47]

Well west of South Carolina, Lieutenant Samuel H. Allyne Jr. commanded the outpost of San Elizario, Texas. As at his former post in Arizona, Apaches were troublesome. The first duty for Allyne was keeping them from raiding government livestock herds. Far better, advised Allyne's commanding officer, to safeguard the herds than make "a hard march in search of the savages." As it turned out, Apaches were the least of Allyne's concerns. Two days before New Year's Day, he rode out on a scout with his men near San Elizario during which Private Robert Kerr of Allyne's company shot the lieutenant in the back and killed him. Kerr fled but was captured and arrested at Socorro, New Mexico Territory and brought back to Texas for court martial. Found guilty, he was executed by firing squad in Franklin, Texas on March 20, 1864. [48]

Allyne's death stood out for its senselessness but was otherwise no different from that of Sandwich's seven other soldiers and sailors who had died in1863. Each was a beloved father, son, husband or brother. The *Barnstable Patriot* editor, in a reflective frame of mind at year's end, wrote, "…the nation has been a deep sufferer in the loss of very many thousands of her fathers and sons, yet she 'still lives.' " Not only did the nation live, the prospect for victory in the war was promising. Clouding that prospect, however, was an implacable enemy that still had left plenty of fight. [49]

Chapter Nine:
John, Did You Catch It Bad?—
January to May 1864

With the arrival of New Year's Day 1864, the war stretched into its fourth year. For the cold and hungry men of the Twenty-ninth Massachusetts, the day was not one of holiday cheer but just another to muddle through at their Tennessee "Valley Forge." To augment the meager ration of a few ounces of flour per man per day Lieutenant Ayling, in command of Company D, sent out Private James Ball to forage. He described Ball as "a big good-natured Irishman with a big round head" who is "not much as a soldier, but as a forager he is great." A native of County Fermanagh Ireland, he came to Sandwich as a twenty-three-year-old in 1859 and worked there as a laborer until he enlisted in 1861. [1]

Amidst the privations, the thirty men remaining from the "first Sandwich Company" (Company D of the Twenty-ninth) were called on to make a major decision—enlistment for another three years. Twenty-four declined and were assigned to finish their three years in the Thirty-sixth Massachusetts. Reenlisting in the Twenty-ninth to perhaps see the war through to its finish were James Ball, Perez Eldridge, David Hoxie and Joseph Madigan. A sad January day it was when those who went to the Thirty-sixth said goodbye to those who stayed with the Twenty-ninth. [2]

Though far from Massachusetts, the men of the Twenty-ninth knew about its October 1863 troop call and January 5th draft deadline. "About the draft," wrote Private O. S. Stearns of Company G, "I will say that I hope every Copperhead in Massachusetts will be drafted—yes! Conscripted and be compelled to serve. All who oppose the draft, likewise." Stearns's hope was not realized because volunteering, at least in Sandwich's congressional district, proceeded well enough that the draft deadline was deferred. [3]

A man from Sandwich who volunteered in the October 1863 call but was credited to nearby Yarmouth was James P. Atkins. He was born and grew up in Spring Hill and in 1850 was employed as a stage driver. He moved to Hyannis around 1852, became a brakeman for the Cape Cod Railroad and was living in West Yarmouth when he volunteered for a new regiment, the Fifty-eighth Massachusetts.

While men in Massachusetts were volunteering, Lieutenant Ayling was adapting to command of a company of just four men. In early February he promoted one of them, Private Madigan, to sergeant. Described by the lieutenant as "a bright little fellow," Madigan was useful in a tight spot. After the regiment made a long march in the rain, Ayling's tent was unavailable so he crawled into Madigan's for the night. Another of Ayling's men, Irishman Ball, was first rate when out foraging but troublesome in camp. He bullied Ayling's black servant boy Frank to the point that Frank would draw a knife and Ayling would have to step in to break up the ruckus. [4]

Another problem required the action of regimental commander Colonel Barnes. Stray horses and "muley plugs" roamed about the camp perimeter, and enlisted men and servant boys such as Frank often jumped on them for a joy ride. "This practice will be stopped," ordered the colonel, adding that enlisted men caught doing it would be punished. The officer's horses, including Major Chipman's, suffered much in the hard winter. Detailed to care for them was another of Ayling's men, Private David Hoxie. He had worked for the Boyden Livery in Sandwich before the war and because of it had equine experience. [5]

Many Civil War horses pulled carriages in their pre-army days. Carriage painter George F. Bruce came to Sandwich around 1860, married local woman Lucy A. Smith and in 1861 was one of the original fifty-eight men who went off to war as the "first Sandwich Company." In July 1862 he was a medical assistant on the hospital steamer *Commodore* and in August was appointed a hospital steward and assigned to the general hospital in Madison, Indiana. In January 1864 he asked to be relieved of his steward position in order to return to field duties, but his request was not acted on and he remained at the hospital. [6]

A hospital patient rather than steward was Benjamin Fuller, one of the twenty-four who entered the Thirty-sixth Regiment. He was admitted to Knoxville's Hospital Number Five February 16th and while there received as visitor another of the twenty-four, Sergeant William H. Woodward. Although Fuller was discharged from the hospital March 21st (so that he could go north with his regiment), he was not well. Consumption ate away at his lungs so that when he was discharged from the service and arrived in Sandwich, Woodward thought he looked feeble and unlikely to live long. Indeed, he was soon dead. His death brought his widowed mother Dorcas much financial and emotional pain. [7]

Sandwich's "second company," Company I of the Fortieth Massachusetts Regiment, was still camped at Folly Island, South Carolina as 1864 began. Of the forty-one men of the town who were part of the company when it formed in 1862, fifteen were now gone to death, disability discharge, resignation or transfer. The remaining twenty-six were about to undergo a major change.

Early in 1864, President Lincoln approved an expedition to Florida that had several objectives, one of which was establishment of a loyal state government. General Quincy Gilmore, in command of Union troops in South Carolina, needed an additional cavalry regiment for the expedition and decided the best means of obtaining it was by having his infantry regiments compete for the choice duty. The winner was the Fortieth Regiment. Little did it seem to matter that many of its men had never ridden a horse. [8]

January 16th was a big day on Folly Island. At the rat-a-tat of a drum, the men of the Fortieth struck their tents, assembled and with band playing and banners flying, marched to the boat landing, took transports and crossed to Hilton Head Island. For the next few weeks, they rode up and down its beaches drilling on their new mounts. In a review just before their February 4th departure for Florida, General Gilmore complimented the men on what seemed an amazing transformation to cavalry proficiency. Unknown to him, many of them were secured to their saddles with gun slings. [9]

The 8,000-man expedition force consisting of one mounted and three infantry brigades landed unopposed at Jacksonville February 7th. Attached to the Fortieth's Mounted or Light Brigade was the Third (Independent) Battalion of the First Massachusetts Cavalry, with William W. Phinney. Within the infantry brigades was the black Fifty-fourth Massachusetts with Surgeon Giles Pease and Private George H. Clark. Altogether, twenty-nine men of Sandwich were in the expedition.

The force moved inland from Jacksonville, initially encountering light resistance. On February 17th the men of the Fortieth exchanged their muzzle loading rifles for the Seventh New Hampshire's Spencer repeating carbines. Resistance increased as the force penetrated more deeply into Florida. In an ill-advised attack of February 20th on well-entrenched enemy at the settlement of Olustee, the federals were defeated and driven back to Jacksonville. [10]

West of Jacksonville on March 1st, a probe by elements of the Mounted Brigade collided with Confederate cavalry. In the hard skirmish that ensued, Fortieth Private William Manley of North Sandwich was shot in the left arm. Machinist Manley, father of four, was first hospitalized in Jacksonville and later taken to South Carolina on the hospital steamer *Cosmopolitan*. Only after nine months of recuperation did he return to the regiment. [11]

Since the Fortieth and First Massachusetts Cavalry were in the same brigade in Florida, men of the two units mingled. On March 16th, Nathan C. Perry of the Fortieth conversed with his Monument neighbor and boyhood friend William W. Phinney of the First Cavalry. An hour later Phinney went out on a scout and was captured. [12]

The winter was as hard for horses in Florida as it was for those in Tennessee.

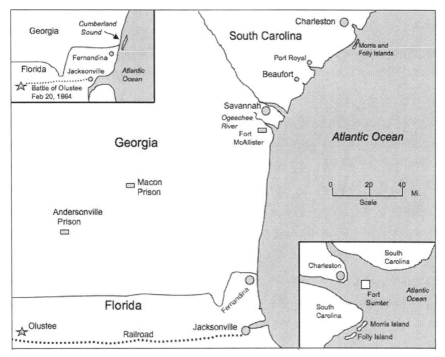

Map 5, South Carolina, Georgia and Florida 1862-1865

On March 19th the colonel of the Fortieth informed his superior that his regiment's horses had received their ration of hay (around twelve pounds per head daily) just once in the past ten days. A month later, "with much regret," the men turned in their horses. With orders for Virginia, not as cavalry but as infantry, they would be foot soldiers again. As for Florida, the Union expedition there that had begun so auspiciously came to an "inglorious termination." The state would remain in the Confederacy. [13]

In Tennessee, brigade after brigade of 9th Corps began leaving Knoxville and vicinity March 21st for the intermediate destination of Cincinnati. One brigade, commanded by Colonel Barnes, consisted of the Twenty-ninth Massachusetts and German-speaking Forty-sixth New York. Another contained the Thirty-sixth Massachusetts and Seventy-ninth New York "highlanders." Men who were shoeless or sick went on the cars to Louisville, then river steamer to the Queen City. The others, many with but remnants of shoes, marched to Cincinnati over the grueling 200 miles of Kentucky mountains. [14]

Major Chipman commanded the Twenty-ninth for the cross-Kentucky trek. The march had no wagons, only mules to carry regimental baggage and food. On some nights it snowed as the men slept on the ground. Roads were at times so steep, officers such as Chipman had to dismount and lead their horses. When the 3,200 men of 9th Corps marched into Cincinnati April 1st, their slog completed, a local newspaper described the men as "very much embrowned" and looking like "real old veterans." While there, the officers lodged at a hotel, the men at an army barracks. Also while there, Private James Cook, who had been hospitalized in Kentucky for some months, rejoined his comrades. [15]

Left behind at Knoxville when 9th Corps departed was John T. Collins. He received an officer commission with the First U. S. Colored Heavy Artillery, making him the fourth Sandwich soldier to command black troops. He recruited one of the first men to enlist in his new unit, twenty-year-old farmer George Roberts of Kentucky. [16]

At Cincinnati, the paths of the Thirty-sixth and Twenty-ninth Regiments diverged. The Thirty-sixth, with twenty-four men of Sandwich, took the cars to and through Pittsburgh and Baltimore and on April 7th arrived at Annapolis where General Burnside was re-organizing his 9th Corps divisions, brigades and regiments. Six days later General Grant, new Union commander of the Army of the Potomac, reviewed the corps. Back at Cincinnati the Twenty-ninth, with six men of Sandwich, hung around awaiting the paymaster. Finally paid off, they boarded the cars April 7th, passed through Cleveland and Buffalo, reached Boston April 9th and on the 11th were dismissed for a thirty-day furlough home, a reward for re-enlisting. [17]

A Sandwich soldier who would never see home by furlough or otherwise was murder victim Samuel H. Allyne Jr. "Alas," lamented his grieving father, "we shall see his face no more in this world." In other matters around town, Attorney Whittemore recorded in his diary that he hired Ann McAlaney to work at $1.25 per week for his family. She was a sister of Private John McAlaney who had declined re enlistment and was serving out his three years in the Thirty-sixth Massachusetts. Whittemore also noted that fourteen-year-old Ann Reilly (Riley), sister of Philip Reilly of the Twenty-fourth Massachusetts and found to be leading a "vagrant life," was sent to the Lancaster Industrial School for Girls in central Massachusetts. [18]

First Lieutenant Obed M. Fish.
The Horse Soldier

Meanwhile, the war went on. At Plymouth, North Carolina a Confederate ironclad steamed down the Roa-

Naval ship Southfield *sinking near Plymouth, NC April 1864.* Harpers Weekly

noke River and on April 19th rammed the Union gunboat *Southfield*. Second class fireman Caleb H. Perry of Monument and the sinking *Southfield* saved himself by climbing aboard a nearby vessel. Less fortunate was former Sandwich saloon and restaurant keeper Obed M. Fish, an officer of the Second Massachusetts Heavy Artillery at Plymouth. He and many of his fellow artillerymen were captured.[19]

While Fish trudged toward a southern prison, a more spirited movement began at Annapolis, where 9th Corps's soldiers took up a line of march. On April 25th its column of infantrymen, wagons, ambulances, artillery batteries, cavalry squadrons and trailing herds of cattle tramped up Pennsylvania Avenue in Washington under the reviewing eye of President Lincoln, who watched from a balcony of Willard's Hotel while throngs on sidewalks below cheered the passing ranks of blue. Within the long procession was the Thirty-sixth Massachusetts and within it Private John McAlaney and his twenty-three comrades of the "first Sandwich company."[20]

Of great interest to the spectators along Washington's streets was a new division of black troops attached to 9th Corps, the first large body of such soldiers to march through Washington. To see these men and their unrestrained joy and exuberance as they marched before the man who had made them free brought tears to the eyes of many in the crowd. In command of the division was General Edward Ferraro.[21]

Ninth Corps's men crossed the Potomac, marched westward and on April

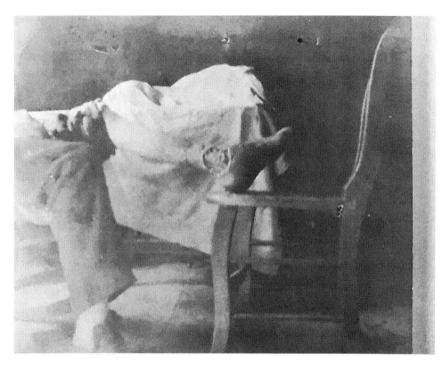

Ulcerated ankle of Francis C. Swift, many years after war. Wound due to gunshot at Battle of Wilderness May 1864. NA

28th camped along railroad tracks at Bristow Station, Virginia. Four days later the new Fifty-eighth Massachusetts Regiment arrived and joined the Thirty-sixth's brigade in 9th Corps. Sandwich men in the Fifty-eighth were James Atkins, Thomas B. Bourne, Roland Holway, Samuel Marvel and John Tinkham.

An advance westward May 5th from Bristow Station brought the men of 9th Corps within hearing of the deep boom of artillery fire emanating from a brushy expanse to the south. Grant had found Lee's army and was taking the fight to him in what would later be called the Battle of the Wilderness. In it Thomas B. Bourne of Monument and brother of transport ship captain Henry A. Bourne was captured. Also captured—for the second time—was Horace Lovell, whose Eighteenth Massachusetts was still attached to 5th Corps. Wounded were Sandwich soldiers Joseph W. Eaton and Francis C. Swift. Eaton, shot through the body, was hospitalized in Washington where he remained until July while Swift, shot in the ankle, was transported by the hospital steamer *Connecticut t*o Washington for a hospital stay lasting into June. [22]

To extricate his army from the confusing Wilderness terrain and continue

Samuel M. Marvel. Photograph of Around May 1864 when Marvel promoted to sergeant. HDS

moving south, Grant maneuvered it over roads that led to Spotsylvania Court House. Spearheading the drive to reach this vital intersection was 5th Corps. Unfortunately, Lee discerned Grant's intent and had his men block the route with a barricade of logs on a low rise later called Laurel Hill. On the morning of May 8th, regiments of 5th Corps including Lieutenant James O'Neill's Irish Ninth Massachusetts assaulted the hill. Born in County Cork, Ireland, O'Neill married Ellen Quinn in 1852 and around 1855 moved with his family and in-laws from Boston to Sandwich where several children were born. He enlisted in 1861, worked his way up from private to lieutenant and in February 1864 came to Boston to see family he had not seen since enlistment. He returned to his regiment in March and on May 8th died leading his company up Laurel Hill. [23]

First Lieutenant James O'Neill.
USAHEC

On May 9th, a day after O'Neill's death, young Henry Knippe, who had chosen in the troop call of October 1863 to enlist for the cavalry over working on Charles Dillingham's farm, was part of a mounted force under General Philip Sheridan that set out to destroy railroads serving Lee's army. Sheridan's column of 10,000 horsemen riding four abreast stretched nearly thirteen miles. Late that day, as darkness approached in unfamiliar territory, Knippe and nineteen others of his First Massachusetts Cavalry comrades mistakenly rode into enemy lines and were captured. Thus, as of May 9th, six men of Sandwich—Knippe, William Phinney, Obed Fish, Thomas Bourne, Horace Lovell and James Gaffney—were in or headed for prisoner of war camps. [24]

The First Massachusetts Cavalry captives spent three weeks at Libby Prison in Richmond and on June 8th they and other captives were crammed sixty-seven men to a boxcar for the six-day trip south to Georgia prisons. The cars had no seats and men could not get off. Nature's calls had to be attended to in the cars and waste thrown out. The stench in them was overpowering. [25]

Early on May 12th, Ninth Corps attacked a protrusion or salient in the Confederate line at Spotsylvania Court House. As John McAlaney and his Thirty-sixth Regiment pressed forward, a minie ball tore through McAlaney's canteen and left side, doubling him up. Francis Woods, close by at the time, asked his old friend and comrade, "John, did you catch it bad?" to which he responded, "Bad enough, I guess." Another friend and comrade, James Cook, carried McAlaney to the rear. Although sore and "pretty well used up" by his wound, McAlaney managed to stay with his unit and out of the hospital. [26]

Killed at Spotsylvania was Ireland-born James Ward who came to Sandwich in the 1850s with younger brother John after their parents died in Boston. The brothers roomed at John and Sarah Montague's boarding house and James worked at the glassworks. The twenty-one-year-old was just days short of completing his three-year enlistment.

With the death of Ward and hospitalization of others of the twenty-four men of Sandwich who left Annapolis in April with the Thirty-sixth Regiment in 9th Corps, eighteen remained after the May 12th battle. Four days later, Corps commander General Burnside wrote a pass for these eighteen and other men with expiring enlistments to proceed to Belle Plain Landing for Potomac River passage to Washington. They left their camp May 17th and reached Washington the next day. [27]

In Massachusetts, the thirty-day furlough of the Twenty-ninth Regiment ended. Major Chipman took the morning train of May 15th from Sandwich to Boston and the next day departed with his regiment for Washington. As luck would have it, its arrival there coincided with that of the eighteen Sandwich men coming north from Spotsylvania. "I saw Sam today," Chipman wrote his wife May 19th, referring to her brother-in-law Private Samuel Hunt, one of the eighteen. "He was well but looking very thin." Also while in Washington, Chipman and his friend Colonel Barnes visited and took tea with Eveline Freeman Clark, daughter of Watson Freeman Sr. and husband of U. S. Capitol architect Edward Clark. [28]

Chipman, Barnes and the regiment went down the Potomac to Belle Plain Landing where on May 21st ten junior officers of the Twenty-ninth who had served three years, including Lieutenants Atherton and Ayling, elected to muster out of the service in compliance with an order from the War Department. Chipman and Barnes disagreed with the order, thinking it ambiguous, and also thinking it wrong to leave the army during active

Lieutenant James H. Atherton.
USAHEC

operations. Their request for clarification on the order went through channels to the War Department but final disposition on it is unknown. Atherton, Ayling and the eight other officers returned to Washington May 22nd, reached Boston the 24th and were mustered out the 26th by a perplexed mustering out officer. [29]

As the Twenty-ninth minus the ten officers made its way south from Belle Plain toward Grant's army, it camped near General Ferraro's black division that had marched through Washington April 25th. "We are now about 8 or 10 miles from the Front encamped near Gen. Ferraro's Division of Niggers," wrote Chipman May 26th. "It seems that none of them have as yet fired a gun notwithstanding all the talk in the Newspapers about their fighting so savagely." Ferraro's men had indeed not fired a gun nor fought in battle; kept at the rear of the army guarding supply trains, they had had opportunity to do neither. [30]

The next day, May 27th, was ordinary for Chipman but special for the eighteen men of Sandwich he had seen in Washington eight days earlier. When they along with Lieutenant Atherton stepped off the cars at Sandwich depot that Friday morning, the town was ready for them. A procession headed by Charles B. Hall and William H. Harper of the "second Sandwich company" escorted them up Jarves Street onto Main. Lining the streets were flag-waving school children. At a stand erected near the post office, dignitaries delivered speeches and the band performed "Home Sweet Home." After "Johnny Comes Marching Home" concluded the ceremonies, Atherton put the eighteen men through a dress parade exercise (Table 3). The crowd then retired to the town hall where all enjoyed a splendid meal. Streamers suspended from the ceiling bore names of battles in which the eighteen men had fought, such as Antietam and Fredericksburg. [31]

Table 3
The Eighteen Returning Men [32]

1. Badger, George W.	10. Hunt, Samuel W.
2. Bumpus, Frank G.	11. McAlaney, John
3. Cook, James	12. McDermott, William
4. Cox, James	13. Robbins, Caleb T.
5. Dalton, Christopher B.	14. Russell, Peter
6. Donnelly, Edward	15. Woods, Francis
7. Fagan, John	16. Woods, James H.
8. Guiney, James	17. Woodward, William H.
9. Hoxie, Charles H.	18. Wright, Anderson

That night the festivities resumed with the ladies of town putting on a ball that was "the largest ever held in Sandwich." Lieutenant Ayling accepted an invitation to attend, arrived on the afternoon train and stayed up until 4 a.m. dancing in what he termed "a pretty lively affair." [33]

To replace these eighteen men and thousands of others across the North leaving service, the War Department issued troop calls such as the one of October 1863. In Massachusetts, however, volunteering fell short of meeting quotas. To deal in part with the shortfall, state officials recruited more than 1,000 black men for the black Fifth Massachusetts Cavalry, almost all from outside the state, in the period January to May 1864. Sandwich received credit for six of these men, two of whom were seamen born in the West Indies. [34]

Despite enlistments of black men and volunteering, deficiencies remained in Massachusetts quotas. Accordingly a second Bay State draft was held in May in which eighteen men of Sandwich received their notices. One was John McAlaney's factory mate Cornelius Donovan while two others were bandleader James H. Dalton and newlywed William H. H. Weston. A fourth, amazingly, was young drummer Thomas Davis who had received a medical discharge from his Twentieth Regiment after nearly dying of wounds at Antietam. His military service of less than two years made him draft-liable. None of the eighteen were held to service but whether this was because of exemptions, procurement of substitutes or selectmen-obtained outside credits is unknown. [35]

A man of Sandwich who did enter service in May was James McNulty. His enlistment, however, probably didn't count against the Sandwich quota because he enlisted in Boston. Irishman McNulty, younger brother of Peter of the "the first Sandwich company," received $325 in bounty money for enlisting and entered the Second Massachusetts Cavalry. In a sense, this was a re-enlistment for him since he deserted in 1862 after collecting bounty from entering the Forty-first Massachusetts Infantry. [36]

The War Department's need for troops in the spring of 1864 was great because it was feeding them into three large offensives. The first was Grant battling Lee in central Virginia, the second Sherman pushing south from Tennessee into Georgia and the third General Benjamin Butler targeting Richmond from the lower James River. It was to the latter campaign that the Fortieth Massachusetts proceeded when it left South Carolina with orders for Virginia.

General Butler's 23,000-man James River force steamed up the river on transports and on May 6th went ashore south of Richmond at Bermuda Hundred. Over the next nine days it advanced slowly toward the city, slowly enough to allow the Confederates to shift troops to a riverside cliff known as Drewry's Bluff.

From out of the early morning fog of May 16th Butler's soldiers discerned, first faintly then unmistakably, the knee-buckling rebel yell. The onrushing enemy soon turned the Federal line and forced Butler's men back to Bermuda Hundred in defeat. The Fortieth's casualties of more than fifty killed and wounded was its most costly battlefield loss to date. During the battle, Fortieth soldier and band member George T. Lloyd performed the customary duty of musicians at such times, that of stretcher bearer. That duty was taxing at Drewry's Bluff because the wounded had to be carried as much as two miles over and through stump-covered fields and ravines. In some cases no stretchers were available and the bandsmen had to improvise and use blankets as litters. [37]

Lloyd might have helped carry from the battlefield two wounded men of Sandwich, Dean Swift and Benjamin Chamberlain. Both were admitted to the Hampton, Virginia Hospital May 19th. Chamberlain's gunshot wounded arm kept him out of action the next four months. Far more serious was Swift's gun shot wound in the leg. He died June 22nd and has markers at Hampton National Cemetery and Sagamore burial ground. His personal effects were haversack, canteen, looking glass, tobacco box and fifty cents money. [38]

Wounded a few days after Swift and Chamberlain was Fortieth soldier Charles E. Ellis of West Sandwich. With shattered right forearm, he was admitted May 23rd to Point Lookout, Maryland Hospital where twenty-one bone fragments were removed. Still a patient there five months later, he asked the hospital chaplain to see if he might be transferred to a hospital in Massachusetts, a request the hospital surgeon refused. Still there in February 1865 and arm wound a running sore, he wrote Secretary of War Edwin Stanton about the transfer and again the surgeon denied the request. Ellis remained at Point Lookout until his army discharge in June 1865. [39]

Arriving in Virginia from Florida and joining the Fortieth's division in the James River campaign was the Twenty-fourth Massachusetts, with Sandwich soldiers Watson Adams, Benjamin Ewer, Phillip Riley, James Dalton and Phineas Gibbs. That regiment, like the Fortieth, sustained heavy casualties at Drewry's Bluff but its five men from Sandwich were spared.

As May ended, General Grant's telegraphed message from the front, that "I propose to fight it out on this line if it takes all summer," was grabbing the attention of the nation. A New York newspaper used the line to open an editorial and the *Barnstable Patriot* borrowed and featured it in its May 24th issue. Grant, assured the editorial, "has set his strong, imperturbable face; he will not give way…" The Union had the man it had long needed. It was time to support him and see the war through to victory.

Chapter Ten:
My Greatest and Best Friend—
June to December 1864

After Spotsylvania and Laurel Hill, Grant maneuvered his army south and east. Lee countered so that the two armies paralleled each other along a diagonal front east of Richmond at the five-road intersection of Cold Harbor. Needing reinforcements, Grant summoned 18th Army Corps (within which was the Fortieth Massachusetts) from General Butler's army at Bermuda Hundred. Embarking on transport vessels, the Fortieth's men steamed to White House Landing where on June 1st they began a thirteen-mile march to Cold Harbor. Musician George T. Lloyd of the Fortieth's band called the march, done under a merciless sun over a road where dust rose like flour with each step and turned blue uniforms yellow "one of the hardest…we ever had." [1]

Upon arrival at Cold Harbor, Lloyd looked across an immense field into a radiant setting sun backlighting the enemy's colors. Among them might have been those of Leonard Hinds's Seventeenth North Carolina Regiment. To cheer on his exhausted men, the colonel of the Fortieth ordered its band to play "Yankee Doodle" in quick time. That seemed to revive them, reported horn player Lloyd. Attached to the Fortieth's 18th Corps at Cold Harbor was an artillery brigade, within which was Isaac Phinney of Battery L, Fourth U.S. Artillery, now commanded by Major Chipman's friend Henry B. Beecher. [2]

Around 6 p.m. of June 1st, the tired men of the Fortieth received orders to charge and and "we went at it," as Lloyd put it, and the air was soon filled with the cries of the wounded and dying. As stretcher bearer, Lloyd worked until well after midnight carrying men to the field hospital. A night later he returned to see some of the wounded. While they were being served beef tea, a hospital steward began to sing "Annie Laurie." Others joined in and before long the song was heard over the entire battlefield. "Tears ran from the eyes of everyone," recalled Lloyd, "and I have never heard that song since that time but what I thought of that night at Cold Harbor." [3]

North of the Fortieth and Battery L in the Cold Harbor battle line were Major Chipman and the Twenty-ninth Massachusetts, fresh from furlough in the Bay State. In repelling an attack by Georgia troops the evening of June 1st

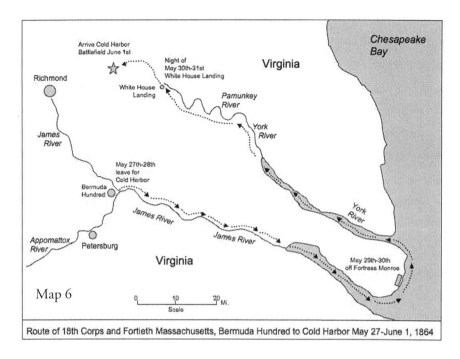

Route of 18th Corps and Fortieth Massachusetts, Bermuda Hundred to Cold Harbor May 27-June 1, 1864

the regiment sustained casualties, one of them Perez Eldridge. "He was shot through the arm," wrote Chipman in a letter home. After several hospital stays, Eldridge recovered sufficiently to return to the regiment. [4]

Grant ordered a general assault at Cold Harbor June 3rd but a waiting, well-entrenched enemy repelled the federals in one the bloodiest Union defeats of the war. Five Cape Cod soldiers were killed, the most ever in one day for the Cape in all its military history. All thirty or so Sandwich soldiers who participated survived. The green Fifty-eighth Massachusetts suffered heavily. On June 4th Samuel Marvel of Monument wrote, "Yesterday we had another battle. It was the worst we have had yet…there were 91 killed and wounded in our Regiment." [5]

The many casualties required lots of surgeons. Physician John Bachelder, who had practiced at Monument in the 1850s, left Massachusetts at the beginning of June with orders to report to the army medical director in Washington. In the next two months he served as a contract surgeon at Washington's Armory Square Hospital, at 9th Corps Hospital near Petersburg and on the hospital transport ship *New World*. [6]

Wounded a day after the June 3rd Cold Harbor battle—and in an unusual way—was Pocasset soldier Leonard E. Howard of the First Maine Heavy Artillery. While cleaning rust off his gun, it discharged sending a round through his left foot. He was hospitalized in Washington where his bed card listed his

Hospital Number Bed 11 Ward 3

Name Leonard E. Howard
Age 26 Nativity American
Married or Single Single
Residence Abbott Maine
Post Office address of wife or nearest relative. Mrs Lewis N Barlow Middletown Conn—
Rank Corp. Co. E Regiment 1, Me, H.A.
When admitted June 8th 1864
From what source the Fields

Diagnosis: *(in surgical cases, state explicitly seat and character of wound or injury.)*

563

Finley G. H.
Washington, D.C.

On what occasion wounded Coale Harbor
Date June 3d
Nature of missile or weapon Minnie ball

Leonard E. Howard bed card at Finley Hospital Washington. NA

sister Bathsheba Howard Barlow of Middletown, Connecticut as his nearest relative. Their brother, Charles L. Howard, died in Union Navy service in 1863. [7]

James P. Atkins survived his Fifty-eighth Regiment's carnage of June 3rd only to be shot and killed while on picket duty June 8th. His death left a widow Helen Davis Atkins and two fatherless children in Yarmouth and grieving father in Spring Hill. Atkins has two markers, one at Cold Harbor and a second at Cape Cod's Centerville South Congregational Church Cemetery that reads, "He died a Christian soldier." [8]

Through the night of June 12th-13th Grant pulled his army out of the foul trenches of the Cold Harbor line and sent it south. The night's march for the men of the Fortieth Massachusetts was one "never to be forgotten." Rapid travel in high humidity and suffocating dust encased the men in an "earthen armor" blessedly removed with a bath in the river at White House Landing. From there, they and the rest of 18th Corps moved against the important railroad city of Petersburg. In action there on June 18th, John M. Perry received a shell wound in the left arm. A month later, with arm still unhealed, surgeons at a Philadelphia hospital amputated it. [9]

Ninth Corps's Twenty-ninth Massachusetts, with Major Chipman at times in command, filed out of the Cold Harbor trenches at 7:30 p.m. of June 12th, crossed two rivers and on June 16th days arrived at Petersburg. The next day its men charged across a one-half-mile-wide oats/cornfield but were repulsed, taking heavy casualties. When Chipman learned the regimental colors had been left on the field he, Sergeant Madigan and several other men retrieved them by unclasping its staff from the death grip of Sergeant Major William F. Willis of the Twenty-ninth, all while under heavy fire. [10]

Soon after Major Chipman made his courageous colors retrieval, he was ordered to take command of the Fourteenth New York Heavy Artillery, in the same brigade as his Twenty-ninth Massachusetts. Ever a stickler for following orders, Chipman hung back on this one. For one thing, the Fourteenth's books were in disorder. For another, his bond with his Twenty-ninth was understandably strong. Finally, he had chronic diarrhea. A surgeon's certificate backed him up on that, in case questions arose. [11]

The Fourteenth New York Heavy Artillery Regiment was raised in central New York in the second half of 1863. Many men enlisted in it under the impression they could not be transferred to infantry and could therefore ride out the war in a safe, comfortable army post. The regiment's men left Park Barracks in New York for Washington in late April expecting to garrison forts there but General Grant needed men to shoulder muskets rather than serve fortress guns and ordered artillerymen such as the Fourteenth to infantry duty in his army in Virginia. [12]

With Washington's artillerymen transferred to Grant in Virginia and its defenses unmanned, the War Department instructed Governor Andrew to forward companies stationed at Massachusetts coastal forts. The companies vigorously protested this move since they had been promised when recruited that they would remain in the Bay State. They should have known that in war promises are both easily made and easily broken. Thus, on May 3, 1864 Sandwich Privates Frederick Norris, George and Seth Gibbs and the rest of their Sixth Unattached heavy artillery company marched out of their New Bedford fort and sailed unhappily for Washington. [13]

After Confederates menaced Washington in July, Massachusetts was asked to raise troops for 100 days service to defend it and other places. The men raised were in several regiments, one of them the Fifth Massachusetts. Lying about their ages to enlist in it were Sands Chipman, Charles Clarke, Alvin Howes and Joseph Phinney. Since they feared their boyish physiques would make the mustering officer reject them, they stuffed hay under their clothing to increase their bulk. All four passed muster. Chipman, Howes and Phinney were from Spring Hill, Clarke from Sandwich Village. Clarke and his brother William F. were Sandwich's youngest Civil War soldiers, both age fourteen at enlistment. They were brothers of Sandwich marine Franklin R. J. Clarke. Their regiment did guard duty at forts in Baltimore. [14]

The Confederates menaced more than Washington in July. The whaling bark *Golconda,* with crewman Cranston W. Nickerson of Monument, was captured and burned off the New Jersey coast by the Confederate raider *Florida* while returning to New Bedford from a five-year cruise. Union blockading vessels sometimes pursued the raiders but more often they went after blockade runners. After the blockading steamer *Metacomet* captured the blockade runner *Donegal* off Florida, a prize crew that included Alonzo Clement of Pocasset brought her to Philadelphia.[15]

Also in July, furniture maker Samuel H. Allyne wrote of two young men of Sandwich, Robert R. Boyden and Gideon Wing. The former, a twenty-five-year-old son of livery and expressman William E. Boyden, died of consumption June 30th. Three days later Allyne wrote, "The bell of the Universe Church is now tolling whilst the body of Robert Boyden is being conveyed to the tomb." He is buried in Sandwich's Bayview Cemetery. Wing, a Quaker of Spring Hill and eldest son of educator Paul Wing, enlisted in the Seventh Indiana Cavalry in that state on December 1st of 1863 and on December 13th was in Sandwich to be married. "The next day," wrote Allyne, "he started for the scene of conflict. I took him by the hand the morning of his departure. 'I go,' he said, 'from a sense of duty.' I said, 'May God bless you…and return you in safety.' We received the tidings a few days since that he was slain in battle." [16]

Gideon Wing moved, possibly in 1862, from Sandwich to Madison Township of Montgomery County, Indiana where lived Quaker relative Allen Davis, a brother of Wing's paternal grandmother Elizabeth Davis Wing. Gideon Wing's reason for enlisting in Indiana is unknown but it may be that his Sandwich Friends Meeting was more opposed to Quaker military service than that of his relative in Indiana. Wing died in a cavalry battle in Mississippi in June of 1864. [17]

While Sandwich was mourning Boyden and Wing in early July, Major Chipman's diarrhea improved and he accepted command of the Fourteenth New York Heavy Artillery at Petersburg. Army life there in the summer of 1864, from command down to the greenest private, was one of grim, filthy trench warfare. In a letter of July 25th, Chipman gave some idea of the conditions: "We had a terrible 'rain storm' last night. It rained hard all night. Our trenches were filled with water. Our men were obliged to stand in water nearly up to their knees all night." [18]

Worse than Union trenches were Confederate ones. Leonard Hinds served in them in his Seventeenth North Carolina Regiment of General Robert Hoke's division. A soldier of that division wrote, "Seldom are men called upon to endure as much as was required of the troops who occupied the trenches of Petersburg during…June, July and August." Apparently having endured enough, Hinds received a pass from his colonel July 18th to go to Petersburg, failed to return and on July 24th gave himself up to some New York cavalry at Suffolk, Virginia. He signed an oath of allegiance to the United States, enlisted in the Fifteenth New Jersey Regiment and holds the distinction of having fought on both sides in the war. [19]

Incessant sharpshooter and mortar fire made Petersburg an inferno. "The [sharpshooter's] bullets," wrote Chipman, "whizz by quite often sounding very much like 'Bumblebees' flying by your ears only passing much faster." Mortars could loft a shell that would explode over an enemy trench. "They don't do much damage usually," he told his wife, then added less reassuringly, "but now and then one bursts just right…" [20]

Pocasset soldier Charles N. Godfrey, serving with the Eleventh New Hampshire Regiment, was shot in the shoulder at Petersburg July 6th and taken to the rear where a surgeon probed the wound and removed bone fragments. Five days later he was one of 700 sick and wounded soldiers packed into the hospi-

Oath of Allegiance signed by ex-Confederate Soldier Leonard Hinds near Norfolk, Virginia in July 1864. NA

tal steamer *Atlantic* for a thirty-hour passage to New York. At a hospital there, his bed card listed older sister Louisa Barlow as his closest relative. The death of Charles's mother Mercy in 1859 had left him an orphan. He died July 19th and is buried in the Cypress Hills National Cemetery in Brooklyn. [21]

Another July 19th death was that of forty-two-year-old Nathaniel S. Ellis of the Fortieth. He died of disease in Philadelphia and was buried in its Odd Fellows Cemetery, leaving a widow and several young children in West Sandwich. His sister Emily F. Gibbs was notified of his personal effects that included five cents money and a portfolio, possibly containing sketches or writings. [22]

With the two sides at Petersburg locked in stalemate and chances of success minimal in ground level assaults, attention turned to below ground possibilities. Union soldiers with mining experience tunneled beneath the Union line toward a salient in the Confederate one, packed the tunnel with black powder and on July 30th detonated it. The blast heaved earth, flame and enemy soldiers 200 feet upward and left a huge crater of smoking rubble.

Although the tunneling and blasting phase of the operation went well, the follow-up assault was a fiasco. Troops had to scramble over parapets and debris, organization broke down and men milled about in confusion in the crater while the dazed Confederates regained their composure and counterattacked. Major Chipman's Fourteenth New York Heavy Artillery, one of the lead assault units, was decimated. He might have been with it in the crater except his diarrhea had recurred and put him off duty. "I could scarcely walk," he wrote. Sandwich Private John W. Tinkham and his Fifty-eighth Massachusetts formed part of the mass of men trying to maneuver through the turmoil. Compounding the situation was General Ferraro's black division of 9th Corps, which advanced under ill-advised orders into the maelstrom. [23]

Chipman, who experienced the battle second-hand, was predictably critical of the black troops. "They took the enemy's works then formed the niggers to charge. They charged a short distance, met a small force…and ran back like sheep…if they had had 500 white men where they had nearly 5000 niggers we should have gone right into Petersburg." He was not alone in such criticism. Other soldiers and even members of the press blamed the black division for the defeat. With more time, though, as pointed out by historian John F. Schmutz, most men from the ranks came to cast blame where it properly lay, with the generals. [24]

John W. Tinkham, who had survived battles at Vicksburg, Spotsylvania and Cold Harbor, was captured along with twelve other Cape Cod soldiers. They and other captives were paraded through Petersburg in an alternating order of four black soldiers and four white to demonstrate the shame of racial equality. From the onlookers came racial taunts and insults. After the "parade," Tinkham and his fellow captives went by rail cars to prison at Danville, Virginia. [25]

Tinkham's confinement brought to six the number of Sandwich soldiers languishing in southern prisons in late July. The others were Thomas Bourne, Obed Fish, Henry Knippe, Horace Lovell and William Phinney. A seventh Sandwich prisoner, James Gaffney, died at the infamous Andersonville, Georgia prison the day Tinkham was captured.

Further west in Louisiana, Lieutenant Robert H. Chadbourne's black Louisiana Native Guards, which had fought at Port Hudson in that state and been recently designated the Eighty-fourth U. S. Colored Infantry, camped at Morganza, Louisiana. On the night of August 8th a black woman wearing a sergeant's uniform entered Chadbourne's tent after dark and remained several hours. He was overheard to ask if he might connect himself with her, to which she replied, "Well, do what you were going to do." Around this time Private Robert Jones of the Eighty-fourth, whose wife was in the tent, asked Colonel William H. Dickey of the regiment if the woman could be gotten out of it. Hearing noises, she slipped out but was soon arrested and put in the guardhouse. In a court martial, Chadbourne was found guilty of conduct unbecoming an officer and sentenced to dismissal from the service and imprisonment. Whether the woman entered the tent at the bidding of Chadbourne or was put up to it by someone who disliked him is unknown. [26]

At Petersburg, the stalemate dragged into August. That month's first Sunday, the 7th, began quietly in 9th Corps's sector. Major Chipman and Colonel Barnes partook of their customary breakfast together and later the former began a letter to his wife. The tranquility, however, ended around 4 p.m. when the enemy unleashed a hail of mortar fire that exploded over 9th Corps. During the barrage, a shell fragment struck Chipman's right temple and felled him. The next day, the gravely wounded Major died. Just how his wife received the news is unknown. Perhaps a dispatch came into Sandwich's telegraph office and a messenger took off on horseback for West Sandwich to deliver the dreaded knock on her door. [27]

Lieutenant Colonel Joseph H. Barnes and Major Charles Chipman, Twenty-ninth Massachusetts Regiment. Photo taken probably Spring of 1864 when both men were in Massachusetts. SHS/SGM

Colonel Barnes was devastated. "He was my greatest and best friend. I am alone in the Army now." From the Peninsula to Petersburg, he and Chipman had shared all the dangers and privations of soldiering. They had gone into battle side by side, slept under the same blanket, drunk from the same canteen, suffered the same maladies. "His merits and character," wrote the heart-broken Barnes, "were known throughout the Corps and everybody mourns." [28]

Chipman's body reached West Sandwich August 13th. Flags flew at half-staff and stores closed for the August 16th funeral, one of the largest ever for Sandwich. At the conclusion of the service at the Unitarian Church, a procession of twenty-two veterans of Chipman's Company D escorted the casket to Freeman Cemetery. Acting as pallbearers were former officer comrades, among them Captain Brady and Lieutenant Kern. [29]

A day after the August 8th death of Chipman, the horrors of Andersonville prison claimed a second Sandwich soldier, Henry Knippe. The deaths of Knippe and James Gaffney reduced the number of Sandwich soldiers imprisoned at Andersonville to three, Thomas Bourne, Horace Lovell and William Phinney. John Tinkham and Obed Fish were in other southern prisons.

Another August death was that of eighteen-year-old Private Roland Holway of the Fifty-eighth Regiment. He took sick with bilious fever at Petersburg, went to Armory Square Hospital in Washington and died August 14th. His personal effects consisted of a testament, letters and photographs. He was buried in Washington August 16th and his body sent home August 18th for reburial at Sandwich Bayview Cemetery. The Holway home was near the Sandwich Alms House. Young Holway's death left his parents Bethia and John in desperate circumstances since he had supported them since 1861 with his $8.00 monthly earnings as a hired out laborer. John Holway died in early 1865. [30]

The trenches of Petersburg also victimized Samuel J. Wood, Sandwich's only Native-american soldier. Married, father of six and member of North Sandwich's Herring Pond Tribe, he had served as officer's cook and barber for the Fortieth Regiment. Small pox and fever so weakened him he couldn't tolerate riding in the ambulance to the general hospital but had to be cared for at the closer 18th Corps one. Henry B. Baker, a comrade of Wood in Company I (second Sandwich company), wrote home for Wood and admitted to his wife Love Wood that though "the Boys in the Reg't do all in their Power for him… we can't take Proper care of him here." [31]

Wood died August 21st. "He was all the life to the Reg't," wrote Baker, who was with his friend Wood when he died. Baker was working as a section master of the Cape Cod Railroad in 1862 when he enlisted. In Company I, he served as company cook and in that capacity made gruel and carried it two miles each morning to the ailing Wood, all to no avail. Wood and his wife were upstanding members of their tribe. Before enlisting he had chopped wood for the poor and she had cared for needy children. The governor's commissioner described the condition of the tribe in 1863 as good and commented that its members "have no firewater among them, nor do they desire it." [32]

With the war dragging on at Petersburg and elsewhere, and with volunteering at a low level, more troop calls came. Massachusetts, which also had low volunteering, tried to answer the calls while at the same time keep its men out of the draft and at home working in its factories. Two congressional measures aided the state in performing this delicate dance. The first, enacted July 4th, empowered northern states to recruit blacks in the occupied south and have them count against troop quotas. Massachusetts took quick advantage of the law, putting it into effect just ten days after congressional passage as general order number twenty-seven. [33]

Under the general order, town selectmen such as those of Sandwich deposited money with state officials which was then used to pay the expenses of recruiting blacks at recruiting agencies in the South. The agency of most relevance to Sandwich was New Bern, North Carolina, where eighteen blacks were enlisted and credited to Sandwich. This number, eighteen, was 25 per cent of Sandwich's quota of seventy-one as of September 1864, the maximum percentage allowed under the order. New Bedford businessman Nathan S. Ellis recruited many of the eighteen. All entered the First North Carolina Colored Heavy Artillery. "She [Massachusetts] has gained quite a reputation in being the pioneer in the recruitment of colored soldiers…" noted a New Bern newspaper of 1864. Some of that reputation arose through the Bay State's success in recruiting its black Fifth Massachusetts Cavalry earlier in 1864. [34]

The second measure that aided Massachusetts as it worked to meet troop quotas in the summer of 1864 related to the navy. From the start of the war, men who had enlisted in that branch of service had not been credited against state quotas. In Massachusetts alone, this amounted to some 22,000 men. The legislation of 1864 corrected this injustice by permitting states to credit such men. In Massachusetts, selectmen submitted sworn lists of men of their towns who had been in the navy, for Sandwich around thirty men. When all the lists were gone over, it was determined that there had been enough naval enlistments to fill quotas and thus permit cancellation of a draft scheduled for September. [35]

In the months before the naval credits question was settled, expectation of a draft ran high in Sandwich and other Cape towns, so high that Sandwich draft eligible men Robert Armstrong, Frank H. Burgess, John M. Covell,

Substitute contract between drafted man John M. Covell of Sandwich and Irishman William Driscoll in September 1864. NA

Paul C. Gibbs, William R. Gibbs, John Q. Miller and Nathan Nye purchased substitutes at New Bedford around August 5th. Their substitutes were mostly seamen of Ireland or Canada who elected to enter the navy. Irishman Armstrong had been an alien in 1863 and thus not draft liable; naturalization later that year made him liable in1864. Ship captain Paul C. Gibbs of Pocasset had served in the navy but not long enough to be draft-protected. Substitutes were not cheap. Storekeeper Abram Swift and stone carver Seth F. Maxim of Monument paid $675 each for one. Details of their substitutes are unknown. [36]

Three of Sandwich's thirty navy men participated in the August 5, 1864 Battle of Mobile Bay Alabama. Christopher H. Foster, whose brothers Josiah Jr. and John D. had served in the army, was an officer aboard the screw sloop *Lackawanna* which sustained casualties of four killed and thirty-five wounded. Aboard the *Richmond* was Major Chipman's brother-in-law Acting Volunteer Lieutenant Charles I. Gibbs. Through long service on that vessel, he had worked his way up to third-in-command. Receiving the most Union casualties in the battle was Admiral Farragut's flagship *Hartford*. One of her officers was William H. Childs. He had seen his share of merchant ship perils; at Mobile Bay he could compare them to naval ones. Captain of marines on the *Hartford* was Chipman's friend Charles Heywood. [37]

Well south of Mobile Bay and a month after the battle, Abram Phinney sailed from Rio de Janeiro for Baltimore in the bark *Mondamin*. Fifteen months earlier he had done the same in the brig *Clarence* and had it captured by the Confederate raider *Florida*. Could South Atlantic lightning strike his decks twice? Amazingly, the answer was yes. On September 26th, the same raider captured and burned the *Mondamin*. The down-on-his-luck Phinney got passage to Baltimore on two different vessels, finally arriving there in November. His losses were books, charts, clothing and wages that included a bag of coffee. [38]

Some September excitement occurred in Sandwich when merchant and provost marshal deputy John Q. Miller—now safe from the draft—apprehended deserter William H. Branch on "the cars." Branch, from the Cape town of Dennis, had been drafted and held to service in 1863 but been on the loose since. Deputy Miller delivered his prisoner to New Bedford and picked up a reward for his police work. [39]

September also marked the return of Private Benjamin Chamberlain to his Fortieth Regiment. If a gunshot wound can be providential, his might have been. Received at Drewry's Bluff in May, it kept him out of the Battle of Cold Harbor and the trenches of Petersburg, since the Fortieth left the latter August

27th and marched with the rest of 18th Corps to new duty at Bermuda Hundred. While recuperating, Chamberlain spent a two-week furlough in Sandwich. When he left for the front, Hannah D. Lloyd, mother of Chamberlain comrade George T. Lloyd, gave Chamberlain a bottle of medicine "of a hot nature" to take to her son to "warm him up" from chills and fever. [40]

When Chamberlain arrived at Bermuda Hundred he went into Lloyd's tent, delivered the medicine and did what he could to cheer up his ailing friend. They had spent their childhoods together in Sandwich and were close. Lloyd had a strong fear of going to the hospital and often told Chamberlain, "I had much rather die with the boys if I must." To honor this wish, Chamberlain got quinine and whiskey from the hospital steward and gave it directly to Lloyd. [41]

Chamberlain may have come from Fortress Monroe to Bermuda Hundred on the hospital steamer *Matilda*. Detailed as a nurse aboard that vessel was Daniel V. Kern of the Fortieth. After the *Matilda's* boiler blew up at the end of September, he was transferred to another hospital steamer, the *Thomas Powell*, where he finished the war. [42]

Unlike the Fortieth Regiment, the Fifty-eighth Massachusetts remained in the Petersburg trenches. On September 30th, it was part of four Union divisions that made a flanking attack at Peeble's Farm south of the city with objective of cutting enemy supply lines. The attack failed and furthermore led to the capture of 1,300 Union soldiers. One of them was eighteen-year-old Sergeant Samuel Marvel of Monument. He and his parents came there from Fairhaven in 1863 and rented a house owned by Henry Blackwell. Samuel worked at Blackwell's store and received credit for rent and groceries as part of his pay. In February 1864 he enlisted in Company H of the Fifty-eighth, which had many men from the Harwich part of the Cape. He had a connection to that place through his mother Eliza, a sister of Harwich abolitionist Loring Moody. [43]

The end of September brought expiration of term of service for twenty-nine men of the Fifth Massachusetts Light Artillery who had done their three years and chosen not to re-enlist. One of them, John H. Alton, was a son of Samuel Alton of Sandwich and brother of Samuel T., who had died at Gettysburg. Lieutenant Ephraim B. Nye, who had served in the Fifth, wrote that the twenty-nine men went aboard their steamer near Petersburg and sailed for home "with light hearts." John H. came home to wife Melissa sick with consumption. She died in December and is buried in Sandwich. [44]

West of Petersburg in the Shenandoah Valley, General Sheridan took command of a Union force that included the Third Massachusetts Cavalry, recently dismounted and fighting as infantry. Three men of Sandwich with the Third were Cornelius Dean, James McKowen and Edward Heffernan. The last survived a major battle at Winchester on September 19th in which the Third sustained many casualties only to be killed in a smaller action three days later at Fisher's Hill in which its casualties were few. Heffernan's burial site is unknown. His death left his fifty-four-year-old mother Abigail in financial straits since her sole support came from his pay and what little she took in from sewing and boarders at her "cheap" house, valued at $500, on Church Street in Sandwich. [45]

The First Massachusetts Cavalry spent the fall of 1864 near the Petersburg front. That September a new surgeon for the First reported, Samuel W. Abbott. In need of an orderly (servant), he looked over the regiment and found the man he wanted, Nathaniel H. Fish, who had re-enlisted some months earlier. He selected Fish because at age thirty-nine he was older than other enlisted men of the regiment and therefore, in Abbott's estimation, more trustworthy. Less fortunate was Joseph A. Baker, also of the First. He was thrown from his horse before the May Battle of the Wilderness and had to be hospitalized in Washington where he developed chronic illness. Upon receiving a month's furlough in September, friends came to Washington and took him to Sandwich where Dr. Leonard treated him. [46]

Sheridan's men had a second major Shenandoah Valley battle on October 19th at Cedar Creek. Captured was Third Cavalry soldier James McKowen, who had a wife and three children in Sandwich. He was imprisoned at Salisbury, North Carolina, joining Samuel Marvel. Salibury, along with Andersonville and Danville, were prisons for enlisted men. By being an officer, Obed M. Fish missed the pleasures of those places. Instead, he was imprisoned at Macon, Georgia and later Columbia, South Carolina (Table 4).

Table 4
Sandwich Prisoners of War 1864

Soldier	Where and When Captured	Status November 1864
1. Thomas B. Bourne	Wilderness, VA May 6, 1864	Prisoner Andersonville, GA
2. Obed M. Fish	Plymouth, NC April 20, 1864	Prisoner Columbia, SC
3. James Gaffney	Unknown	Died Andersonville Jul 30, 1864
4. Henry H. Knippe	Near Richmond, VA May 9, 1864	Died Andersonville Aug 9, 1864
5. Horace H. P. Lovell	Wilderness VA May 6, 1864	Prisoner Andersonville, GA
6. Samuel Marvel	Petersburg, VA Sep 30, 1864	Prisoner Salisbury, NC
7. James McKowen	Cedar Creek, VA Oct 19, 1864	Prisoner Salisbury, NC
8. William W. Phinney	Near Jacksonville, FL Mar 1864	Prisoner Andersonville, GA
9. John W. Tinkham	Petersburg, VA July 30, 1864	Prisoner Danville, VA

Enlisted men prison camps—especially Andersonville—were vile beyond belief but officer ones were not much better. To illustrate, on October 6, 1864 Fish and other captives arrived at the Columbia prison. They had gone without food several days and a hungry Lieutenant Horace L. Clark, who had served and been captured with Fish, received permission from a guard to purchase a melon from a civilian. To do so, Clark stepped over a boundary line which caused another guard to rush at Clark and bayonet him severely in the back. He had to be carried away to a hospital where he eventually recovered. [47]

West of the Carolinas in Tennessee, Captain John T. Collins took a furlough from his duties with the First U. S. Colored Heavy Artillery and made an October visit to Sandwich where his widowed mother was caring for her four daughters. While visiting, his rheumatism flared up and he had to be treated by the busy Dr. Leonard. [48]

In November, President Lincoln was re-elected. In Sandwich he received 444 votes to 119 for his opponent, General McClellan. "Well," wrote Susan P. Runnells of Monument in a letter to her brother, "we have 'Uncle Abe' again for President. I hope we shall not have war the next four years as many predict, though it is better so than peace on dishonorable terms." She was a daughter of Captain Thomas C. Perry, who had kept his sons out of the war, and wife of physician Andrew J. Runnells. [49]

Susan's sister Clementine (Clem) married Union Army officer Isaac C. Hart of New Bedford in September. In October, General Butler named him as acting ordnance officer of artillery for 18th Corps. This staff position entitled him to a cabin and two black servants. In early December, Clem left Monument to be with her husband near Richmond and live in the cabin, making her the only Sandwich woman to reside in the war zone. [50]

The Catholic Religious Society women of Sandwich Village had a busy December, putting on a fair. The much anticipated event began December 15th and continued five days. Conceived by Mary Swansey Cole, it was held at the town hall and featured raffling of prizes ranging from a barrel of flour to a parian marble tobacco box. Adorning the hall were loops of evergreen and American, Irish, English, French and Italian flags. The fair was a great success, raising more than $1600. That the poorest religious society in Sandwich, the Catholic one, could pull off such a feat was a source of amazement. On Saturday evening, December 17th, when the hall was at its most crowded, Charles B. Hall read a dispatch just received announcing General Sherman's capture of Savannah, which drew three large cheers. [51]

The year ended on a sad note with the death of Samuel Marvel at the Salisbury, North Carolina prison. Sandwich prisoners surviving into the new year were Thomas Bourne, Obed Fish, Horace Lovell, James McKowen, William Phinney and John Tinkham. Would 1865 bring them the sweet aroma of freedom?

Chapter Eleven:
It Seemed Like a Dream—
1865 and End of War

The task before the Union Army and Navy in 1865 was straightforward—finish off a tottering Confederacy and bring the war to an end. The task for Sandwich's six prisoners of war who made it into the new year was also a straightforward one—survival. Each day was a test of hanging on to get to the next. Unfortunately the weather did them no favors. Old man winter brought temperatures so low that the Dan River froze solid outside John Tinkham's Danville prison. Inside, 6,500 prisoners shivered and often died in threadbare vermin-infested rags. [1]

January marked the tenth month of imprisonment for William W. Phinney. On January 9th Thomas C. Perry of Monument wrote Union prison officials inquiring if they knew anything of the young man's whereabouts. Since his capture, the family had had but one letter from him, one of nine months earlier from Andersonville. Perry couldn't have known when he wrote that Phinney, Thomas B. Bourne and many other Andersonville prisoners had been moved to Florence, South Carolina, a move necessitated by the advance of General Sherman's Union Army into Georgia. [2]

Confined in a different sort of prison in January was Private James McNulty of the Second Massachusetts Cavalry. After coming to Sandwich on furlough and overstaying his leave, he was arrested in Boston and sent to Alexandria, Virginia's Prince Street Military Prison. A court martial found him guilty and sentenced him to be returned to his regiment under guard and forfeiture of pay. Several court martials and desertions blemished the military records of him and his brother Peter. [3]

After General Sherman made Georgia "howl," as he put it, his army rolled into South Carolina. To throw off the enemy, he had the navy make a diversionary move into Charleston harbor. In so doing the ironclad *Patapsco* struck a mine January 15th and blew up causing great loss of life. One sailor lost was Ansel C. Fifield, who had transferred from the army to the navy in 1864. His death was sad because his 1858 to 1860 prison stay had turned him from lawbreaker in Massachusetts to law enforcer on the *Patapsco*, i.e., its master at arms. [4]

A week after Fifield's death, Willard Weeks Jr. of Pocasset and the Fortieth Regiment died. He was the second son of Willard and Eunice Weeks to succumb to war-related disease. Eldest son John died in 1861. In 1864 Willard and Eunice moved to Nova Scotia where Willard worked as a fisherman. It was there that they received news of Willard Jr.'s death. The Weeks's are the only Sandwich family who lost two sons in the war. [5]

On the day of Weeks Jr.'s January 23rd death, Andersonville prisoner of war Horace H. P. Lovell transferred to the Confederate Tenth Tennessee Infantry under Colonel John G. O'Neill. This move got Lovell outside the stockade walls; once there he escaped and reached Union lines at Charleston. A few months later he returned to duty with his regiment. Also returning to his regiment, except from Boston, was Private Hiram B. Ellis of the Thirtieth Massachusetts. His mother, Eliza Ellis of West Sandwich, thinking he might need additional clothing to ward off the cold winter, wrapped an overcoat and flannel shirt in brown paper and forwarded it on January 25th on William E. Boyden's Cape Cod Express. To make sure it was delivered, she had neighbor Isaac N. Keith write Boston authorities about it. [6]

Concerned about neither weather nor winter clothing but rather a perceived waywardness of Sandwich citizens was furniture maker Samuel Allyne. "I assure you," he wrote in a January letter to his son, "the moral tendencies here seem to be downward." Supporting him in this contention was Unitarian minister Thomas W. Brown who declared that Sandwich had taken the lead among the Cape towns in level of drunkenness. Even store owner Thomas C. Sherman, according to Allyne, was often seen inebriated on the streets. Working vigorously to suppress liquor sales and put Sandwich on the straight and narrow were the town selectmen. [7]

In late January Charles H. Little of Pocasset was in Boston to enlist in the Sixty-first Massachusetts, which trained at nearby Galloup's Island. This was his second enlistment. He had enlisted first in 1862 in the Fortieth Massachusetts, from which he received a disability discharge. Enlisting with him was his neighbor, Thomas M. Gibbs, who lied about his age (saying he was twenty) to enlist when only seventeen. His mother Ann Maria Gibbs had a pass to take a boat to visit her son at Galloup's Island but whether she used it is unknown. [8]

Concern continued regarding prisoner of war William W. Phinney. On February 6th the young man's father, ship captain George O. Phinney, wrote President Lincoln asking how soon a prisoner exchange might occur. The anxious father also relayed to the President the substance of what his son had written

Pass for Ann Maria Gibbs to visit her son in training at Galloup's Island Boston. Bourne Historical Society

him, that he and other prisoners were kept in "filthy prisons and treated like dogs." Two weeks later the War Department replied to Captain Phinney that plans for a general prisoner exchange were proceeding as rapidly as possible. [9]

Prisoner Obed M. Fish didn't have to await an exchange to gain his freedom. After incarcerations at Macon, Georgia and Charleston, South Carolina, he escaped from Camp Asylum officer prison on the grounds of the South Carolina state lunatic hospital in Columbia, probably in February as Sherman's army approached the city. He returned to his heavy artillery regiment but was so debilitated from his escape he was granted a month's furlough in Massachusetts. [10]

The general prisoner exchange was finally worked out and William Phinney was exchanged near Wilmington, North Carolina at the end of February. He was so weak by that time he had to be admitted to that place's Sherman Hospital. It appears he died around the end of March on a transport ship steaming between Wilmington and Fortress Monroe, Virginia, the death going unrecorded. His Monument neighbor Thomas B. Bourne was also exchanged near Wilmington at the end of February but he was too deranged of mind to be aware of Phinney. Still another prisoner exchanged near Wilmington at the end of February was cavalryman James McKowen. Like William Phinney, he was admitted to the hospital at Wilmington and apparently died aboard a transport ship at the end of March. As with Phinney, no death record exists. [11]

Exchange for Danville prisoner John Tinkham began around February 20th when Confederates packed him and fellow prisoners into freight cars bound for Richmond. After a few days there, they steamed down the James River to Boulware's Landing near City Point. From there they walked to waiting Union vessels. Tinkham was so ill with lung disease he had to be admitted to a hospital at Annapolis. Upon discharge, he went to Sandwich on furlough, then rejoined his Fifty-eighth Regiment at City Point, near where he had been exchanged.[12]

Camped at Chapin's Farm, Virginia near the James River prisoner exchange site was the Fortieth Massachusetts with fifteen Sandwich soldiers. The surgeon of the Fortieth visited the site and found a pathetic scene of almost naked exchanged prisoners so weak from starvation as to be barely able to crawl. On February 22nd, news of the fall of Charleston and Columbia, South Carolina reached the soldiers camped at Chapin's Farm. In response a noon salute of 100 guns rent the air. The Fortieth continued to win interregimental competitions. After winning one in South Carolina in 1864, it took first place honors in others at Chapin's farm in 1865.[13]

South of the James River, the stalemate at Petersburg continued. In a desperate attempt to break Union lines, Confederates mounted a surprise attack March 25th at Fort Stedman garrison. Killed in the attack was artilleryman Lieutenant Ephraim B. Nye. He had served several years in the Fifth Massachusetts Battery and in 1864 received a lieutenant commission and transfer to the Fourteenth Massachusetts Battery. Captured in the attack was James Ball of the Twenty-ninth Massachusetts Regiment, defending a sector just south of the garrison. He was exchanged six days later. Lieutenant Joseph Madigan of the Twenty-ninth was wounded.[14]

*Lieutenant Ephraim B. Nye.
Courtesy Brian P. Murphy*

Ephraim Nye was born in Pocasset in 1826, married Elizabeth Howard of that place in 1848 and had a grocery business in New Bedford when he enlisted in 1862. Because he touched off two cannon to alert the Union line of the attack before he fell, he was hailed as a hero. His brother William F., serving as sutler to the Fourth Massachusetts Cavalry, brought Ephraim's body to New Bedford where a funeral procession passed through streets thronged with citizens paying their respects. Provost Marshall A. D. Hatch accompanied the remains in a

Ensign Ezra Bassett of ironclad Kickapoo. *Note single sleeve stripe of ensign.* HDS

mourning cloth-draped car of the Cape Cod Railroad to Cataumet Cemetery for burial. [15]

Lieutenant Madigan also distinguished himself at Fort Stedman and in recognition received a twenty-day furlough beginning March 27th. On the fourteenth day of his leave, April 9th, he was injured in Springfield, Massachusetts when jumping onto a railroad car while the train was in motion. He recuperated from this injury in Sandwich until the first of May, when he returned to his regiment. [16]

One of the few targets left to Union military forces in March 1865 was Mobile, Alabama but standing in the way were several forts. A campaign to neutralize them began March 11th when West Gulf Squadron Commander Henry Thatcher boarded the dispatch boat *Glasgow* and from her signaled the ironclad *Kickapoo* and other vessels as they fired at one of the forts. Four men of Sandwich were officers of the *Glasgow* and *Kickapoo*, Masters Mates John F. Baker and William H. Childs on the former and Lieutenant Charles I. Gibbs and Ensign Ezra Bassett on the latter. Gibbs was also executive officer of the *Kickapoo*. Operations near the forts were dangerous because of mines in the waters. When one exploded beneath the ironclad *Milwaukee*, the *Kickapoo* sent all her boats to her and brought on board seventy-two men plus hammocks and small arms. After a month's-long campaign, Union troops occupied Mobile April 11th. [17]

John F. Baker was born in Maine in 1840 and came to Sandwich with his family in 1842. His father Thomas worked as an overseer at the glassworks. According to the 1863 enrollment list, John was whaling that year. He was drafted, perhaps in late 1863, but in the meantime applied for and received a Masters Mate position in the Navy. Because of this, the War Department authorized Provost Marshal Hatch in New Bedford to relieve Baker of his draft obligation so that he could accept his Navy position. [18]

Ezra Bassett, born in 1837 in East Sandwich, had a close association with the Holways of that place. He went to school with Hepsa Holway who was his age and in April 1864, a few months before he received his navy appointment, married Hepsa's sister Elizabeth. The marriage made him a brother-in-law of Quaker Edward W. Holway who a year earlier had refused military service for religious reasons. [19]

Willing enough to serve save for health and home front problems was cavalryman Joseph A. Baker. Despite a medical furlough in Sandwich in 1864 and care from Dr. Leonard, he had a relapse in 1865 and had to be re-hospitalized in Washington. While there on April 1st he asked the surgeon for another furlough to Sandwich because his mother, fifty-year-old Priscilla Baker Pardey, was sick and had no one to provide for her. "By obtaining a short furlough," he explained, "I can prevent her removal to the alms house." [20]

Like Charles Little, Irishman John W. Campbell enlisted for a second time in 1865. He first enlisted in 1861 with the "first Sandwich company" but deserted at the Battle of Antietam in 1862 and vanished afterward. Some time in the next few years he showed up at Sandwich and told his family he had been discharged from the army. Perhaps fearing arrest, he moved his family to Delaware and on April 3, 1865 enlisted at Wilmington, Delaware in the First Delaware Infantry as a substitute for Episcopal minister William A. Newbold of South Christiana, Delaware. [21]

When Leonard Hinds re-enlisted, it was not just from one unit into another but from Confederate into Union army. Since this meant he could be executed as a turncoat if captured and found out, he changed his name to John Baker. He remained in the unit in which he "re-enlisted," the Fifteenth New Jersey Regiment, until the spring of 1865 when his commanding officers told him that General Grant had ordered that former Confederate soldiers in

Union regiments could not remain in Virginia. Accordingly, in early April, Hinds (Baker) was sent west to Camp Reno at Milwaukee and three weeks later to Camp Ridgeley in western Minnesota where he joined the First Regiment U. S. Volunteers. [22]

The First U. S. Volunteers consisted mostly of captured Confederate soldiers who had taken an oath of allegiance to the United States. Since their loyalty was somewhat suspect, they were sent to places distant from military action, such as Fort Ridgeley. Although Hinds's (Baker's) assignment to the First U. S. Volunteers was not from prisoner of war status, the fact that he was nonetheless assigned to that unit would qualify him for membership in that somewhat exclusive fraternity of Civil War soldiers of the First and other U. S. volunteer units popularly known as Galvanized Yankees.

Charles Little and Thomas Gibbs arrived in Virginia in late March just in time to join their Sixty-first Massachusetts Regiment for one of the war's final battles, the Fort Mahone sector of the Petersburg line. On April 2nd its men charged the fort, drove back the enemy and on April 3rd entered an evacuated Petersburg and planted their colors on the courthouse. [23]

Richmond was also evacuated April 3rd. Word of it reached General Charles Devens early that morning at Chapin's Farm. In command of the Third Division of 24th Army Corps (within which was the Fortieth Massachusetts), he ordered an immediate advance by the division and thus the Fortieth with its fifteen Sandwich soldiers became one of the first Union infantry regiments to enter the city. Later that day the Sixty-first Massachusetts assisted in escorting 8,000 captured Confederate soldiers from Petersburg to City Point. Along the way Gibbs, Little and the rest of the regiment heard of the evacuation of Richmond and a great cheer went up. "…it seemed like a dream," wrote the Sixty-first's surgeon, —"Richmond fallen, that city for which we had been so long contending, for which so many precious lives have been sacrificed." [24]

Clementine Perry Hart's artillery officer husband Isaac was also attached to the Third Division of 24th Corps. He collected enemy cannon as the division entered Richmond. Clem could have gone into Richmond but declined as the weather was hot. The cabin in which she and Isaac resided was at Chapin's Farm, probably not far from the Fortieth's camp. During an enemy bombardment of a nearby fort, her cabin and bed trembled but she was not alarmed. In fact, she was described as a braver "soldier" than the men guarding her camp. [25]

In another division of 24th Corps, the first, was the Twenty-fourth Massachusetts Regiment. Early in the war it had had nine Sandwich soldiers but in 1865 it had but one, Thomas Gibbs's father Phineas. Father and son saw each other around April 6th near City Point. In a letter to his mother, Thomas wrote, "Farther [sic] looks old and dride up and black as night." Little wonder. Phineas Gibbs had been soldiering for three and a half years when he saw his son that April. The Twenty-fourth Massachusetts received orders April 8th to proceed from near City Point to Richmond where it made its headquarters in a tobacco factory and began, along with the Fortieth Massachusetts, doing guard duty in the city. [26]

A day later, April 9th, Lee surrendered his army at Appomattox. In Sandwich and other Cape towns an exultant citizenry celebrated with ringing of bells and firing of cannons. Guns were also fired at Mobile Bay. As part of a 100-gun noon salute, the *Kickapoo* discharged her four guns, the *Glasgow* her three and the rest of the fleet theirs. [27]

The joy turned to sadness a week later with the death of President Lincoln on Saturday April 15th from an assassin's bullet. At Sandwich, Sunday church services of April 16th were cancelled and the stunned townspeople gathered in large number at post office square for singing, prayers and scripture reading. Afterward, the latest telegraph dispatches were read. [28]

Seaman Warren Keene of Monument felt Lincoln's death in a personal way. After service in the coast survey, he had joined the crew of the government chartered transport steamer *Ranger*, which operated between Washington and City Point. One morning, perhaps in 1864, while walking in Washington he encountered the President, also out walking. He approached young Keene, shook his hand, said, "How are you, my boy?" and continued on his way. Months later, as Keene looked upon the *Ranger's* flag drooping at half-mast to denote the President's death, he felt once again the clasp of his warm friendly hand. [29]

Since the whereabouts of Lincoln assassin John Wilkes Booth were unknown on April 15th, all escape routes were searched, including the Potomac River. Sailing down the river early that morning from Washington were West Sandwich ship captain Russell Gibbs and his trusted crewman Stillman Ellis, from the same community. After a naval vessel ordered Captain Gibbs to heave to, naval officers came aboard, spotted Ellis who resembled Booth and shouted, "There he is!" Gibbs knew better and in a moment of quick thinking had Ellis show his hands. Examination revealed the calloused work-worn hands of a sailor, not the soft ones of an actor, and Gibbs was allowed to proceed on his way. [30]

Naval vessels at Mobile Bay observed the death of Lincoln on April 22nd. "Fleet set flags at half-mast per order of the admiral as a mark of respect at the death of the President of the United States," recorded *Kickapoo* watch officer

Ezra Bassett in that day's log. Off Florida's west coast, Ensign James P. Montague's blockading bark *Restless* honored the President by firing a gun every half hour commencing at sunrise and ending at sunset. [31]

The fighting might have been over but not the marching. "Tomorrow," wrote Thomas Gibbs in a mid-April letter to his mother, "we are going to march 100 miles. I will hate that. My feet will be sore." The 100 miles was from City Point to Burkeville, Virginia where the Union army had a supply depot, troop staging area and collecting point for surrendered Confederate weapons. On arrival there, the Sixty-first joined 5th Army Corps. [32]

More marching followed. From Burkeville, 5th Corps joined by 2nd marched north and at dawn on May 6th began crossing the James River on a pontoon bridge and entering Richmond. All day these 40,000 soldiers passed through the city. Standing on streets and sidewalks to watch respectfully as they passed was 24th Corps, meaning Phineas Gibbs stood and watched as his son Thomas passed by. Also standing and watching that day were Sandwich's soldiers of the Fortieth Massachusetts. [33]

Ensign James Montague of bark Restless. USAHEC

The destination of the marchers was Washington and the May 23rd grand review of the victorious Union army. For weeks leading up to it, soldiers such as those of the Sixty-first Massachusetts camped on hills outside the city. At night they lit candles, fixed them to their guns and marched about, making a spectacular illumination. On the day of the review 150,000 veteran soldiers gathered at the Capitol. General Grant led the parade, which made the mile-long march down Pennsylvania Avenue to the White House. The troops marched shoulder to shoulder, 200 feet wide, the width of the street. As they marched, their bayonets flashed and when they shifted arms their guns glistened like diamonds. Part of the parade were Thomas Gibbs, Charles Little and probably a few other soldiers of Sandwich. [34]

On June 15th, three weeks after the review, Gibbs was admitted to a hospital in Alexandria, Virginia with typhoid fever. Ten days later both he and Little were at Augur Hospital in Alexandria with that disease. Although a patient, Little wrote Ann Maria Gibbs on June 28th that he was looking after her son and that there were laddes (ladies) at Augur to care for the sick. He also asked her to give his love to his mother Sarah Little. Gibbs died July 4th and has a stone at Pocasset Cemetery. Little recovered and received his army discharge July 14th. [35]

The end of the war brought demobilization of the army. The Twenty-ninth Massachusetts Regiment was mustered out of service July 29th near Washington and marched on Broadway in New York on the way home. That march was said to be the last parade of Union troops in the city. Of the fifty-eight men who made up the "first Sandwich company" of 1861 and became Company D of the Twenty-ninth, but one man, David A. Hoxie, mustered out with the regiment and marched with it on Broadway. [36]

The Fortieth Massachusetts Regiment mustered out at Richmond June 17th and also marched on Broadway on its way to Massachusetts. Of the forty-one men who made up the "second Sandwich Company," Company I of the Fortieth, just fifteen mustered out with the regiment (Table 5). In what was the final time George T. Lloyd would play his horn as a soldier, the band of the Fortieth led the regiment past cheering crowds as it marched up Broadway June 20th. [37]

Table 5
The Fifteen Returning Men [38]

1. Rodman Avery
2. Luke Burbank
3. Benjamin F. Chamberlain
4. Abner Ellis
5. Abraham Healey
6. John T. Huddy
7. John F. Johnson
8. George T. Lloyd
9. William Manley
10. Barzillai Manimon
11. Patrick McMahon
12. Henry Perry
13. Nathan C. Perry
14. Charles E. Swift
15. William H. Swift

With the war over and still no news of prisoner of war William W. Phinney, Thomas Perry resigned himself to reality, writing to his son May 7th, "Nothing is heard of William Wallace and I fear nothing will be." In a final attempt to learn something, Reverend Jacob J. Abbott of the U. S. Christian

Commission wrote the commissary general of prisoners. The response, if any, is unknown. Perry's May 7th letter also reported Monument news. Thirty-year-old Seth Swift had gone to New York State to take the water cure for consumption. With health failing, he started for home and made it to New York City from which place his parents Ellis and Betsy Swift were telegraphed to come at once if they wished to see him alive. They left immediately, found him in a low state and brought him home April 21st. He died two days later. Also, forty-year-old Mary Coffin Wing, an unmarried widow for the past eight years, had delivered a child and whisperings centered on her son-in-law, twenty-eight-year-old Henry W. Weeks, as the father. [39]

Word that the war had ended was slow in reaching ships at sea. Thus, their war went on. Off Russia's Kamchatka peninsula on May 27th the Confederate raider *Shenandoah* captured the *Abigail,* whose captain Ebenezer F. Nye of Pocasset had been whaling and trading in that vessel in the North Pacific for three years. During that time he had advanced around $15,000 to crewmen. All this he lost when the purser of the *Shenandoah* threw Nye's account books overboard. After an imprisonment of twenty-eight days on the *Shenandoah,* Nye was put aboard a ship bound for San Francisco. [40]

Nye's brother William F. manufactured and bottled cordials, ales and other liquors before becoming an army sutler in 1862. When the *Abigail* under brother Ebenezer sailed that year from New Bedford for the North Pacific, she had on board forty-two gallons of William's rum and forty-four of his whiskey, all of which was lost in the 1865 capture. [41]

Word that the war was over was also slow to reach the taskmaster commanding officer of the Third Massachusetts Heavy Artillery. He had his men laboring in a hot July sun eleven hours daily pushing wheelbarrow loads of earth to fortify Washington's Fort Lincoln. At length, nineteen men of George F. Gibbs's Company B refused to work, were arrested and jailed. Gibbs's remark that the nineteen were "bully fellows" for their action got him court-martialed for insubordination. Found guilty and sentenced to confinement for a year with a twelve-pound ball attached to his leg by a six-foot chain, he deserted before the sentence could be carried out. [42]

Sandwich's Civil War saga closed with the activities of soldier-sailor Nathan B. Fisher. This son of Nathan and Joanna Fisher of South Sandwich was born in 1832 and served a nine-month army enlistment in 1862-1863. In late 1864 former whaler Fisher enlisted in the navy and was assigned to the screw sloop *Wachusett* where he was quartermaster in a crew of 175 men. The *Wachusett* left Boston in March 1865 with orders to seek the raider *Shenandoah* in the Pacific but a month later when the war ended was no further than the West Indies.

As the Navy adjusted to peacetime, it formed an East India Squadron to watch over American interests in that region. Assigned to the squadron was Fisher's *Wachusett*. From the West Indies she steamed for squadron headquarters in Hong Kong but in February 1866 had gotten only as far as Manila, indeed a slow boat to China! At Manila, an ailing Fisher was condemned by a medical survey and sent home on the clipper ship *Santee,* which arrived in New York in June 1866. He died a month later. [43]

Twenty-seven days before Fisher's July 31st death, Sandwich celebrated Independence Day 1866. Having had a year to assimilate the 1861 to 1865 war, the day was a time for the town to remember the past and look to the future. *Barnstable Patriot* editor Sylvanus Phinney noted the honorable record of Sandwich in the late war, then turned to the future, offering a sentiment both eloquent and powerful:

> "Now that war is ended and Peace resumes her benignant sway, may that Divine Providence which has never failed this people, so direct the councils of our Rulers that sectional strife and discord shall forever cease, and this Nation become once more in reality as in name, The United States of America." [44]

Sandwich's soldiers, sailors and sons had done their part to end strife and unite the states, at least in their time. Their war was over.

Epilogue

After the war, Sandwich's population went through a steady decline that only in the mid-twentieth century began to rebound. Part of this decline was because of closure of the glassworks in 1888. Strikes and competition from midwestern glassworks using cheaper fuels doomed it. Disputes between the Cape Cod Bay and Buzzard's Bay sides of Sandwich led to a division of the town in 1882 in which the latter side formed the new town of Bourne. West Sandwich, no longer part of Sandwich, took the new name of Sagamore, North Sandwich became Bournedale and Monument's center shifted south to become Monument Beach.

In 1882 the veteran soldiers of Sandwich formed the Charles Chipman Post of the Grand Army of the Republic, the first such chapter on Cape Cod. Samuel W. Hunt served as its first commander. Five years later, Sandwich's women formed an auxiliary women's relief corps. It first president was Emily M. Jones, a sister-in-law of veteran Daniel V. Kern. A GAR post was also formed in Bourne.

With business opportunities scarce in post-war Sandwich, many veterans moved away to seek employment in nearby towns or other parts of the country. The following is an accounting of the post-war lives of a few of Sandwich's Civil War personalities.

Samuel H. Allyne: Furniture maker Allyne, who operated his furniture business from the Sandwich Town Hall and taught John W. Pope the trade, died in Sandwich May 30, 1883 at age eighty. Allyne daughter Helen married Josiah Stanford, brother of California Governor Leland Stanford, in 1861. Her personal papers are at Stanford University Special Collections Library, Stanford, California.

James H. Atherton: After three years in the Twenty-ninth Massachusetts, Atherton did brief service in the Fourth Massachusetts Heavy Artillery as a First Lieutenant. After the war he worked as a compositor for New York newspapers and died of suicide May 30, 1883.

James Ball: Irishman Ball, who spent four years in Company D of the Twenty-ninth Massachusetts, settled in Dixon County, Nebraska around 1885 where he worked as a laborer and wood chopper. After friends wrote the Pension Bureau for him, he began receiving a well-deserved $8.00 per month pension. He never married and died May 22, 1904, around age sixty-eight.

Joseph H. Barnes: Major Chipman's close friend Colonel Barnes left the army in October of 1864. In 1866 he married Anna Stickney of Boston. They had daughters Annette E. and Clara W. and son Joseph S. Barnes. The family lived many years at 191 Trenton Street in East Boston. He served several years on Boston's city council and died January 16, 1906 having never applied for nor received a pension. A school in East Boston is named for him.

Undated photograph of Bourne Post of GAR members. Sailor Wilder Booth at far left can be identified because he always carried an umbrella. Bourne Historical Society

John W. Campbell: After serving in the First Delaware Regiment, Campbell and his wife Catherine were in Philadelphia in 1870. Around 1880, he was living in Wheeling, WV with his son James and she was still in Philadelphia. In 1887, despite being a deserter, he was admitted to the Hampton, Virginia Soldiers Home. He died there February 16, 1893.

Robert H. Chadbourne: He wrote Secretary of War Stanton in the spring of 1865 from prison at Fort Jefferson, Florida appealing his sentence and was released in May by order of General Butler. Later that year he married Mary Jane Delware in Louisiana. He became a Louisiana state senator and died near New Orleans in July 1876.

Elizabeth Gibbs Chipman: The recipient of Charles Chipman's letters, she and her mother Excie lived in their West Sandwich house (no longer standing) until 1866 when they moved into one on School Street in Sandwich that Charles I. Gibbs built for them. That house still stands. In 1867 Congress approved $125 for her for a horse Chipman lost in military service on August 18, 1863. She moved to New Bedford around 1905 to live with her daughter Sarah. Never remarrying, she died at age ninety-one March 20, 1920 at Sarah's home and was buried at Freeman Cemetery in Sandwich.

John T. Collins: After being brevetted as a lieutenant colonel in 1866, he became collector for the port of Brunswick, Georgia in 1868 and kept that position until 1884. His letter books for that period are at the University of Georgia Special Collections Library. His later life was spent in business in New York City, where he died April 19, 1911.

Perez Eldridge: His gunshot wound entitled him to an $8.00 per month pension. By the 1890's he was a widower. A drinking habit afforded him numerous visits to the cells of the Barnstable County jail. Since he couldn't be trusted to spend his monthly pension judiciously, a guardian was appointed to allot the money to him. He died January 6, 1903 at seventy-five at the Soldiers Home in Chelsea and was buried in Sandwich.

Charles E. Ellis: His wounded right arm reduced greatly his productivity in his old profession of farming. Living in West Barnstable in 1867, he married widow Nancy Wright Swift of West Sandwich. Two years after her death in 1875 he married Isabella Sears of Marstons Mills. He received a monthly pension of $6.00 for many years and died in Barnstable December 18, 1904.

George F. Gibbs: After deserting in Washington, DC in 1865, Gibbs was a farm laborer in Contra Costa, CA in 1870 and farmer in Cloud County, KS in 1875. Around 1883 he married Persis Johnson in Cloud County. They had daughters Persis and Olive. Gibbs and his wife were listed as photographers in 1900 in Enid, OK and a few of their photos can be seen on the internet. They apparently divorced around 1902. Nothing more is known of Gibbs.

Francis Freeman Jones: A grandson of Charles Chipman, Jones was born in New Bedford, Massachusetts in 1892. After graduating from Dartmouth College he became a navy lieutenant in World War I. In 1966 his stepson Stanton Garner edited and published the letters of Chipman's sister Mary in *The Captain's Best Mate: The Journal of Mary Chipman Lawrence on the Whaler Addison 1856-1860*. Garner's work may have motivated Jones to find a place of permanent safekeeping for Charles Chipman's letters, a goal realized around 1972 when he donated them to the Carlisle Barracks army facility, now U.S. Army Heritage and Education Center, in Carlisle, PA. Posterity gratefully acknowledges his generosity and foresight.

Thomas Hollis: After suffering a severe forearm wound at the Battle of Antietam in 1862, Hollis received a disability discharge in 1863. He returned to his native Birmingham, England, where he married and fathered children in 1868 and 1872. He returned to Massachusetts and practiced glass blowing until around 1881 when he could no longer handle the tools of that trade. He moved to San Francisco around 1882, became a letter carrier, was naturalized in 1885 and died there February 2, 1892 at age fifty-six.

Charles H. Hoxie: He was living at the Massasoit House Hotel in Atchison, KS in 1870, and working there at billiards in 1872. After fire destroyed the hotel in 1873 he operated saloons in Atchison. He began living in the Old Soldiers Home in Milwaukee in 1884 and died there February 2, 1902.

David A. Hoxie: One of twelve children, Hoxie married married Laura Small of Provincetown in 1868 and settled in the Forestdale section of Sandwich where he farmed. He wrote poems which he read on Memorial Day at the graves of veterans. He died in the Cotuit part of Barnstable February 22, 1910.

Samuel Wells Hunt: He married Mary A. Nichols of Sandwich in 1866. Around that time he engaged in the shoe business in Sandwich with his brother-in-law Charles Gibbs. An article in the February 8, 1881 issue of the *Barnstable Patriot* reported that Hunt had a flag presented to Company D by *Patriot* editor Phinney in 1861. Its whereabouts are unknown. Hunt died at his home on Main Street in Sandwich September 10, 1929.

Charles H. Little: Charley, as he was known, worked in the sea trades after the war. He arrived in Indianola, TX around 1874 and began boating with Albert Rohre in nearby waters of Matagorda Bay. Little married Mary Armstrong in 1876 and died in 1908 in Wimberly, TX.

Horace H.P. Lovell: Lovell was married in 1867 and fathered ten children. He began receiving a pension of $8.00 monthly in 1887 but was dropped from pension rolls in 1893 when his brief transfer to the Confederate Army was discovered. The pension was later re-instated. Sandwich Overseer of Poor Benjamin Chamberlain wrote in 1893 that Lovell received town aid of $150 yearly. He died in Attleboro, MA September 2, 1918.

James McKowen: Catherine McKowen, wife of James swore in March 1872, just before her July 1872 death, that she had not heard from her husband since his 1864 capture and that she fully believed he was dead. Yet, he is in the membership list of the East Boston post of the G.A. R. meaning he might have survived the war. No further information can be found about him.

Ebenezer F. Nye: Captain Nye became a whaler at around age nine in 1831 and was a whaling captain much of his life. He made many whaling voyages to the arctic, the last in the *Mount Wollaston,* which left New Bedford in June 1879 and became locked in arctic ice later that year. In 1881, his wife Joanna Godfrey Nye would not permit his will to be probated as she thought he might be still alive. He has a stone at the Cataumet Cemetery.

Giles M. Pease: Surgeon Pease moved from Boston to San Francisco in 1873. He was divorced in 1888 for objecting to his wife's use of face powder to lighten her complexion. He was troubled with chronic bowel and rectal disease, probably war related, and died December 14, 1891 in San Francisco after almost twenty years of practice there.

Caleb T. Robbins: Robbins worked in the U.S. Coast Survey under Alexander M. Harrison of Plymouth before and after the war. In 1870 he married Anna Baker, with occupation at the time given as surveyor. He became a salesman for Sandwich glass and lived in Plymouth much of his post-war life. He died there December 18, 1933 at age ninety-three, the last of Sandwich's Civil War veterans to die.

Francis H. Swift: Pocasset native Swift fell into a gulley in early 1863 while his Fortieth Regiment was at Miner's Hill, Virginia. With injured leg he had to be hospitalized in Washington, unable to go with his regiment in mid-April to Suffolk, Virginia. In July he received his discharge. He tried farming in Pocasset and working in a shoe factory in Boston area but could do neither due to his injury. In late 1863 he went to Galloup's Island in Boston harbor to enlist in the Veterans Reserve Corps but was rejected because he could not march five miles. He returned to Pocasset and in 1867 moved to New Bedford where he died March 12, 1927.

Appendix A—
Military Roster of Sandwich Civil War Soldiers

Italicized names are men who died of disease during or immediately after the war, were killed in action or died of wounds. Age is age when enlisted. Rank is highest one obtained. Unit is infantry unless denoted Cav (Cavalry), Heavy Artillery (HA) or Light Artillery (LA). Col is Colored Troops. Remarks is means of or reason for cessation of service. Dow is died of wounds, kia is killed in action, dod is died of disease.

Name	*Age*	*Rank*	*Unit*	*Remarks*
1. Adams, Asa R.	28	Pvt.	4th MA, Co C	disch. Aug 28, 1863
2. Adams, Isaiah M.	22	Pvt.	24th MA, Co A	disch. disab. Sep 22, 1863
3. Adams, Watson F.	19	Pvt.	24th MA, Co A	disch. Oct 16, 1864
4. Allen, Jesse H.	42	Pvt.	24th MA, Co A	disch. disab. Sep 8, 1862
5. *Allyne, Sam'l H. Jr.*	23	1st Lt.	1st CA Cav, Co A	murd'd Texas Dec 29, 1863
6. Alton, John H.	26	Pvt.	5th MA LA	disch. Oct 3, 1864
7. Alton, Joseph B.	19	Pvt.	5th MA LA	disch. Jun 12, 1865
8. *Alton, Samuel T.*	23	Pvt.	2nd MA, Co B	dow Gettysb. Jul 17, 1863
9. Atherton, Jas H.	22	1st Lt.	29th MA, Co D	disch. Jun 17, 1865
10. *Atkins, James P.*	32	Pvt.	58th MA, Co A	kia VA Jun 8, 1864
11. Avery, Rodman	18	Pvt.	40th MA, Co I	disch. Jun 16, 1865
12. *Avery, Watson D.*	21	Pvt.	40th MA, Co I	dod VA Oct 27, 1862
13. Badger, George W.	22	Pvt.	29th MA, Co D	disch. Aug 15, 1864
14. Badger, Gustavus	21	Pvt.	29th MA, Co D	disch. disab. May 14, 1863
15. Baker, Henry B.	27	Pvt.	40th MA, Co I	disch. May 30, 1865
16. Ball, James	25	Pvt.	29th MA, Co D	disch. May 26, 1865
17. Ball, Michael A.	30	Music.	28th MA, band	disch. Aug 17, 1862
18. Ball, Thomas	29	Pvt.	1st MA, Co C	disch. disab. Mar 13, 1863
19. Ball, Thomas A.	18	Pvt.	40th MA, Co I	disch. disab. Feb 22, 1864
20. *Benson, Henry F.*	37	Pvt.	45th MA, Co D	dow NC Dec 28, 1862
21. Bent, Francis	23	Pvt.	3rd MA HA, Co K	disch. Sep 18, 1865
22. *Blake, David A.*	20	Pvt.	1st ME Cav	died injuries Feb 13, 1862
23. *Bourne, Isaac D.*	23	Pvt.	5th RI HA, Co E	dod NC May 23, 1862
24. Bourne, Joshua W.	23	Capt.	7th MO, Co K	disch. Jun 15, 1864
25. Bourne, Thos. B.	21	Sgt.	58th MA, Co I	disch. July 14, 1865
26. Boyer, James	22	Pvt.	54th MA, unass.	transf. to navy Apr 2, 1864
27. Brady, Charles	38	Capt.	29th MA, Co D	resigned Dec 5, 1862
28. Brady, Edward	36	Sgt.	29th MA, Co D	disch. disab. Dec 28, 1862
29. Breese, William	29	Sgt.	29th MA, Co D	disch. May 30, 1864
30. Bruce, George F.	22	Cpl.	29th MA, Co D	disch. Aug 21, 1865

Name	Age	Rank	Unit	Remarks
31. Bumpus, Frank G.	21	Pvt.	29th MA, Co D	disch. Sep 2, 1864
32. Burbank, Luke P.	18	Pvt.	40th MA, Co I	disch. Jun 16, 1865
33. Burgess, Elisha H.	24	Pvt.	24th MA, Co D	disch. disab. May 28, 1863
34. Burgess, Geo. A.	18	Pvt.	45th MA, Co D	disch. Jun 20, 1865
35. Burgess, Howard	21	Pvt.	3rd MA, Co K	disch. Jul 22, 1861
36. Burgess, Theoph. J.	23	Pvt.	3rd MA, Co A	disch. Jun 26, 1863
37. Campbell, John W.	38	Pvt.	29th MA, Co D	deserted Sep 17, 1862
38. Chadbourne, John	18	Pvt	28th MA, Co I	disch. May 5, 1865
39. Chadbourne, Rbt.	22	1st Lt.	84th U.S. Col	dismissed Nov 24, 1864
40. Chamberlain, B. F.	23	Pvt.	40th MA, Co I	disch. Jun 16, 1865
41. Chase, Ebenezer W.	32	Pvt.	15th MA LA	disch. 1864
42. Cheval, Alfred	32	Pvt.	29th MA, Co D	disch. disab. Feb 7, 1863
43. *Chipman, Charles*	31	Major	29th MA, Co D	dow Aug 8, 1864
44. Chipman, Howard	18	Corp.	45th MA, Co D	disch. Jul 7, 1863
45. Chipman, Jas. F.	37	Capt.	33rd MA, Co D	disch. Jun 11, 1865
46. Chipman, Jos. P.	23	Pvt.	45th MA, Co D	disch. Jun 27, 1865
47. Chipman, Samuel	38	Pvt.	45th MA, Co D	disch. Jul 7, 1863
48. Chipman, Sands K.	18	Pvt	5th MA, Co A	disch. Nov 16, 1864
49. Clancy, Patrick C.	23	Pvt.	29th MA, Co D	deserted May 1, 1863
50. Clark, George H.	40	Pvt.	54th MA, Co H	disch. Aug 20, 1865
51. Clarke, Charles S.	14	Pvt.	5th MA, Co A	disch. Nov 16, 1864
52. Clarke, Frank. R. J.	21	Sgt.	22nd MA, Co K	deserted Oct 1, 1862
53. Clarke, William F.	15	Pvt.	22nd MA, Co K	disch. disab. Oct 3, 1862
54. Collins, John T.	18	Capt.	1st U.S. Col HA	disch. Mar 31, 1866
55. Connell, James G.	19	Pvt.	43rd MA, Co E	disch. Jul 30, 1863
56. Cook, Ebenezer R.	38	Pvt.	1st MA LA	disch. disab. April 4, 1863
57. Cook, James	18	Pvt.	29th MA, Co D	disch. Sep 2, 1864
58. Corliss, Jos. S.	22	Pvt.	6th MA, Co A	disch. Oct 27, 1864
59. Cox, James	21	Corpl.	29th MA, Co D	disch. Aug 16, 1864
60. *Crocker, Horace L.*	20	Pvt.	13th MA, Co I	dod VA Mar 30, 1862
61. Dalton, Christ. B.	18	Music.	29th MA, Co D	disch. Aug 15, 1864
62. *Dalton, James*	45	Pvt.	24th MA, Co H	dod 1867
63. Dalton, William B.	31	Music.	28th MA, Band	disch. Aug 17, 1862
64. *Davis, Benjamin*	28	Pvt.	20th MA, Co I	kia VA Oct 21, 1861
65. Davis, Thomas	20	Pvt.	20th MA, Co I	disch. disab. Jan 13, 1863
66. Dean, Cornelius	18	Pvt.	3rd MA Cav, Co E	disch. May 20, 1865
67. Dean, Timothy	41	Pvt.	29th MA, Co D	disch. disab. Aug 2, 1862
68. Dean, Warren P.	19	Pvt.	29th MA, Co D	disch. disab. Apr 27, 1863
69. Denson, Otis E.	20	Pvt.	1st MA HA, Co E	disch. Jun 28, 1865
70. Dillaway, George E.	26	Pvt.	1st MA, Co E	disch. May 25, 1864
71. Dillingham, Naaman H.	25	Pvt.	38th MA, Co H	disch. Aug 16, 1864
72. *Donnelly, Edward*	22	Pvt.	29th MA, Co D	dod Sandw. Oct 1, 1865
73. *Eaton, Joseph W.*	19	Pvt.	29th MA, Co D	dod Sandw. Jul 15, 1869

Name	Age	Rank	Unit	Remarks
74. Eldridge, Perez	38	Pvt.	29th MA, Co D	disch. Jun 29, 1865
75. Ellis, Abner	35	Pvt.	40th MA, Co I	disch. Jun 16, 1865
76. Ellis, Charles E.	25	Pvt.	40th MA, Co I	disch. Jun 9, 1865
77. Ellis, Elisha J.	22	Pvt.	44th IN, Co G	disch. Sep 14, 1865
78. Ellis, Josiah Bartlett	26	Pvt.	18th MA, Co C	disch. disab. Sep 11, 1862
79. Ellis, Nathan B. Jr.	27	1st Lt.	20th MA, Co K	disch. disab. Jul 29, 1864
80. *Ellis, Nathaniel S.*	41	Pvt.	40th MA, Co I	dow Philad. Jul 19, 1864
81. *Ellis, Thomas*	24	Pvt.	40th MA, Co I	dod VA Aug 11, 1864
82. *Emerson, Wm. L.*	28	Pvt.	22nd MA, Co H	kia VA Jun 18, 1864
83. Ewer, Benjamin	38	Pvt.	24th MA, Co A	disch. Oct 4, 1864
84. Fagan, John	19	Pvt.	29th MA, Co D	disch. Aug 16, 1864
85. *Fifield, Ansel C.*	31	Pvt.	32nd MA, Co A	kia SC Jan 15, 1865
86. Fifield, Watson H.	43	Pvt.	45th MA, Co D	disch. Jul 7, 1863
87. Fish, Ephraim W.	20	Pvt.	2nd MA HA, Co E	deserted Nov 4, 1863
88. Fish, Henry S.	22	Pvt.	33rd MA, Co C	disch. Jun 11, 1865
89. *Fish, John F.*	22	Pvt.	24th MA, Co A	dod Sandw. Oct 5, 1862
90. Fish, Nathaniel H.	36	Pvt.	1st MA Cav, Co G	disch. June 26, 1865
91. Fish, Obed M.	26	Capt.	2nd MA HA, Co G	disch. Aug 19, 1865
92. *Fish, Sumner B.*	20	Pvt.	5th MA, Co K	missing VA Jul 21 1861
93. Fisher, Calvin G.	26	Capt.	Miss. Marine Brig.	disch. Feb 1, 1865
94. Fisher, Nathan B.	30	Pvt.	47th MA, Co F	disch. disab. Mar 7, 1863
95. Foster, John D.	27	Pvt.	45th MA, Co D	disch. Jul 7, 1863
96. Foster, Josiah Jr.	28	Pvt.	12th NY, Co D	disch. Aug 5, 1861
97. Freeman, Geo. H.	22	Pvt.	3rd MA, Co L	disch. Jul 22, 1861
98. Freeman, Hartwell	20	1st. Lt.	81st Col, Co I	disch. May 27, 1865
99. *Freeman, Wm. N.*	29	Pvt.	1st MA, Co I	dod Philad. Jan 5, 1863
100. Fuller, Benjamin	20	Pvt.	29th MA, Co D	disch. Aug 16, 1864
101. *Gaffney, James*	41	Pvt.	11th MA, Co K	dod GA Jul 30, 1864
102. Geisler, Francis C.	18	Pvt.	20th MA, Co D	disch. disab. Mar 11, 1864
103. Gibbs, Bradford	39	Corp'l	6th MA LA	disch. Aug 7, 1865
104. Gibbs, George F.	18	Corp'l	3rd MA HA, Co B	deserted Jul 20, 1865
105. Gibbs, Phineas	42	Pvt.	24th MA, Co B	disch. Jan 20, 1866
106. Gibbs, Seth F.	18	Pvt.	3rd MA HA, Co B	disch. Sept 18, 1865
107. *Gibbs, Thos. M.*	20	Pvt.	61st MA, Co K	dod DC Jul 15, 1865
108. *Godfrey, Charles*	18	Pvt.	11th NH, Co G	dod NY, NY Jul 19, 1864
109. Greene, Henry C.	28	Pvt.	45th MA, Co D	disch. Jul 7, 1863
110. Guiney, James	19	Pvt.	29th MA, Co D	disch. Aug 16, 1865
111. *Hackett, Thomas*	38	Pvt.	45th MA, Co D	dow Sandw. Dec 30, 1874
112. Haines, Geo. F. W.	25	Pvt.	9th MA LA	disch. Jun 6, 1865
113. Haines, George L.	21	Corp'l	45th MA, Co D	disch. Jul 7, 1863
114. *Haines, Jas. G. B.*	19	Pvt.	29th MA, Co D	dod Sandw. Jul 26, 1862
115. Hamlen, Benj. H.	18	Corp'l	29th MA, Co D	disch. Aug 16, 1864
116. Hamlen, Ezra	25	Pvt.	45th MA, Co D	disch. Jul 7, 1863

Name	Age	Rank	Unit	Remarks
117. *Hammond, Luther*	27	Pvt.	40th MA, Co I	dod SC Dec 15, 1863
118. Harkins, Charles	19	Pvt.	29th MA, Co D	disch. disab. Nov 22, 1862
119. Harlow, James	44	Pvt.	40th MA, Co I	disch. disab. Feb 21, 1863
120. Harmon, Persia B.	30	Pvt.	18th MA, Co C	disch. disab. Dec 9, 1862
121. Harper, Wm. H.	42	Capt.	40th MA, Co I	resigned June 27, 1863
122. Hathaway, Jas. E.	42	Pvt.	40th MA, Co I	disch. disab. Jun 24, 1865
123. *Heald, James H.*	22	Pvt.	29th MA, Co D	dod MD Oct 11, 1862
124. Healy, Abraham	28	Pvt.	40th MA, Co I	disch. Jun 16, 1865
125. *Heffernan, Edward*	25	Pvt.	3rd MA Cav, Co E	kia VA Sep 22, 1864
126. Heslin, Michael	19	Pvt.	29th MA, Co D	disch. disab. Nov 4, 1861
127. Hinds, Leonard	18	Pvt.	15th NJ, Co I	disch. Jun 27, 1865
128. Hobson, Geo. H.	28	Pvt.	1st MA Cav, Co D	disch. Oct 3, 1864
129. Hollis, Thomas	24	Sgt.	20th MA, Co I	disch. disab. Mar 6, 1863
130. Holmes, Herman	25	Pvt.	3rd MA, Co I	disch. Oct 27, 1865
131. Holmes, Thomas F.	18	Pvt.	45th MA, Co K	disch. Jul 7, 1863
132. Holway, Augustus	22	Pvt.	45th MA, Co D	disch. Jul 7, 1863
133. Holway, Edw. W.	28	Pvt.	22nd MA, Co E	disch. Nov 6, 1863
134. *Holway, Roland G.*	28	Pvt.	58th MA, Co C	dod DC Aug 14, 1864
135. Holway, Thomas E.	18	Pvt.	45th MA, Co D	disch. Jul 7, 1863
136. Howard, Leon. E.	24	Corp.	1st ME HA, Co E	disch. Jun 4, 1865
137. Howes, Alvin C.	18	Pvt.	5th MA, Co A	disch. Nov 10, 1864
138. Howes, Charles A.	21	Pvt.	18th MA, Co D	disch. Sep 2, 1864
139. Hoxie, Charles H.	18	Pvt.	29th MA, Co D	disch. Aug 15, 1864
140. Hoxie, David A.	21	Pvt.	29th MA, Co D	disch. Sep 2, 1864
141. Hoxie, Nath'l C.	38	Pvt.	45th MA, Co D	disch. Jul 7, 1863
142. Hoxie, Zenas H.	19	Pvt.	29th MA, Co D	disch. Sep 2, 1864
143. Huddy, John T.	18	Pvt.	40th MA, Co I	disch. Jun 16, 1865
144. Hunt, Samuel W.	18	Pvt.	29th MA, Co D	disch. Aug 16, 1864
145. Johnson, John F.	18	Pvt.	40th MA, Co I	disch. Jun 16, 1865
146. *Jones, Charles E.*	20	Pvt.	29th MA, Co D	killed VA Feb 11, 1862
147. Jones, Solomon H.	24	Pvt.	4th MA Cav, Co L	disch. Jun 21, 1865
148. Jones, James T.	19	Pvt.	45th MA, Co D	disch. Jul 7, 1863
149. Kelly, James H.	32	Pvt.	9th MA, Co C	disch. Jun 11, 1864
150. Kelley, William P.	36	Pvt.	33rd MA, Co I	disch. Jul 24, 1865
151. Kern, Daniel V.	19	Pvt.	40th MA, Co I	disch. disab. Jun 5, 1865
152. Kern, Henry A.	27	1st Lt.	29th MA, Co D	disch. May 30, 1862
153. Kern, Martin L. Jr.	19	Sgt.	29th MA, Co D	disch. May 21, 1864
154. *Knippe, Henry H.*	19	Pvt.	1st MA Cav, Co K	dod GA Aug 9, 1864
155. Lane, Andrew J.	26	Pvt.	20th MA, Co H	deserted Jul 1, 1863
156. *Lawrence, Edward*	19	Pvt.	40th MA, Co I	dod SC Nov 26, 1863
157. Lincoln, Ensign	21	Pvt.	40th MA, Co I	disch. disab. Jan 11, 1864
158. Little, Charles H.	18	Pvt.	40th MA, Co I	disch. Jul 11, 1865
159. Lloyd, George T.	20	Pvt.	40th MA, Co I	disch. Jun 16, 1865
160. *Long, Patrick*	20	Pvt.	29th MA, Co D	dod VA Aug 9, 1862

Name	Age	Rank	Unit	Remarks
161. Lovell, Fred. U.	36	Pvt.	45th MA, Co D	disch. Jul 7, 1863
162. Lovell, James A.	21	Corp'l	2nd MA HA, Co K	disch. Sep 3, 1865
163. Lovell, Horace H.	22	Pvt.	32nd MA, Co C	disch. Jun 29, 1865
164. Madigan, Joseph J.	20	1st Lt.	29th MA, Co D	disch. Aug 9, 1865
165. Magoon, Davis	28	Pvt.	40th MA, Co I	disch. Jun 10, 1865
166. Manimon, Barzillai	28	Corp'l	40th MA, Co I	disch. Jun 16, 1865
167. Manimon, Seth T.	26	Pvt.	40th MA, Co I	disch. disab. Feb 21, 1863
168. Manley, William	38	Pvt.	40th MA, Co I	disch. Jun 16, 1865
169. *Marvel, Sam'l M.*	20	Sgt.	58th MA, Co H	dod NC Dec 29, 1864
170. Mason, Thomas	28	Pvt.	3rd MA Cav, Co E	disch. disab. Aug 29, 1863
171. McAlaney, John	37	Corp'l	29th MA, Co D	disch. Sep 2, 1864
172. McCabe, John	38	Pvt.	28th MA, Co C	disch. disab. Oct 11, 1862
173. McDermott, Wm.	20	Pvt.	29th MA, Co D	disch. Aug 16, 1864
174. McElroy, Patrick	30	Pvt.	29th MA, Co D	disch. disab. Oct 24, 1862
175. *McGirr, Edward*	19	Pvt.	5th NY, Co F	dow DC Oct 3, 1862
176. McGirr, Patrick	35	Pvt.	9th MA, Co C	disch. disab. Mar 28, 1863
177. McKenna, Michael	22	Pvt.	29th MA, Co D	deserted Jun 8, 1863
178. *McKenna, Peter*	24	Pvt.	20th MA, Co I	kia VA Oct 21, 1861
179. McKeon, Henry	18	Pvt.	22nd MA, Co C	disch. Jun 29, 1865
180. McKowen, Francis	21	Pvt.	2nd MA Cav,unass	deserted Sep 19, 1863
181. *McKowen, James*	27	Pvt.	3rd MA Cav, Co E	died 1865?
182. McLaney, Thos. J.	21	Pvt.	7th MA LA	no further record
183. McMahon, Patrick	30	Corp'l	40th MA, Co I	disch. Jun 16, 1865
184. McNulty, James	21	Pvt.	2nd MA Cav, Co I	deserted Nov 29, 1864
185. McNulty, Peter	18	Pvt.	29th MA, Co D	deserted Jun 13, 1863
186. Murphy, Terrance	33	Pvt.	20th MA, Co I	disch. disab. Dec 2, 1863
187. Norris, Fred. A.	18	Pvt.	3rd MA HA, Co B	disch. September 18, 1865
188. *Nye, Ephraim B.*	35	1st Lt.	14th MA LA	kia VA Mar 25, 1865
189. Nye, Oliver C.	39	Pvt.	4th MA Cav, Co I	disch. May 15, 1865
190. Nye, Samuel H.	25	Pvt.	45th MA, Co D	disch. Jul 7, 1863
191. *O'Neill, James*	34	2nd Lt	9th MA, Co B	kia VA May 8, 1864
192. *Packard, Charles*	26	Sgt.	11th RI, Co A	dod Sandw. Oct 30, 1866
193. Pease, Giles M.	24	Surg.	54th MA	resigned May 28, 1864
194. Perry, David Jr.	27	Pvt.	40th MA, Co I	disch. disab. May 26, 1863
195. *Perry, George R.*	29	Pvt.	95th PA, Co I	kia VA May 1863
196. Perry, Henry	22	Pvt.	40th MA, Co I	disch. Jun 16, 1865
197. Perry, John M.	18	Pvt.	40th MA, Co I	disch. disab. Nov 12, 1864
198. Perry, Nathan C.	19	Corp'l	40th MA, Co I	disch. Jun 16, 1865
199. Phinney, Isaac H.	19	Pvt.	4th US Art, Co L	disch. disab. Dec 28, 1865
200. Phinney, Joseph W.	19	Corp'l	5th MA, Co A	disch. Nov 16, 1864
201. Phinney, Prince A.	19	Pvt.	25th MA, Co D	disch. Sep 19, 1864
202. Phinney, Sylv. O.	19	Pvt	3rd MA, Co K	disch. Jul 22, 1861
203. *Phinney, Wm. W.*	21	Corp'l	4th MA Cav, Co K	dod VA Apr 1, 1865

Name	Age	Rank	Unit	Remarks
204. Regan, Barthol. F.	20	Pvt.	12th MA, Co B	disch. July 8, 1864
205. Riley, Phillip J.	21	Pvt.	24th MA, Co A	disch. Oct 11, 1864
206. Riordan, Geo.W.	23	Sgt.	11th MA, Co A	disch. Jun 24, 1864
207. Riordan, Wm. C.	21	Sgt.	11th MA, Co A	deserted Nov 1, 1862
208. Robbins, Caleb T.	19	Pvt.	29th MA, Co D	disch. Sep 2, 1864
209. Russell, Peter	19	Pvt.	29th MA, Co D	disch. Aug 16, 1864
210. Russell, Phillip	29	Pvt.	29th MA, Co D	deserted Jun 13, 1863
211. Sampson, Samuel	30	Pvt.	40th MA, Co I	disch. disab. May 23, 1863
212. Scobie, John G.	24	Pvt.	40th MA, Co E	disch. Jun 1, 1865
213. *Shaw, Colin*	30	Pvt.	11th MA, Co I	dow Gettysb. Aug 6, 1863
214. Shevlin, James	20	Pvt.	7th U.S., Co E	disch. Jul 13, 1867
215. Shurtleff, Nath. H.	37	Sgt.	9th VT, Co B	disch. Jul 7, 1865
216. Simpson, Thos. O.	40	Pvt.	45th MA, Co D	disch. disab. Apr 4, 1863
217. Smith, Jas. William	26	Pvt	29th MA, Co D	deserted May 24, 1863
218. Stephens, Edw. R.	37	Pvt.	20th MA, Co A	disch. disab. May 20, 1863
219. Stimpson, Chas. H.	21	Pvt.	45th MA, Co D	disch. Jul 7. 1863
220. Swift, Charles E.	27	Pvt.	40th MA, Co I	disch. Jun 16, 1865
221. Swift, Clark	33	Pvt.	40th MA, Co I	disch. May 25, 1865
222. *Swift, Dean W.*	32	Pvt.	40th MA, Co I	dow VA Jun 23, 1864
223. Swift, Francis C.	30	Pvt.	29th MA, Co D	disch. Sep 2, 1864
224. Swift, Francis H.	19	Pvt.	40th MA, Co I	disch. disab. Jul 30, 1863
225. Swift, Major A.	22	Pvt.	51st IL, Co G	disch. July 1864
226. Swift, Thacher H.	17	Pvt.	40th MA, Co I	disch. Jun 26, 1865
227. Swift, William H.	19	Pvt.	40th MA, Co I	disch. Jun 16, 1865
228. Tinkham, John W.	24	Pvt.	58th MA, Co A	disch. Jul 14, 1865
229. Turner, Joseph	38	Pvt.	29th MA, Co D	disch. Mar 11, 1863
230. *Ward, James*	19	Pvt.	29th MA, Co D	kia VA May 12, 1864
231. *Weeks, John*	21	Pvt.	29th MA, Co D	dod VA Oct 20, 1861
232. Weeks, Stephen	18	Pvt.	20th MA, Co I	disch. disab. Apr 27, 1863
233. *Weeks, Willard*	23	Pvt.	40th MA, Co I	dod VA Jan 23, 1865
234. Wheeler, Albert	21	Pvt.	45th MA, Co D	disch. Jul 7, 1863
235. *Wheeler, Thos. Jr.*	22	Pvt.	28th MA, Co C	kia VA Aug 30, 1862
236. *White, Thomas F.*	33	Pvt.	12th IL, Co A	kia TN Feb 15, 1862
237. *Wing, Gideon*	22	Pvt.	7th IN Cav, Co I	kia MS Jun 12, 1864
238. Wood, John	26	Pvt.	20th MA, Co H	disch. disab. Apr 22, 1863
239. *Wood, Samuel J.*	31	Pvt.	40th MA, Co I	dod VA Aug 21, 1864
240. *Wood, William H.*	35	Pvt.	29th MA, Co D	dod VA Jan 16, 1862
241. Woods, Bernard	41	Pvt.	28th MA, Co D	disch. disab. Nov 22, 1862
242. Woods, Francis	21	Pvt.	29th MA, Co D	disch. Sep 2, 1864
243. Woods, James H.	19	Pvt.	29th MA, Co D	disch. Sep 2, 1864
244. Woods, John	19	Pvt.	29th MA, Co D	disch. disab. Jan 14, 1863
245. *Woodward, E. L.*	24	Pvt.	20th MA, Co I	dow VA Dec 13, 1862
246. Woodward, W. H.	20	Sgt.	29th MA, Co D	disch. Aug 15, 1864
247. Wright, Anderson	21	Pvt.	29th MA, Co D	disch. Sep 2, 1864

Name	Age	Rank	Unit	Remarks
248. Wright, Charles S.	20	Pvt.	29th MA, Co D	disch. Jun 27, 1865
249. Wright, Stillman	44	Pvt.	45th MA, Co D	disch. Jul 7, 1863

Appendix B—
Personal Roster of Sandwich Civil War Soldiers

Starred names are native born or first generation Irish. Lived at is that community of Town of Sandwich where soldier resided around the year 1860 as reported in the 1860 Massachusetts census or other sources.

Name	Lived at	Parents
1. Adams, Asa R.	Pocasset	Thomas and Jedidah (Raymond)
2. Adams, Isaiah M.	Greenville	Bethuel and Sarah (Fish)
3. Adams, Watson F.	Greenville	Bethuel and Sarah (Fish)
4. Allen, Jesse H.	South Sandwich	Samuel and Phebe (Hoxie)
5. Allyne, S. Howard	Sandwich Village	Sam'l H. and Sophronia (Winslow)
6. Alton, John H. *	Sandwich Village	Samuel and Elizabeth (May)
7. Alton, Joseph B. *	Sandwich Village	Samuel and Elizabeth (May)
8. Alton, Samuel T. *	Sandwich Village	Samuel and Elizabeth (May)
9. Atherton, James H.	Sandwich Village	James M. and Phebe F. (Swift)
10. Atkins, James P.	East Sandwich	James and Deborah (Foster)
11. Avery, Rodman	Pocasset	Gilbert and Reliance (Taylor)
12. Avery, Watson D.	Pocasset	Gilbert and Reliance (Taylor)
13. Badger, George W.	Sandwich Village	John M. L. and Mary A. (Collins)
14. Badger, Gustavus A.	Sandwich Village	John M. L. and Mary A. (Collins)
15. Baker, Henry B.	Sandwich Village	b. NH, Stephen and Roxane (Lane)
16. Ball, James *	Sandwich Village	Unknown
17. Ball, Michael A. *	Sandwich Village	Michael and Mary (Stapleton)
18. Ball, Thomas *	Sandwich Village	Thomas and Mary (?)
19. Ball, Thomas A.*	Sandwich Village	Thomas and Ellen (Lonergan)
20. Benson, Henry F.	Sandwich Village	David and Maria (Swift)
21. Bent, Francis	North Sandwich	Wilson and Phoebe (Cahoon)
22. Blake, David A.	West Sandwich	Thomas D. and Hannah (Norton)
23. Bourne, Isaac D.	North Sandwich	Charles and Louisa (Shiverick)
24. Bourne, Joshua W.	Monument	Joshua T. and Mary Ann (Cady)
25. Bourne, Thomas B.	Monument	Henry and Sarah (Haskell)
26. Boyer, James	Monument	Henry and Ophelia (Johnson)
27. Brady, Charles *	Sandwich Village	James and Alice (?)

Name	Lived at	Parents
28. Brady, Edward *	Sandwich Village	William and Mary (?)
29. Breese, William	Sandwich Village	born England, Samuel and Mary (?)
30. Bruce, George F.	Sandwich Village	George W. and Isabella (Morrison)
31. Bumpus, Frank G.	Sandwich Village	Hosea and Mary (Bennett)
32. Burbank, Luke P.	Sandwich Village	William S. and Abigail (Perkins)
33. Burgess, Elisha H.	Monument	Jabez and Rebecca (Bassett)
34. Burgess, George A.	West Sandwich	James and Betsy O. (Robbins)
35. Burgess, Howard	Monument	Hunnewell and Rebecca (Phinney)
36. Burgess, Theophilus	Pocasset	Resolved and Susan (Eldridge)
37. Campbell, John W. *	Sandwich Village	Unknown
38. Chadbourne, John	Sandwich Village	Paul C. and Alice (Swansey)
39. Chadbourne, Rbt. H.	Sandwich Village	Paul C. and Alice (Swansey)
40. Chamberlain, Benj.	Sandwich Village	Ebenezer and Hannah (Foster)
41. Chase, Ebenezer W.	Sandwich Village	John L. and Lydia (?)
42. Cheval, Alfred	Sandwich Village	born Montreal, parents unknown
43. Chipman, Charles	West Sandwich	Jonathan E. and Celia (Bassett)
44. Chipman, Howard	Sandwich Village	Barnabas and Elizabeth (Hinckley)
45. Chipman, James F.	Sandwich Village	Jonathan E. and Celia (Bassett)
46. Chipman, Joseph P.	Sandwich Village	Thomas and Elmira (Jones)
47. Chipman, Samuel	Spring Hill	Samuel and Nancy (Churchill)
48. Chipman, Sands K.	Sandwich Village	Thomas and Elmira (Jones)
49. Clancy, Patrick C. *	Sandwich Village	b. Ireland, Walter and Margaret (?)
50. Clark, George H.	Sandwich Village	b. Boston, William and Margaret (?)
51. Clarke, Charles S.	Sandwich Village	John and Ann (Bradfield)
52. Clarke, Robert J.	Sandwich Village	John and Ann (Bradfield)
53. Clarke, William F.	Sandwich Village	John and Ann (Bradfield)
54. Collins, John T. *	Sandwich Village	Patrick and Mary (Irwin)
55. Connell, James G.	West Sandwich	John and Jerusha (Tripp)
56. Cook, Ebenezer R.	West Sandwich	John L. and Lydia (Raymond)
57. Cook, James	Sandwich Village	James and Bridget (?)
58. Corliss, Joseph S.	Sandwich Village	Charles and Rebecca (Collins)
59. Cox, James	Sandwich Village	b. Birm. Eng, Rob't and Ann (Botts)
60. Crocker, Horace L.	South Sandwich	Asa and Temperance (Crocker)
61. Dalton, Christop.B.*	Sandwich Village	Christopher and Mary (Bergen)

Name	Lived at	Parents
62. Dalton, James *	Sandwich Village	James and Ann (?)
63. Dalton, William B. *	Sandwich Village	Christopher and Mary (Bergen)
64. Davis, Benjamin	Sandwich Village	b. Birmingham, Engl., parents unkn.
65. Davis, Thomas *	Sandwich Village	Edward and Catherine (?)
66. Dean, Cornelius F.	Sandwich Village	William and Margaret (Haviland)
67. Dean, Timothy	Sandwich Village	Freeman and Desire (Kilburn)
68. Dean, Warren P.	Sandwich Village	William and Margaret (Haviland)
69. Denson, Otis E.	Sandwich Village	William F. and Patience (Ellis)
70. Dillaway, George E.	Sandwich Village	Enoch S. and Harriet (Farrar)
71. Dillingham, Naman	Sandwich Village	Freeman B. and Paulina (Freeman)
72. Donnelly, Edward *	Sandwich Village	Hugh and Catherine (?)
73. Eaton, Joseph W.	Sandwich Village	Frederick and Catherine (Kern)
74. Eldridge, Perez	Sandwich Village	Leonard and Nancy (Roberson)
75. Ellis, Abner	West Sandwich	Bartlett and Maria (Swift)
76. Ellis, Charles E.	West Sandwich	Eleazer and Lydia (Cahoon)
77. Ellis, Elisha J.	Monument	Shalmanezer and Lydia (Jones)
78. Ellis, Josiah Bartlett	West Sandwich	William B. and Eliza (Gibbs)
79. Ellis, Nathan B. Jr.	Monument	Nathan B. and Sabrina (Crowell)
80. Ellis, Nathaniel S.	West Sandwich	Bartlett and Maria (Swift)
81. Ellis, Thomas	West Sandwich	William B. and Eliza (Gibbs)
82. Emerson, William L.	Monument	born Boston, William and Mary (?)
83. Ewer, Benjamin	East Sandwich	Benjamin and Rebecca (Burgess)
84. Fagan, John *	Sandwich Village	Peter and Alice (Toner)
85. Fifield, Ansel C.	Sandwich Village	Abednego and Cynthia (Chadwick)
86. Fifield, Watson H.	Sandwich Village	Abednego and Cynthia (Chadwick)
87. Fish, Ephraim W.	Sandwich Village	Ansel C. and Abigail (Fish)
88. Fish, Henry S.	East Sandwich	Moody and Rhoda (Goodspeed)
89. Fish, John F.	South Sandwich	Jeduthan D. and Keziah (Adams)
90. Fish, Nathaniel H.	Sandwich Village	Braddock Jr. and Susan (Fish)
91. Fish, Obed M.	Sandwich Village	Braddock Jr. and Susan (Fish)
92. Fish, Sumner B.	Sandwich Village	Braddock Jr. and Susan (Fish)
93. Fisher, Calvin G.	South Sandwich	Calvin and Martha (Adams)
94. Fisher, Nathan B.	South Sandwich	Nathan and Joanna (Fish)
95. Foster, John D.	Sandwich Village	Josiah and Susan (Howes)

Name	Lived at	Parents
96. Foster, Josiah Jr.	Sandwich Village	Josiah and Susan (Howes)
97. Freeman, George H.	Sandwich Village	David C. and Jane (Newcomb)
98. Freeman, Hartwell	Sandwich Village	Frederick and Isabella (Williams)
99. Freeman, William N.	East Sandwich	Henry W. and Mehitable (Bassett)
100. Fuller, Benjamin	Sandwich Village	Nathaniel and Dorcas (Myrick)
101. Gaffney, James *	Sandwich Village	Unknown
102. Geisler, Francis C.	Sandwich Village	James and Elizabeth (Heineman)
103. Gibbs, Bradford	West Sandwich	Pelham and Mary (Crowell)
104. Gibbs, George F.	Sandwich Village	Thomas and Mary (Lovell)
105. Gibbs, Phineas	Pocasset	Phineas and Anna Maria (Raymond)
106. Gibbs, Seth F.	Sandwich Village	Freeman B. and Isabella (Swift)
107. Gibbs, Thomas M.	Pocasset	Phineas and Anna Maria (Cushman)
108. Godfrey, Charles N.	Pocasset	Christopher and Mercy (Barker)
109. Greene, Henry C.	Pocasset	Zebedee and Betsy (Swift)
110. Guiney, James *	Sandwich Village	Michael and Bridget (?)
111. Hackett, Thomas *	Sandwich Village	James and Rebecca (?)
112. Haines, George F. W.	Sandwich Village	Benjamin and Elizabeth (Gordon)
113. Haines, George L.	Spring Hill	Edward and Chloe (Vaughn)
114. Haines, James G. B.	Spring Hill	Edward and Chloe (Vaughn)
115. Hamblen, Benj. H.	Sandwich Village	Ezra and Paulina (Allen)
116. Hamblin, Ezra	Sandwich Village	Cornelius and Martha (Monroe)
117. Hammond, Luther T.	Monument	Noah and Zilpha (Maxim)
118. Harkins, Charles *	Sandwich Village	Unknown
119. Harlow, James	Sandwich Village	Benjamin and Lavinia (Shurtleff)
120. Harmon, Persia B.	Monument	Nathaniel and Hannah (Goding)
121. Harper, William H.	Sandwich Village	Unknown
122. Hathaway, James E.	Monument	Jacob and Mary (?)
123. Heald, James H.	Sandwich Village	Hiram and Sophronia (Hersey)
124. Healy, Abraham	Sandwich Village	Eng., Jos. and Rachel (Birchenough)
125. Heffernan, Edward *	Sandwich Village	Edward and Abigail (Burgess)
126. Heslin, Michael	Sandwich Village	Unknown
127. Hinds, Leonard	Pocasset	Heman and Nancy (Parker)
128. Hobson, George H.	Sandwich Village	William and Ann (Lane)
129. Hollis, Thomas	Sandwich Village	Engl., Edward and Mary (Stevens)

Name	Lived at	Parents
130. Holmes, Herman G.	North Sandwich	Thomas and Hannah (Gurney)
131. Holmes, Thomas F.	North Sandwich	Thomas and Hannah (Gurney)
132. Holway, Augustus	Spring Hill	Alvah and Lydia (Freeman)
133. Holway, Edward W.	Spring Hill	Stephen and Abigail (Wing)
134. Holway, Roland G.	Sandwich Village	John A. and Bethia (Fish)
135. Holway, Thomas E.	Spring Hill	Russell and Caroline (Eldred)
136. Howard, Leonard E.	Pocasset	Charles and Mary (Swift)
137. Howes, Alvin C.	Spring Hill	Nathaniel P. and Anna (Allen)
138. Howes, Charles A.	Spring Hill	Nathaniel P. and Anna (Allen)
139. Hoxie, Charles H.	East Sandwich	Charles A. and Rebecca (Ames)
140. Hoxie, David A.	South Sandwich	Allen and Delpha (Handy)
141. Hoxie, Nathaniel C.	Sandwich Village	Peleg and Phoebe (Allen)
142. Hoxie, Zenas H.	South Sandwich	Allen and Delpha (Handy)
143. Huddy, John T.	Pocasset	William and Mary S. (Tillinghast)
144. Hunt, Samuel W.	Sandwich Village	Henry and Eliza (Jenny)
145. Johnson, John F.	Sandwich Village	John and Eliza (Waters)
146. Jones, Charles E.	Sandwich Village	Unknown
147. Jones, Solomon H.	South Sandwich	Saul and Sarah (Hoxie)
148. Jones, James T.	East Sandwich	Eliphalet and Minerva (Fuller)
149. Kelly, James H. *	Sandwich Village	b. Ireland, Michael and Mary (?)
150. Kelley, William P.	Sandwich Village	Allen and Rebecca (Slauford?)
151. Kern, Daniel V.	Sandwich Village	Francis and Elmira (Badger)
152. Kern, Henry A.	Sandwich Village	William E. and Tabitha (Hamblin)
153. Kern, Martin L. Jr.	Sandwich Village	Martin L. and Cyrene (Hamblin)
154. Knippe, Henry H.	Sandwich Village	Henry H. and Isabella (?)
155. Lane, Andrew J.	South Sandwich	b. Maine, John and (?)
156. Lawrence, Edward J.	Pocasset	Edward D. and Elizabeth (Howard)
157. Lincoln, Ensign	Sandwich Village	Charles and Anna (French)
158. Little, Charles H.	Pocasset	Anthony and Sarah (Adams)
159. Lloyd, George T.	Sandwich Village	Samuel and Hannah (Danforth)
160. Long, Patrick *	Sandwich Village	Thomas and Bridget (Toner)
161. Lovell, Frederick U.	Sandwich Village	Ezekiel and Martha (Cahoon)
162. Lovell, James A.	Sandwich Village	Horace P. and Delia (Hammond)
163. Lovell, Horace H. P.	Sandwich Village	Horace P. and Delia (Hammond)

Name	Lived at	Parents
164. Madigan, Joseph J.	Sandwich Village	John and Margaret (Ford)
165. Magoon, Davis	Monument	Nathaniel and Hannah (Perry)
166. Manimon, Barzillai	Monument	Hugh and Salome (Pierce)
167. Manimon, Seth T.	Monument	Hugh and Salome (Pierce)
168. Manley, William	Monument	John C. and Sarah (Stevens)
169. Marvel, Samuel M.	Monument	Bradford and Eliza (Moody)
170. Mason, Thomas	Sandwich Village	Born Maine, James and Mary (?)
171. McAlaney, John *	Sandwich Village	Thomas and Susan (Campbell)
172. McCabe, John *	Unknown	Unknown
173. McDermott, Wm.*	Sandwich Village	Thomas and Mary Ann (?)
174. McElroy, Patrick *	Sandwich Village	Unknown
175. McGirr, Edward *	Sandwich Village	Patrick and Margaret (Matthewson)
176. McGirr, Patrick *	Sandwich Village	Unknown
177. McKenna, Michael *	Sandwich Village	John and Mary (McGirr)
178. McKenna, Peter *	Sandwich Village	John and Mary (McGirr)
179. McKeon, Henry *	Sandwich Village	John and Mary Ann (McGrath)
180. McKowen, Francis *	Sandwich Village	John and Mary Ann (McGrath)
181. McKowen, James *	Sandwich Village	John and Mary Ann (McGrath)
182. McLaney, Thos. J.*	Sandwich Village	John and Susan (Campbell)
183. McMahon, Patrick *	Sandwich Village	Patrick and Susan (?)
184. McNulty, James *	Sandwich Village	Peter and Ann (Burke)
185. McNulty, Peter *	Sandwich Village	Peter and Ann (Burke)
186. Murphy, Terrance *	Sandwich Village	Mark and Margaret (?)
187. Norris, Frederick A.	West Sandwich	Benjamin and Mary (Swift)
188. Nye, Ephraim B.	Pocasset	Ebenezer and Syrena (Dimmock)
189. Nye, Oliver C.	Sandwich Village	Bethuel and Bethia (Paddock)
190. Nye, Samuel H.	East Sandwich	Samuel and Sarah (Rea)
191. O'Neill, James *	Sandwich Village	James and Mary (?)
192. Packard, Charles M.	Monument	Joseph W. and Rosanna (Cahoon)
193. Pease, Giles M.	Sandwich Village	Giles and Mabel (Moseley)
194. Perry, David Jr.	Pocasset	David and Fanny (Gibbs)
195. Perry, George R.	Pocasset	David and Fanny (Gibbs)
196. Perry, Henry	Pocasset	David and Fanny (Gibbs)
197. Perry, John M.	Sandwich Village	Joseph and Meribah (Tinkham)

Name	Lived at	Parents
198. Perry, Nathan C.	Pocasset	David and Fanny (Gibbs)
199. Phinney, Isaac H.	Sandwich Village	John C. and Chloe (Hoxie)
200. Phinney, Joseph W.	Spring Hill	Warren and Henrietta (Smith)
201. Phinney, Prince A.	Sandwich Village	John C. and Chloe (Hoxie)
202. Phinney, Sylvester O.	Monument	George O. and Betsey (Fisher)
203. Phinney, William W.	Monument	George O. and Betsey (Fisher)
204. Regan, Barthol. F.	North Sandwich	Patrick and Ellen (O'Neill)
205. Riley, Phillip J. *	Sandwich Village	James and Mary (?)
206. Riordan, Geo. W. *	Sandwich Village	Titus P. and Ann (Kelley)
207. Riordan, William C.*	Sandwich Village	Titus P. and Ann (Kelley)
208. Robbins, Caleb T.	Sandwich Village	Thomas and Jane (Nye)
209. Russell, Peter *	Sandwich Village	Patrick and Mary (Mannix)
210. Russell, Philip *	Sandwich Village	William and Catherine (Sheehan)
211. Sampson, Samuel	Sandwich Village	Samuel and Isabel (?)
212. Scobie, John G.	West Sandwich	George and Lydia (Wheldon)
213. Shaw, Colin	Sandwich Village	Donald and Mary (Campbell)
214. Shevlin, James *	Sandwich Village	Phillip and Elizabeth (McParlin)
215. Shurtleff, Nathan H.	Sandwich Village	David and Waitsill (Hammond)
216. Simpson, Thomas O.	Spring Hill	William and Sally (Riddell)
217. Smith, Jas. William *	Sandwich Village	George and Elizabeth (?)
218. Stephens, Edward R.	Monument	born England, Edward H. and (?)
219. Stimpson, Charles H.	Sandwich Village	Andrew and Lydia (Chipman)
220. Swift, Charles E.	Pocasset	Charles and Zebia (Hewins)
221. Swift, Clark	West Sandwich	Ellis C. and Ruhama (Dean)
222. Swift, Dean W.	West Sandwich	Ellis C. and Ruhama (Dean)
223. Swift, Francis C.	West Sandwich	Clark and Sarah (Spring)
224. Swift, Francis H.	Pocasset	Nathan B. and Pamelia (Cowing)
225. Swift, Major A.	Pocasset	Bartlett H. and Mary (Fish)
226. Swift, Thacher H.	Pocasset	Joseph L. and Elizabeth (Rugg)
227. Swift, William H.	Pocasset	Wayman S. and Lucy (Freeman)
228. Tinkham, John W.	Sandwich Village	Micah and Hannah (Proaty)
229. Turner, Joseph	Sandwich Village	born England, Joseph A. and (?)
230. Ward, James *	Sandwich Village	Lawrence and Mary (Larkin)
231. Weeks, John	Pocasset	Willard and Eunice (Mills)

Name	Lived at	Parents
232. Weeks, Stephen	Pocasset	Willard and Eunice (Mills)
233. Weeks, Willard Jr.	Pocasset	Willard and Eunice (Mills)
234. Wheeler, Albert	Sandwich Village	Levi and Betsy (Fuller)
235. Wheeler, Thomas Jr.	Sandwich Village	Thomas and Joanna (Burgess)
236. White, Thomas F.	Pocasset	Bela and Celia (Gardner)
237. Wing, Gideon	Spring Hill	Paul and Laura (Soule)
238. Wood, John	Unknown	Unknown
239. Wood, Samuel J.	North Sandwich	Samuel and Eliza (?)
240. Wood, William H.	Sandwich Village	Richard and Louisa (Collins)
241. Woods, Bernard *	Sandwich Village	Unknown
242. Woods, Francis *	Sandwich Village	Bernard and Ann
243. Woods, James H. *	Sandwich Village	John and Delia (?)
244. Woods, John *	Sandwich Village	Michael and Sarah (?)
245. Woodward, Ezekiel	West Sandwich	Charles and Rosetta (Lovell)
246. Woodward, Wm. H.	Sandwich Village	William and Marietta (Newcomb)
247. Wright, Anderson	Pocasset	Stillman and Zipha (Hammond)
248. Wright, Charles S.	Pocasset	Luther T. and Eliza (Avery)
249. Wright, Stillman	Pocasset	Zadock and Jane (Tillson)

Appendix C— Roster of Sandwich Civil War Navy Sailors

Italicized names are men who died in the war. Names with superscripted A denote men who also served in the army. Duty ships only are listed. Training ships are not listed. Several men served on more than two duty ships but limited space permitted no more than two to be listed.

Name	*Highest Rank*	*Principal Ship or Ships*	*Years in Navy*
1. Baker, John F.	Acting Masters Mate	*Glasgow*	1864-1865
2. Bassett, Chas. H.	Ordinary Seaman	*Florida, State of Georgia*	1863-1865
3. Bassett, Ezra	Acting Ensign	*ironclad Kickapoo*	1864-1865
4. Bassett, John B.	Second Class Fireman	*Massasoit*	1864-1865
5. Bent, Francis [A]	Seaman	*Sumpter, Bienville*	1862-1863
6. Black, John	Boatswain's Mate	*Minnesota*	1862-1863
7. Booth, Wilder	Ordinary Seaman	*Ino*	1864-1865
8. Bourne, John H.	Coxswain	*Harriet Lane, Corwin*	1861-1865
9. Bourne, Samuel C.	Seaman	*Augusta*	1862-1863
10. Bowes, Robert	Quartermaster	*Hetzel*	1861-1864
11. Boyer, Henry	Ordinary Seaman	*Wachusett, Satellite*	1862
12. Boyer, James [A]	Ordinary Seaman	*Sabine, Fort Donelson*	1861-2, 1864
13. Childs, William H.	Acting Masters Mate	*Hartford*	1863-1865
14. Clement, Alonzo F.	Ordinary Seaman	*R.R. Cuyler, Metacomet*	1862-1864
15. Connell, John H.	Quarter Gunner	*Wabash*	1861-1864
16. Crocker, Zenas A.	Ship's Cook	*Powhatan, Mystic*	1861-1864
17. Doty, James E.	Ordinary Seaman	*W. G. Anderson*	1861-1862
18. Ellis, Charles C.	Ordinary Seaman	*Ino*	1861-1862
19. Ewer, George W.	Acting Master	*Seneca, ironclad Catskill*	1861-1864
20. Ewer, John	Acting Master	*Sabine, ironclad Lehigh*	1861-1863
21. *Fifield, Ansel C.* [A]	Seaman	*ironclad Patapsco*	1864-1865
22. Fisher, Daniel F.	Landsman	*Ohio*	1863
23. Fisher, Edgar W.	Landsman	*Tuscarora, Newbern*	1863-1864
24. Fisher, Nathan B. [A]	Quartermaster	*Wachusett*	1864-1866

Name	Highest Rank	Principal Ship or Ships	Years in Navy
25. *Flaherty, Thomas*	Gunner	*Richmond*	1861-1862
26. Foster, Christopher	Acting Masters Mate	*Lackawanna*	1864
27. Freeman, Isaac C.	Boatswain's Mate	*Curlew, Potomska*	1861-1864
28. Freeman, Watson Jr.	Acting Master	*ironclad Sangamon*	1862-1863
29. Gibbs, Charles I.	Act. Vol. Lieutenant	*Richmond*	1861-1865
30. Gibbs, Paul C.	Acting Master	*R .R. Cuyler*	1862-1863
31. Gibbs, William C.	Acting Master	*Brooklyn*	1862-1863
32. Godfrey, John W.	Acting Master	*Wabash, Darlington*	1861-1863
33. Haines, Geo. F. [A]	Landsman	*Relief*	1861-1862
34. Harlow, William S.	Landsman	*R. R. Cuyler, Emma*	1862-1864
35. Hathaway, Jos. T.	Acting First Engineer	*Vixen, ironclad Montauk*	1862-1864
36. Holmes, Heman [A]	Acting Masters Mate	*Fort Henry*	1864-1865
37. *Howard, Charles L.*	Ordinary Seaman	*Sabine*	1862-1863
38. Johnson, Anthony	Landsman	*North Carolina*	1862
39. Jones, Solomon [A]	Ordinary Seaman	*Nahant*	1862-1864
40. Kilmartin, Daniel	Landsman	*Susquehanna*	1861-1863
41. Lane, Andrew J. [A]	Seaman	*Midnight*	1861-1862
42. Little, Francis	Ordinary Seaman	*Kingfisher, Fernandina*	1861-1862
43. McGirr, Patrick [A]	Ordinary Seaman	*Sunflower*	1863-1864
44. McKenna, John	Ordinary Seaman	*Unadilla, Sangamon*	1861-1863
45. McParlin, John	Unknown	*Sabine*	Unknown
46. Montague, James P.	Acting Ensign	*San Jacinto, Two Sisters*	1863-1865
47. Nickerson, John	Seaman	*New Ironsides*	1861-1863
48. Nightingale, Chas.	Captain of Hold	*Vermont, N. Hampshire*	1862-1864
49. Norris, William W.	Landsman	*Western World, Dragon*	1863-1864
50. O'Neil, Peter	Unknown	*Colorado*	1862-1865
51. Parker, David J.	Landsman	*Rhode Island, Guard*	1862-1864
52. Pease, Giles M. [A]	Surgeon	*Bohio*	1861-1862
53. Perry, Caleb H.	Seaman	*Southfield, Miami*	1862-1865
54. Perry, Joseph M.	Landsman	*Colorado*	1861-1862
55. Phinney, George E.	Landsman	*Colorado*	1861-1862
56. Phinney, Jesse F.	Landsman	*Colorado*	1861-1862

Name	Highest Rank	Principal Ship or Ships	Years in Navy
57. Pierce, William F.	Ordinary Seaman	*Monongahela, Richmond*	1864-1865
58. Pope, John	Commodore	*Richmond*	1861-1864
59. Ryder, Andrew J.	Landsman	*Hunchback*	1861-1864
60. Tinkham, John [A]	Ordinary Seaman	*Benton*	1861-1863
61. Weston, Daniel	Acting Third Engineer	*Somerset, Honduras*	1864-1865

Notes

Abbreviations

1. BC Barnstable County
2. *BP Barnstable Patriot*
3. *Boston DA Boston Daily Advertiser*
4. *CCANI Cape Cod Advocate and Nautical Intelligencer* of Sandwich
5. CWDC Civil War Document Collection
6. FNEPN FamilySearch New England Petitions for Naturalization
7. MF Microfilm
8. MNGMA Massachusetts National Guard Museum and Archives
9. MSA Massachusetts State Archives
10. NA National Archives
11. NCSM Non-population Census Schedules Massachusetts
12. ORA Official Records Union Army, followed by Series, Volume, Part and Page.
13. ORN Official Records Union Navy, followed by Series, Volume and Page.
14. PR Pension Records (at National Archives)
15. RG Record Group at National Archives
16. SA Sandwich Archives
17. SR Service Records (at National Archives)
18. USAHEC U.S. Army Heritage and Education Center

Chapter One. A Pre-War Town

1. *Boston Columbian Centinel*, October 29, 1825; Harriet Barbour. Sandwich The Town That Glass Built. Augustus M. Kelly. 1976, 112; R. A. Lovell Jr. Sandwich. A Cape Cod Town. Town of Sandwich, MA. 1996, 284. The Jarvesville section of Sandwich Village retains that name. A Jarvesville National Register Historic District was created in 2008.
2. Raymond B. Burgoin. The Catholic Church in Sandwich 1830-1930. Boston: E. L. Grimes Printing. 1930, 6, 17 and 19. The terms "B and S," "factory" and "glassworks", unless otherwise specified, will refer henceforth to the Boston and Sandwich Glassworks.
3. Statistical Information Relating to Certain Branches of Industry in Massachusetts 1855; *Middleboro Gazette*, "Sandwich," July 18, 1856; NCSM (BC Manufacturing Sandwich 1860).
4. *Middleboro Gazette*, "Jaunt Over the Cape Cod RR," June 12, 1858;

Wareham Transcript and Advertiser, "A Visit to Agawam Nail Works," July 20, 1855.

5. Barbour, Sandwich, 174. Barbour, page 62, suggests that friction existed between Sandwich Village's Puritan and Irish populations. With but one possible exception, the author found no instances of it. In pension records of John W. Tinkham, Mary Sutton Tinkham wrote that Micah and Adaline Tinkham of Sandwich opposed her marriage to Tinkham son John in 1861. "It [the opposition] made a feeling between us," wrote Mary. Mary Sutton was a poor Irish girl who lived in the household of William H. Gibbs, possibly as a servant. The Tinkham's were of Puritan descent.

6. Lovell, Sandwich, 259 and 286; *BP*, "Manomet Iron Works," October 29, 1850.

7. *Middleboro Gazette*, "Pocasset Correspondence," January 20, 1858 and "Pocasset," December 8, 1860; Statistical Information 1855; NCSM (BC Manufacturing Sandwich 1860).

8. *Sandwich Mechanic*, "Carriage Manufactory," December 3, 1851; NCSM (BC Manufacturing Sandwich 1860); *BP*, "Marble Foot Manufactory," September 18, 1860.

9. Jonathan Bourne Correspondence. Bourne to Dillingham, July 26, 1860.

10. *New Bedford Mercury*, "Port of New Bedford," July 3, 1857 and August 7, 1857; From Pocasset to Cataument. Bourne Historical Society. 1988, 38-39; *Sandwich Independent*, "Mrs. Lucinda E. Phinney," September 21, 1917.

11. *New Bedford Mercury*, "Mansion House Sandwich," July 1, 1842; *BP*, "Sandwich Hotel," August 15, 1854 and "Representative Convention," October 30, 1860.

12. *BP*, "Sportsman's Retreat Sandwich," October 11, 1848, "Marston's Hotel, "April 5, 1853 and "Pictures from my Camera," June 19, 1855; *CCANI*, "Marston's Hotel," October 20, 1855.

13. *CCANI*, "Washington House," April 14, 1860; MSA Letters Sent, Vol. 29, Frederick Freeman to Governor Andrew, March 1863.

14. *CCANI*, "Oyster Saloon!" November 21, 1855.

15. *Sandwich Observer*, "Look at This," February 6, 1847; *BP*, "Daguerreotypes," August 30, 1853 and "Pictures from my Camera," March 27, 1855; *CCANI*, "Wanted! Wanted!" October 20, 1855 and "Notice Extra," August 28, 1858. Joseph Blackwell was also a physician. According to a note in the pension file of John McAlaney, he practiced in Sandwich from 1843 to 1868.

16. *CCANI*, "Sandwich Circulating Library," February 17, 1857; *BP* July 27, 1858. Isaac N. Keith of West Sandwich learned telegraphy in 1858 but whether he was an operator in Sandwich is unknown. In May 1861 he went to Washington to join the army telegraph corps but apparently did not stay

(*Boston Herald*, "The Army Telegraph Corps," May 10, 1861).

17. *CCANI*, "Dr. Parkinson," November 21, 1857; *New York Times*, "Lucy Amanda Swasey," July 2, 1905.

18. *CCANI*, "Notice," November 21, 1855.

19. *BP*, "Funeral at Brewster," July 24, 1849, "Sandwich Brass Band," June 17, 1851 and "Sandwich Cotillon Band," January 27, 1852.

20. NCSM (BC Social Statistics Sandwich 1860); Lovell, Sandwich, 285.

21. *CCANI*, "Jarvesville District," April 14, 1860.

22. SA. Sandwich Academy Folder; NCSM (BC Social Statistics Sandwich 1860); *BP*, "Apple Grove Family School," January 11, 1859; *New Bedford Mercury*, "Sandwich Female Seminary," March 27, 1846.

23. *BP*, "Sandwich Collegiate Institute," March 25, 1846 and December 5, 1849; NCSM (BC Mortality Sandwich 1860).

24. *Sandwich Observer*, "Bonnet Rooms," May 19, 1849; *Sandwich Mechanic*, "Millinery Goods," December 3, 1851; *CCANI*, "Sandwich Directory," August 28, 1858.

25. George H. Winchester Journal.

26. Winchester Journal.

27. *Whalemen's Shipping List*, "Passengers," March 20, 1849; *New York Weekly Herald*, "Arrived at San Francisco," December 29, 1849; Winchester Journal.

28. *BP*, "Installation in Sandwich," October 31, 1854 and "Called," December 16, 1856.

29. John M. Erle. Report of the Governor and Council, Indians of the Commonwealth. Boston, 1861; Sandwich Massachusetts Citizens to Abraham Lincoln (Petition Endorsed by Seth Ewer).

30. SA. Sandwich Anti-slavery Collection; *Liberator*, "Conventions in Barnstable County," August 12, 1844.

31. *Boston Emancipator and Republican*, October 15, 1843; *BP*, "Death of Joseph Marsh," May 30, 1887.

32. *Sandwich Observer*, "Miss Lucy Stone," December 22, 1849; Winchester Journal.

33. *BP*, "Abolitionism," February 10, 1862; *Liberator* March 26, 1851; *Sandwich Observer*, March 9, 1850; SA. Sandwich Anti-slavery Collection; *Liberator*, "Treasurer's Account," January 24, 1840; SA. Kern Family Folder; Dorothy Porter Wesley and Constance Porter Uzelac, eds. William Cooper Nell Selected Writings 1832-1874. Baltimore: Black Classic Press. 2002, 309 and 389.

34. *BP*, "Temperance Meeting," July 6, 1852.

35. Reports of Cases Argued and Determined in the Supreme Judicial Court of Massachusetts. Vol. 1.1855, 1-5; *BP*, "Four Barrels of Liquor Seized and Destroyed!" August 10, 1852.

36. *BP*, "Court of Common Pleas," August 5, 1856 and "Justice's Court, September 13, 1859; BC Superior Court Records (Thomas Ball, 1857).

Chapter Two. A Pre-War Heritage

1. One of the 294 men did not volunteer. Edward Holway was drafted.
2. Family Search Petitions for Naturalization Barnstable County Common Pleas 1827-1886, 4-6 (Daniel Fogarty); Raymond E. Barlow and Joan E. Kaiser. The Glass Industry in Sandwich. 5. Kaiser Barlow Publishing. 1999, Roster of Personnel (Fogarty).
3. Naturalization Petitions, 17-18 (Patrick McGirr); *BP*, "Sandwich Town Officers," April 12, 1852 and "The Liquor Law Pronounced," March 20, 1854. McGirr abandoned his family around 1855 and in the next few years his wife and children Edward and Catherine moved to New York City—NA. Civil War "Widow's Pensions" (Edward McGirr).
4. Naturalization Petitions, 31 (Benjamin Tewks), 33-34 (Samuel Alton) and 35-36 (Christopher Dalton).
5. Naturalization Petitions, 25-26 (John Montague) and 41-42 (Edward Heffernan); Barlow-Kaiser Roster (Edward Heffernan).
6. Naturalization Petitions, 47 (Titus P. Riordan); *CCANI*, "Titus P. Riordan," October 20, 1855.
7. *BP*, "Homicide in Sandwich," December 29, 1857.
8. PR Edward Heffernan.
9. Barlow-Kaiser Roster (Patrick Collins); *Sandwich Mechanic*, "Groceries and Provisions," December 3, 1851; BC Probate Records (Patrick Collins, 1855); *BP*, "Administrator's Sale," November 11, 1856.
10. *BP*, "Justice's Court," June 23, 1857, May 10, 1859, September 13, 1859 and "Fire," December 17, 1861; BC Superior Court Records (James Gaffney, 1858).
11. BC Superior Court Records (James H. Woods, 1860); *BP*, "Justice Court in Sandwich," April 24, 1860.
12. PR Edward Brady.
13. PR Thomas Hackett and John McAlaney.
14. Barlow-Kaiser Roster (Samuel Lloyd); PR George T. Lloyd.
15. *Sandwich Observer*, "Rev. Benjamin Haines," March 20, 1888; Naturalization Petitions, 13 (Benjamin Haines).
16. PR James Cox; Birmingham England Baptisms 1813-1912, 55 and 396; Barlow-Kaiser Roster (James Cox). Cox's mother-in-law Emma (Dean) Heviland, daughter of Samuel Dean and Ann (Cox) Dean, was born and christened in Birmingham in 1824 and in 1840 married Jacob Heviland at Sandwich. She died at the home of Cox in Belmont County, Ohio on January

21, 1901. The Heviland, Dean and Cox families have entwined family trees at Birmingham and Sandwich. The Eaton family of Sandwich, related to the latter families by marriage, are from Hednesford, Staffordshire.

17. PR Joseph Turner.

18. *Boston Herald*, "Coroner's Inquest," November 21, 1854; PR Henry H. Knippe.

19. Naturalization Petitions, 79 (Francis Geisler); PR Francis C. Geisler; Barlow-Kaiser roster (Geisler).

20. Kathryn Grover. The Fugitive's Gibraltar: Escaping Slaves and Abolitionism in New Bedford, Massachusetts. Amherst: University of Massachusetts Press. 2001, 185-88; *Whalemen's Shipping List*, "Crew Lists," September 27, 1853; *CCANI*, "Crew Lists," November 21, 1857.

21. Charles Chipman Papers and Letters.

22. *BP*, "Representative Nominations," October 26, 1858 and "State Legislature," September 13, 1859.

23. *BP*, "The Fourth in Sandwich," June 26, 1860 and "The Sandwich Celebration," July 17, 1860. James Atherton's grandfather Daniel Atherton, apparently a Massachusetts gunsmith, became assistant armorer at the Virginia Manufactory of Arms at Richmond in 1802 and served in that capacity until his death in 1820. A Virginia governor in this period was James Monroe and this may be why James Atherton's father was named James Monroe Atherton.

24. *BP*, "Breckenridge and Lane," July 10, 1860 and "Delegates to the State Convention," September 11, 1860.

25. *CCANI*, "Republicans of Sandwich!" October 20, 1855.

26. PR Charles I. Gibbs; SA. Charles I. Gibbs Folder; *Honolulu Friend*, August 19, 1856; Stanton Garner, ed., Mary Chipman Lawrence. The Captain's Best Mate: The Journal of Mary Chipman Lawrence on the Whaler *Addison* 1856-1860. Providence: Brown University Press. 1966, 287; *Boston Herald*, August 15, 1857; *New York Times*, January 29, 1858.

27. *Salem Register*, July 2, 1860; *Philadelphia Inquirer*, July 26, 1860.

28. *Boston DA*, "American Brig Seized by British Steamer," July 26, 1858; Parliamentary Papers, House of Commons and Command, Vol. 34, 218; Thirty-Sixth Congress. 2nd Session. House Executive Documents. Vol. 4. No. 7, 316-19.

29. PR Zenas H. Hoxie; NCSM (BC Agriculture Barnstable 1860).

30. PR Benjamin Fuller and Thomas Wheeler Jr.

31. Allyne Family Papers, Joseph W. Allyne to Father, January 30, 1849 and Samuel H. Allyne Jr. to Sister April 17, 1852; *Boston Daily Courier*, "Passengers," November 27, 1852; *Liberator*, "Obituary," September 15, 1854; *Sacramento Daily Union*, "Teachers," November 13, 1854.

32. *BP*, "Deaths," June 3, 1856.

33. PR Benjamin Ewer; *Berkshire County Whig*, Pittsfield, September 28, 1848.
34. *Whaleman's Shipping List*, "Brig Amelia," August 1, 1854; *Boston Traveler*, "East Cambridge," February 20, 1858.
35. Microfilmed Log of Brig *Ocean* 1856-1857.
36. *Boston Herald*, "Whaling Tragedy," September 4, 1851.
37. PR William H. Childs; Henry C. Kittredge. Shipmasters of Cape Cod. Hyannis: Parnassus Imprints. 1963, 261-63; *B. P.* "Disasters," Jun 10, 1862.
38. James Montgomery Rice. Peoria City and County Illinois. Vol. 2. 1912, 563; *BP*, "Information Wanted," August 30, 1853.
39. Jonathan Bourne Correspondence. Bourne to Benjamin Bourne March 29, 1854; BC Probate Records (Joshua T. Bourne, 1854); Rice. Peoria etc., 563.
40. PR Davis Magoon.
41. PR Watson D. Avery.
42. PR Francis H. Swift; NCSM (BC Agriculture Sandwich 1860).
43. PR Leonard Hinds.
44. *Charleston Courier* October 12, 1850, December 28, 1853, March 24, 1854 and May 1, 1855; *Monthly Nautical Magazine, and Quarterly Review*. 1855, 287. Captain Godfrey was not the only Cape Cod ship captain to benefit from the South's slave economy in the pre-war years. A number of Cape captains engaged regularly in the coal and flour trade in the James River at Richmond, Virginia, in lumber commerce along Georgia's Satilla River and in miscellaneous trade at Mobile, Alabama and Galveston, Texas. A study of the importance of such trade to the Cape Cod economy would be insightful.
45. *Boston Traveler*, May 15, 1856; J. M. Selfridge. "In Memoriam—Dr. Giles M. Pease." *The Homeopathic Physician* XII, No. 6 (June 1892): 260. The most plausible times at which Pease might have acted with Booth are in 1859 and 1860 when the latter had extended performances at Boston's Howard Anthenaeum and Museum Theaters.
46. PR David A. Blake

Chapter Three. To Virginia's Sacred Soil—pril to December 1861

1. Dorothy G. Hogan-Schofield. "A Civil War Diary." *The Acorn, Journal of the Sandwich Glass Museum* (Fall 2011): 10.
2. *Boston DA*, "Meeting of Adopted Citizens," April 17, 1861; *Boston Herald*, "Patriotic Meeting of the Adopted Citizens," April 17, 1861 and "Irish Brigade," April 22, 1861.

3. *Boston Evening Transcript*, "War Preparation," April 18, 1861; *BP*, "Grand Mass Meeting" and "Barnstable County Awake," April 23, 1861; *Yarmouth Register*, "Cape Cod in the Field," April 26, 1861.

4. PR Leonard Hinds; Fred M. Mallinson. The Civil War on the Outer Banks. Jefferson, NC: McFarland and Company. 1998, 25.

5. MNGMA, Adjutant-General's Letterbook #1, April-December 1861; William H. Osborne. The History of the Twenty-ninth Regiment of Massachusetts Volunteer Infantry. Boston. 1877, 32; *Yarmouth Register*, "The Sandwich Volunteers," May 10, 1861.

6. *Boston Daily Journal*, "Volunteers to be Enlisted for Three Years," May 7, 1861; *Boston Daily Journal* May 9, 1861; *Boston DA*, "Military Matters," May 9, 1861 and "The Steamer Pembroke," May 10, 1861; *BP*, "The Sandwich Volunteers," May 14, 1861; MSA Executive Letters Vol. 170, Day to Andrew May 13, 1861 and Vol. 34, November 25, 1861. The United States Hotel was along Beach Street, in present China Town section of Boston.

7. Richard F. Miller. "For His Wife, His Widow and His Orphan: Massachusetts and Family Aid During the Civil War." *Massachusetts Historical Review* 6 (2004), 78.

8. "A Bit of 1861 History," Sandwich Historic Society GAR Folder 19; *Boston Daily Courier*, "Troops for Fort Monroe," May 20, 1861; *BP*, "Departure of the First Cape Cod Volunteers," May 21, 1861; PR John McAlaney; Charles Chipman to Wife May 19, 1861.

9. SR Perez Eldridge; Chipman to Wife June 4, 1861.

10. *New York Herald*, "Our Fort Monroe Correspondence," May 25, 1861; Chipman to Wife May 24, 1861; PR Edward Brady; George H. Freeman Diary of May 22, 1861; Benjamin Butler Correspondence, Box 5. Martin Monahan was age forty-one in 1861. He may have been rejected for evidence of consumption, since he died of that in 1865. Henry Parks was exempted from the draft in 1863 because of varicose veins.

11. Chipman to Wife August 6, 1861.

12. SR William H. Wood; Chipman to Wife June 16, 1861.

13. NA. RG 52. Entry 22. Medical Journals of Ships (*Minnesota* June 1861).

14. *Boston Globe*, "Col C. G. Fisher Dead," March 14, 1908; SR Calvin G. Fisher and Joshua W. Bourne; ORA II, 10, 116.

15. PR James H. Kelley; Christian B. Samito, ed. Commanding Boston's Irish Ninth: The Civil War Letters of Colonel Patrick R. Guiney, Ninth Massachusetts Volunteer Infantry. New York: Fordham University Press. 1998, 8; *Boston Pilot*, "The Irish Regiment," June 29, 1861; *Washington Daily National Intelligencer*, "Local Matters," July 2, 1861.

16. *New York Herald*, "Duryee's Zouaves," May 24, 1861.

17. PR Jesse F. Phinney.

18. NA. RG 76. Records Court of Commissioner Alabama Claims. Dockets 3271-3283.
19. *BP*, "Letter from the Seat of War," July 23, 1861.
20. Alfred S. Roe. The Fifth Massachusetts Volunteer Infantry. 1911, 55, 56 and 70; *Boston Traveler*, "Charlestown," June 7, 1862.
21. NA. RG 153. Records of the Office of JAG. Folder II 447; Chipman to Wife August 13 and September 14, 1861.
22. PR William McDermott; *BP*, "Our Army Correspondence" and "News from the Sandwich Company," September 9, 1861.
23. SR Samuel H. Allyne Jr.
24. PR John F. Fish and Isaiah M. Adams; *BP*, "Osterville," April 5, 1920.
25. PR Isaiah M. Adams and Benjamin Ewer.
26. *Boston Pilot*, "Second Irish Regiment," October 5, 1861.
27. PR Willard Weeks; *BP*, "Another Member of the Sandwich Company Dead," October 29, 1861.
28. PR Francis Little.
29. Chipman to Wife October 30, 1861 and November 29, 1861; *New York Times*, "Affairs at Fortress Monroe," June 26, 1861. Sutlers sold goods to soldiers.
30. Chipman to Wife November 7, 1861.
31. Chipman to Wife October 11, 1861 and January 7, 1862. Swift was apparently also a horse dealer. In 1860, he and William Swift Jr. were sued by Oliver B. Jones of Barnstable for fraudulent representation of a horse Jones purchased from the Swifts. Jones paid $100 for the horse which was diseased, unsound and worth less than $20.00—BC Superior Court Records (Francis C. Swift).
32. Haines Letters. George Haines to Sister November 10, 1861.
33. *Yarmouth Register*, "The Patriotic Ladies of Sandwich," November 22, 1861; Chipman to Wife November 7, 1861.
34. *BP*, "Contributions for U. S. Hospitals," November 26, 1861 and "Patriotic Ladies of West Sandwich," December 17, 1861.
35. Civil War Records. Sandwich Town Offices.
36. MSA Executive Letters Vol. 34, Massachusetts Battalion, and Day to Andrew Vol. 34, November 25, 1861.
37. NA. RG 153. Office of JAG. Folder II 743.
38. NA. RG 153. Office of JAG. Folder KK 121; Missouri State Archives Provost Holding File, Fisher to General J. M. Schofield November 27, 1861 and Fisher to Colonel E. C. Catherwood December 4, 1861.
39. *Boston Daily Courier*, "Military Matters," December 16, 1861; SR Charles Chipman; Chipman to Barnes December 20, 1861 and to Wife September 26, 1861.

40. Chipman to Barnes December 20, 1861; *Boston Evening Transcript*, "Grand Cavalry Parade," December 19, 1861; Benjamin W. Crowinshield. A History of the First Massachusetts Cavalry Volunteers. Baltimore: Butternut and Blue. 1995, 47.
41. MNGMA. Twenty-ninth Regiment Box. Hall to Schouler December 27, 1861; Chipman toWife December 29, 1861.
42. NA. RG 153. Office of JAG. Folder II 773.
43. Thomas F. Darby Letters. Darby to Miss Mary Ann, January 3, 1862.
44. *BP*, "Cape Cod Railroad," December 31, 1861.

Chapter Four. Not Much of a Celebration— January to June1862

1. Civil War Box, Bourne Historical Society. Anderson Wright to Noah January 26, 1862.
2. Chipman to Wife January 10, 1862. "That Chamberlain girl" may be fifteen-year-old Abby Chamberlain who delivered a child January 27, 1862 and about which the Sandwich town clerk affixed the note "male illegitimate." The identity of Crocker is unknown.
3. Chipman to Wife January 10, 1862; Charles F. Herberger, ed., A Yankee at Arms: The Diary of Lieutenant Augustus D. Ayling. Knoxville: University of Tennessee Press. 1989, 19-20.
4. Chipman to wife January 10, 1862; Ayling. Yankee at Arms, 18.
5. Barlow and Kaiser. Glass Industry. 1, 49; Chipman to Wife January 15, 1862.
6. Chipman to Wife January 16, 1862; *New Bedford Standard* January 29, 1862; *BP*, "A Well Deserved Gift," February 11, 1862; *Yarmouth Register*, "Death of a Sandwich Volunteer," January 31, 1862.
7. Chipman to Wife January 16, 1862; Darby Letters. Darby to Ellen M. January 10, 1862.
8. *Boston Evening Transcript*, "Bad Usage of the Mass. 28th Regiment," January 15, 1862; Darby Letters. Darby to Miss Mary Ann January 5, 1862.
9. USAHEC. CWDC. Solomon Beals to Brother June 19, 1862.
10. ORA I, 9, 100; PR Jesse H. Allen; *BP*, "Letter From Roanoke Island," February 25, 1862; *New York Herald*, "The Naval Section," February 15, 1862.
11. Darby Letters. Darby to Miss Marie February 9, 1862; *Yarmouth Register* February 21, 1862.
12. Eben S. Whittemore Diary; Kendall D. Gott. "They Fought at Fort Donelson: The Story of the Units and Commanders of the Battle of Fort Donelson, February 1862." Unpublished manuscript, circa 2005, 75-76.

13. Chipman to Wife January 30, February 4 and February 12, 1862.
14. Edward P. Tobie. History of the First Maine Cavalry 1861-1865. Boston. 1867, 15; PR David A. Blake.
15. SA. Barlow Family Folder.
16. John D. Hayes, ed. Samuel Francis Du Pont: A Selection from his Civil War Letters. Ithaca, NY: Cornell University Press. 1. 1969, 330; NA. Deck Log of *Ottawa* March 1, 1862.
17. *Charleston Daily Courier* January 15, 1862.
18. PR Samuel C. Bourne and Charles W. Nightingale.
19. *BP*, "Abolitionism," February 11, 1862 and "The 22nd in Sandwich," February 25, 1862; Chipman to Wife March 6, 1862. E. S. Whittemore noted in his diary that on April 3, 1862 the Reverend Henry Kimball preached "a warm anti-slavery sermon."
20. PR Thomas Wheeler; *Boston Pilot*, "Letter From the 28th Regiment," April 5, 1862.
21. Chipman to Wife November 15, 1861 and March 11, 1862.
22. Chipman to Wife March 11, 1862; PR Alfred Cheval.
23. Chipman to Wife March 20, 1862.
24. Darby Letters. Darby to Miss Ellen March 21, 1862; *Boston Pilot*, "Twenty-eighth Regiment," April 12, 1862.
25. MNGMA. Cogswell to Dear Doctor. Military Officer Letters. Vol. 2, 1862; PR Benjamin Hamblin; Chipman to Wife April 21, 1862.
26. PR Thomas Ball.
27. Whittemore Diary April 26, April 30, May 4 and May 10, 1862; *BP*, "In Memoriam," January 21, 1862 and "Business in Sandwich," May 20, 1862. Dentist N.C. Fowler had hours in Sandwich each Monday. On other days he was in his Yarmouthport office—*CCANI* August 25, 1862.
28. Chipman to Wife February 1, 1862; MSA Executive Letters. Vol. 34, (Henry A. Kern); *Yarmouth Register* June 20, 1862.
29. MSA Executive Letters, James M. Atherton.
30. George L. Haines to Sister June 26 and July 21, 1862.
31. NA. RG 92. Entry 1403. "Vessel Files." Box 8, *Ellen Bernard*; *New York Times*, "From Key West," July 3, 1862 and "Capt. Henry A. Bourne," April 21, 1899.
32. Samuel Howard Allyne Jr. to Brother June 25, 1862.
33. Isaac Henry Taylor Letter June 12, 1862.
34. Henry H. Robbins Letters. Antietam Battlefield File of Twenty-ninth Massachusetts June 10, 1862; Osborne. Twenty-ninth Regiment, 141; *Boston Daily Evening Transcript*, "The Late Richmond Battle," June 28, 1862; Thomas Darby to Miss E. Marie June 25, 1862.
35. Darby Letters. Darby to Miss E. Marie June 25, 1862.

36. PR Caleb T. Robbins.
37. Osborne. Twenty-ninth Regiment, 141-43; Ayling. Yankee at Arms, 41-44; ORA I, 11, Part III, 228-29; PR Patrick McElroy.
38. Chipman to Wife June 23, 1862.
39. PR George Dillaway.
40. USAHEC. CWDC. William H. Peacock to Sarah May 31, 1862.
41. Ayling. Yankee at Arms, 51.

Chapter Five. Reinforcements Now Appearing—July to December 1862

1. Ayling. Yankee at Arms, 54.
2. Ibid., 53.
3. Whittemore Diary; *BP*, "The Meeting at Sandwich," July 22, 1862.
4. PR Stephen Weeks.
5. *BP*, "War Meetings," July 19, 1862; Samuel H. Allyne to John July 24, 1862.
6. *CCANI*, "Appointments," August 23, 1862; George L. Haines to Sister August 17, 1862; Sandwich Enrollment List 1863 on Ancestry. Com (Matthew Quinn); Civil War Records. Sandwich Town Offices.
7. *BP*, "War Meeting," September 9, 1862 and "Presentation," September 23, 1862.
8. BC Superior Court Records (James McKowen, 1862).
9. MSA Executive Letters and Letters Sent (Vol. 29).
10. Perry Family Collection. T. C. Perry to George August 8, 1862.
11. Eben Whittemore Civil War Draft Documents.
12. *BP*, "Cape Cod out of the Draft," October 28, 1862; George L. Haines to Sister August 17, 1862; Sandwich Historical Society Civil War Boxes. Of the Twenty-five volunteers, twenty-one were mustered into and remained with Company D of the Forty-fifth. George A. Burgess was discharged for disability before the Forty-fifth went south while Nathan B. Fisher and Thomas F. Holmes were in a different company or regiment. William C. Riordon has a curious service record. He and his brother George enlisted at Boston June 13, 1861 for three years in the Eleventh Massachusetts Regiment. William injured his back at Yorktown, Virginia and on September 5, 1862 received a disability discharge at a hospital in Newark, New Jersey, with the comment that his disability made him worthless to the service. Nevertheless, he was mustered into Company D of the Forty-fifth at their Massachusetts training camp on October 29, 1862 and two days later deserted, perhaps having made off with his enlistment bounty of $150.00. His whereabouts after desertion are unknown (SR William C. Riordon).

13. Sandwich 1862 Enrollment in Civil War Box Bourne Historical Society; MSA M-AR 129X Register for Travel Permission.
14. ORA I, 11, Part III, 228-29; ORA I, 11, Part I, 210-12; NA. RG 94. Entry 534. Carded Medical Records Peter McNulty, Gustavus Badger, Patrick McElroy and Patrick McGirr; SR William Breese; *Philadelphia Inquirer*, "Arrival of the Vanderbilt," August 8, 1862.
15. ORN I, 19, 105; Deck Log of *Midnight*.
16. Sandy Barnard. Campaigning with the Irish Brigade: Private John Ryan, 28th Massachusetts, Terre Haute: AST Press. 2001, 55; Civil War Memoirs of Jesse Pollard 28th Massachusetts (on-line); USAHEC. CWDC. William Fairbanks to Sister April 22, 1862.
17. SR Edward McGirr.
18. ORA I, 11, Part III, 747; Osborne. Twenty-ninth Regiment, 179; PR John Campbell, Warren P. Dean and Charles Brady.
19. Marion V. Armstrong Jr. Unfurl Those Colors! McClellan, Sumner and the Second Army Corps in the Antietam Campaign. Tuscaloosa: University of Alabama Press. 2008, 25; PR Charles Brady.
20. MSA Executive Letters, Vol. 44; PR Josiah L. Elder.
21. PR John Fagan and Joseph Turner.
22. Armstrong Jr. Unfurl Those Colors! 136; Richard F. Miller. Harvard's Civil War: A History of the Twentieth Massachusetts Volunteer Infantry. Hanover, NH: University Press of New England. 2005, 165-66.
23. PR Thomas Hollis and Thomas Davis; Daniel McAdams, A Short History.
24. PR Edward Brady.
25. Armstrong Jr. Unfurl Those Colors! 166 and 220; PR John W. Campbell and Caleb T. Robbins.
26. PR and SR Christopher B. Dalton. PR John Fagan and Edward Brady.
27. Samuel W. Hunt Diary September 17 and 19, 1862. Only two pages of this diary exist.
28. NA. RG 94. Entry 800. Correspondence of New England Soldiers Association. Book 5, No. 68.
29. John L. Smith. Antietam to Appomattox with the 118th Penna. Vols. Corn Exchange Regiment. Philadelphia: J. L. Smith, 1892. 87-89; Bibbins Family Papers. Newton Bibbins to Ones at Home October 3, 1862.
30. Bibbins to Sister October 13 and 19, 1862, to Parents November 16, 1862; SR Horace H. P. Lovell.
31. PR Stephen Weeks.
32. SR Patrick Long; Whittemore Diary October 2, 1862.
33. *BP*, "Another Death in the Sandwich Guards," October 14, 1862; SR James H. Heald; James H. Heald Find a Grave Memorial Internet Site.
34. PR Watson D. Avery; NA. RG 94. Fortieth Massachusetts Regimental Book, Vol. 3.

35. Chipman to Wife October 30, 1862.
36. Ibid.
37. Ibid., November 4, 1862.
38. *BP*, "Co. D, Cadet Regiment," September 23, 1862 and "Who Knows Where the Codfish Carried in the 45th Regiment is?" February 12, 1895.
39. *Boston Evening Transcript*, "The 45th (Cadet) Regiment," November 13, 1862.
40. PR John Woods.
41. Osborne. Twenty-ninth Regiment, 203; Ayling. Yankee at Arms, 78; PR William W. Phinney.
42. Osborne. Twenty-ninth Regiment, 210; Chipman to Wife November 20, 1862; SR Charles Chipman; Carded Medical Records Charles Chipman.
43. *Boston Pilot*, "Letter From the Ninth Mass." November 22, 1862.
44. Alden C. Ellis Jr. The Massachusetts Andrew Sharpshooters: A Civil War History and Roster. Jefferson, NC: McFarland. 2012, 50-51; Miller. Harvard's Civil War, 199.
45. ORA I, 21, 314; Ayling. Yankee at Arms, 81-85.
46. NA. RG 153. Office of JAG. Folder NN-3890.
47. George L. Haines to Sister December 25, 1862 and January 29, 1863.
48. PR Thomas Hackett.
49. Craig L. Symonds, ed. A Year on a Monitor and the Destruction of Fort Sumter. Columbia: University of South Carolina Press. 1987, 9.
50. Keene Family Box (Warren P. Keene Memoirs).

Chapter Six. Hard Tack and Mule Beef—January to May 1863

1. Darby Letters. Darby to Miss Mary Ann January 4, 1863 and Miss Ellen M. January 20, 1863; Osborne. Twenty-Ninth Regiment, 213.
2. Darby to Miss Mary Ann February 7, 1863.
3. PR George F. W. Haines; History of the Fifth Massachusetts Battery. Boston: Luther E. Cowles. 1902, 550.
4. ORN I, 13, 544.
5. NA. RG 52, Entry 31, Certificates of Death, Disability, Pension and Medical Surveys (Box 5 Charles L. Howard).
6. Benjamin L. Fessenden. "The Yankee Clipper and the Cape Cod Boy." *The American* Neptune 43, No. 4 (October 1963): 264-269. After the war Fessenden won a claim for lost time and nautical instruments amounting to $1,800.00.
7. NA. RG 24. Deck Log of *Sunflower* September 1, 1863.
8. From Slavery to Freedom. Civil War 150. Reader Number 4. Library of

America, 55-56; Dorothea Dix Folder. Dix to Lincoln February 4, 1863.
9. PR Davis Magoon; Carded Medical Records John T. Collins.
10. Oliver Ricker Diary March 14, 17 and 18, 1863.
11. *New York Times*, "Sick and Wounded Soldiers," March 26, 1863; Ricker Diary March 22, 1863.
12. PR Davis Magoon and Stephen Weeks.
13. *BP*, "Personal," March 31, 1863; Carded Medical Records James H. Atherton and Anderson Wright; SR James H. Atherton.
14. Ayling. Yankee at Arms, 109.
15. MSA Executive Letters and Letters Sent (Vol. 29).
16. SR Hartwell W. Freeman; *New York Herald*, "Departure of General Ullman and His Brigade," April 10, 1863; *BP*, "Personal," March 31, 1863.
17. PR Isaiah Adams; NA. RG 94. Entry 561. Medical Officers Papers (John M. Davies). Portsmouth Hospital in North Carolina should not be confused with Portsmouth Grove Hospital in Rhode Island. The Tarheel State's first hospital, Portsmouth was built in 1847 for sailors. It was a Confederate hospital in 1861.
18. Henry F. Wellington to Abby January 27, 1863; PR James T. Jones and Ezra Hamblin.
19. PR Henry Knippe; Henry F. Wellington to Abby April 15, 1863; George Haines to Sis April 15, 1863.
20. SR George H. Hobson. The so-called First and Second Battalions (Hobson and Fish) of the First Massachusetts Cavalry came to Virginia from South Carolina in August 1862 while the Third Battalion (William W. Phinney) remained behind.
21. *Salem, MA Register*, "War Items and Incidents," May 11, 1863.
22. SR Frederick Norris, Seth F. and George F. Gibbs.
23. George Haines to Sis May 13, 1863.
24. Eben T. Hale to Mother May 5, 1863; Haines to Sis May 13, 1863.
25. ORA I, 10, 372 and 697.
26. ORA I, 24, Part 1, 720; NA. RG 24. Deck Log of *Benton* May 22, 1863.
27. NA. RG 111. Entry 14. Orders of Signal Corps and Entry 17. Synopses of Military Histories of Officers 1860-1867.
28. PR Daniel F. Fisher; *Philadelphia Inquirer*, "Arrived on Monday," May 27, 1863.
29. NA. RG 76. Alabama Claims. Dockets 290, 291, 537 and 686; ORN I, 2, 330.
30. Darby Letters. Darby to Miss E. M. June 3, 1863.
31. Osborne. Twenty-ninth Regiment, 228; Darby Letters. Darby to Miss E. M. June 3, 1863; Chipman to Wife June 1, 1863.
32. Perry Family Collection. Thomas C. Perry to William June 13, 1863.

Chapter Seven. Only Son of a Widow—

The Draft of Summer 1863

1. *BP*, "War News," May 5, 1863.
2. Massachusetts Register 1862, 115; *BP*, "Sandwich," January 24, 1916 and "Citizen's Meeting," September 3, 1861; Simeon Deyo. History of Barnstable County. New York: H. W. Blake. 1890, 300. An alphabetized list of Barnstable County's Class One enrolled and drafted men of summer 1863 can be found in *Barnstable County Massachusetts Civil War Soldiers, Enrolled Men and Drafted Men 1861-1863*, published by Cape Cod Genealogical Society. A list of hired substitutes is at National Archives, Waltham, MA in RG 110, Entry 855, Descriptive Books of Drafted Men and Substitutes.
3. Ancestry. com New York Passenger Lists 1820-1957 (Colclough and Neiter) and Naturalization Records (Parry); Barlow-Kaiser Roster.
4. *BP*, "Christmas Festival in Sandwich," January 5, 1863.
5. Deyo. History of Barnstable County, 278.
6. *BP*, "Dancing," November 3, 1863 and "Sandwich Cotillon Band" January 27, 1852; Whaling Crew Lists Internet Site. The spelling of the surname Marston is sometimes Marstin or Marstins.
7. Jonathan Bourne Correspondence. Bourne to Dillingham July 26, 1860 and Bourne to Tobey August 9, 1860; *Whaleman's Shipping List*, "Crew Lists of Vessels Sailed," August 21, 1860.
8. *BP*, "Exhibition at West Sandwich," May 13, 1862 and "Interesting Trial," April 17, 1866.
9. ORA III, 3, 132-33.
10. *BP*, "The New Standard Time," November 20, 1883 and "Marriages" October 15, 1861; PR Horace L. Crocker.
11. Report of the Directors of American School for the Deaf Hartford, 1887; 1855 Massachusetts Census (Shadrach F. Swift).
12. Ancestry. com Naturalization Records (Patrick Fagan).
13. NA. RG 204. Entry 1A. Pardon Case Files # 242409. The Papers of Abraham Lincoln.
14. Darby Letters. Darby to Miss Mary Anne July 31, 1863; *New Bedford Daily Mercury*, "Substitutes!" July 28, 1863 and "Conscripts," July 30, 1863.
15. *Boston DA*, "Local Matters," September 3, 1863; *Milwaukee Sentinel*, "Items About the Draft," September 7, 1863.
16. *Boston Herald*, "Affairs About Home," September 9, 1863; *Boston DA*, "Local Matters," September 7, 1863; The Record of a Quaker Conscience: Cyrus Pringle's Diary. New York: MacMillan. 1918, 91-92.

Chapter Eight. Do You See the Beginning of the End—

June to December 1863

1. Chipman to Wife June 3, 1863.
2. Chipman to Wife June 7 and 9, 1863.
3. ORN I, 25, 77-79; PR Calvin G. Fisher.
4. NA. RG 52. Entry 22. Medical Journals of Ships (*Benton*); *Boston Daily Traveller*, "Recruiting for the Negro Regiments in Louisiana," June 5, 1863; SR Hartwell W. Freeman.
5. *BP*, "The Reception of the Forty-fifth Regiment," July 7, 1863.
6. Chipman to Wife June 24, 1863.
7. Miller. Harvard's Civil War, 250-254.
8. Ancestry. com Naturalization Records (Samuel Alton); SR Samuel T. Alton.
9. Ancestry. com Naturalization Records (Titus P. Riordan).
10. *Salem Register*, "War Items and Incidents," July 13, 1863 and "Deaths," August 8, 1863; Greg Marquis. In Armageddon's Shadow: The Civil War and Canada's Maritime Provinces. Montreal: McGill University Press. 1998,118.
11. John J. Hennessy, ed. Fighting With the Eighteenth Massachusetts: The Civil War Memoir of Thomas H. Mann. Baton Rouge: Louisiana State University Press. 2000, 179.
12. Fifth Massachusetts Battery, 623-647.
13. NA. Civil War "Widow's Pensions" (Jules Allen).
14. *Salem Register*, "Died," July 27, 1863. Gettysburg National Military Park historian John Heiser provided information on Alton's hospital and burial site. Alton was disinterred at an unknown time and reburied at Sandwich November 15, 1863.
15. *BP*, "The Forty-third Regiment," July 14, 1863.
16. *BP*, "Business in Sandwich," July 7, 1863; *New Bedford Daily Mercury*, "Boston and Sandwich Glass Co.," July 21, 1863.
17. Robert E. Jameson Diary July 7 to 11, 1863; Ayling. Yankee at Arms, 148.
18. Chipman to Wife July 17, 1863.
19. Chipman to Wife August 4, 1863; PR Samuel W. Hunt.
20. PR Charles E. Swift; Fifth Massachusetts Battery, 520, 698, 702.
21. James H. McKee. Back "In War Times." History of the 144th New York Infantry. 1903, 111-12; *Salem Register*, "The Fortieth Regiment," July 23, 1863.
22. PR George W. Scobie, Charles H. Little and Henry Perry; Rebellion Record Town of Barnstable. Diary of Corporal William D. Holmes, July 16, 1863; George H. Buck. A Brief Sketch of Company G Fortieth Massachusetts Infantry 1862-1865; William Watts Folwell Civil War Diary, 434-35

(Accessible through Fiftieth New York Regiment Internet Site). Berlin is now Brunswick, Maryland.
23. George H. Gordon. A War Diary of Events. Boston: James R. Osgood. 1882, 163-65; NA. MF 1523. Proceedings of U. S. Army Court Martials and Military Commissions of Union Soldiers Executed by U. S. Authorities 1861-1866.
24. USAHEC. CWDC. William H. Peacock to Sarah September 13, 1863.
25. Thomas F. Harrington. The Harvard Medical School: A History, Narrative and Documentary. Lewis Publishing. 1905. 2, 958; SR Giles M. Pease.
26. Gordon. War Diary, 224-26; McKee. Back "In War Times." 132-33.
27. NA. RG 24. Muster Roll of *Nahant*.
28. PR Thomas A. Ball and Josiah L. Elder.
29. PR Francis Woods; Register of Sick and Wounded at Hickman Bridge Hospital, Camp Nelson, Kentucky.
30. Chipman to Wife September 10, 12 and 19, 1863.
31. Chipman to Wife September 12, October 16 and November 1, 1863; *Boston DA*, "Died," October 23, 1863.
32. John M. Deane. Civil War Diaries. Freetown, Massachusetts Historical Society. 2005, 190-191; Chipman to Wife September 19, 1863.
33. SR Francis McKowen; Charles A. Howes Diary in Howes Family Papers.
34. PR Calvin G. Fisher.
35. *New York Times*, "Arrivals and Departures," November 20, 1860; *Charleston Mercury*, "Arrived Charleston," December 18, 1860; Commercial Relations of the United States Year Ending September 30, 1860. 36th Congress. 2nd Session. Exec. Doc. # 6, 372-73.
36. *Worcester National Aegis*, "The New Marshall," March 23, 1853.
37. Chipman to Wife October 4 and 16, 1863.
38. Chipman to Wife November 1, 1863; *BP*, "Postmaster in Sandwich," May 28, 1861.
39. *BP*, "300,000 More," October 27, 1863.
40. NA. RG 153. Office of JAG. Folder LL-1813; PR and SR Giles M. Pease; "War Letters of Charles P. Bowditch." *Massachusetts Historical Society Proceedings* 57 (May 1924): 451.
41. Alfred S. Roe. The Twenty-Fourth Regiment Massachusetts Volunteers. 1907, 240.
42. Edward A. Miller. "Angel of Light: Helen L. Gilson, Army Nurse." *Civil War History* 43, No. 1 (March 1997): 30; NA. RG 94. Fortieth Massachusetts Regimental Book, Vol. 3.
43. Haines to Sister November 29, 1863. Carlton Hall was the upper story of William F. Lapham's store along Jarves Street. The Hall's windows gave a commanding view to the east (*Sandwich Observer* June 30, 1849).

44. PR Joseph A. Baker and Henry Knippe.
45. SR George H. Clark; Lewis F. Emilio. History of the Fifty-fourth Regiment of Massachusetts Volunteers. Boston. 1894, 147; SR James Boyer; Deane Diaries, 204.
46. Ayling. Yankee at Arms, 187-89.
47. PR Luther T. Hammond.
48. NA. RG 94. First California Cavalry Regimental Book, Vol. 3, Letter of September 24, 1863; SR Samuel Howard Allyne; NA. RG 94. MF 1523. Proceedings of U. S. Army Court Martials (Robert Kerr); Robert L. Alotta. Civil War Justice: Union Army Executions Under Lincoln. Shippensburg, PA: White Mane Publishing. 1989, 103-104.
49. *BP*, "The New Year," December 29, 1863.

Chapter Nine. John Did You Catch it Bad—January to May 1864

1. Ayling. Yankee at Arms, 197; Osborne. Twenty-ninth Regiment, 276; PR James Ball; NA. RG 94. Twenty-ninth Massachusetts Regimental Book, Vol. 2.
2. Ayling. Yankee at Arms, 202.
3. O. Scott Stearns to Mother January 17, 1864; *BP*, "Volunteering in Barnstable Co'y," January 12, 1864.
4. Ayling. Yankee at Arms, 205, 207.
5. NA. RG 94. Twenty-Ninth Massachusetts Regimental Book. Vol. 3, February 8 and 9, 1864; PR David Hoxie. The Boyden Livery owned ten horses in 1860, the most of any person or establishment in Sandwich (NCSM BC Agriculture Sandwich 1860).
6. Fold 3 Internet Site. Army Registers of Enlistments 1798-1914. "Hospital Stewards" and "Letters Received by the Commission Branch of Adjutant General's Office 1863-1870."
7. NA. Civil War "Widow's Pensions" (Benjamin Fuller).
8. Marcus R. Erlandson. Guy V. Henry: A Study in Military Leadership. Master's Thesis 1985, 19-20.
9. NA. RG 94. Fortieth Massachusetts Regimental Book, Vol. 3; *Boston Herald*, "A Regiment Never Whipped," September 9, 1891.
10. Henry F. W. Little. The Seventh New Hampshire Volunteers in the War of the Rebellion. Concord, NH. 1896, 216; Erlandson. Guy V. Henry, 21.
11. Carded Medical Records William Manley.
12. PR William W. Phinney.
13. NA. RG 94. Fortieth Massachusetts Regimental Book, Vol. 3; Crowninshield. First Massachusetts Cavalry, 265.

14. History of the Thirty-sixth Massachusetts Volunteers 1862-1865. Boston. 1884, 131-32.
15. Osborne. Twenty-ninth Regiment, 285-87; Ernest Mettendorf. Between Triumph and Disaster: The History of the Forty-sixth New York Infantry. Eden, NY. 2012, 81-82; *Boston Daily Courier*, "The News," April 11, 1864; PR James Cook.
16. NA. RG 94. First U.S. Colored Heavy Artillery Regimental Book, Vol 1.
17. History Thirty-sixth Massachusetts, 133-34; Ayling. Yankee at Arms, 122-24.
18. Samuel H. Allyne to John March 23, 1864; SA. Whittemore Folder.
19. Report of the Secretary of the Navy, 1864. 107.
20. History Thirty-sixth Massachusetts, 140-41.
21. Augustus E. Woodbury. Major General Ambrose E. Burnside and the Ninth Army Corps: A Narrative. Providence: S.S. Rider. 1867, 368-69.
22. PR Joseph W. Eaton and Francis C. Swift.
23. SR James O'Neill.
24. Gordon C. Rhea. The Battles for Spotsylvania Court House and the Road to Yellow Tavern May 7-12, 1864. Baton Rouge: Louisiana State University Press. 1997, 100; Crowninshield. First Massachusetts Cavalry, 206. Gaffney of the Eleventh Massachusetts may have been captured in May. If so, the circumstances are unknown.
25. PR John A. Goodwin and John G. Woodruff.
26. PR John McAlaney.
27. Osborne. Twenty-ninth Regiment, 294-96; *Boston Daily Courier*, "Military," May 24, 1864.
28. Chipman to Wife May 19, 1864.
29. Ayling. Yankee at Arms, 227-28; NA. RG 94. Twenty-ninth Massachusetts Regimental Book. Vol. 3, June 21, 1864.
30. Osborne. Twenty-ninth Regiment, 298; Chipman to Wife May 26, 1864.
31. *BP*, "Sandwich Guards!" May 31, 1864; *Yarmouth Register*, "Reception of the Sandwich Guards," June 3, 1864.
32. There is no list of the eighteen returning men. This one, based on service records, seems most correct.
33. *BP*, "Sandwich Guards!" May 31, 1864; Ayling. Yankee at Arms, 229.
34. SR Richard Colwell and Charles Riley, Fifth Massachusetts Cavalry.
35. *BP*, "The Draft For This District," May 17, 1864.
36. NA. RG 153. Office of JAG. Folder OO-0377
37. PR Nelson Cushman.
38. PR Benjamin F. Chamberlain; SR Dean W. Swift.
39. MNGMA. Fortieth Massachusetts Regiment, Box 1; SR Charles E. Ellis.

Chapter Ten. My Greatest and Best Friend—

June to December 1864

1. Erlandson. Guy V. Henry, 37; NA. RG 94. Fortieth Massachusetts Regimental Book, Vol. 3; *New Bedford Evening Standard*, "Death of a Veteran," May 17, 1916.
2. PR George T. Lloyd; "Death of a Veteran."
3. "Death of a Veteran."
4. Osborne. Twenty-ninth Regiment, 298-300; Gordon C. Rhea. Cold Harbor Grant and Lee May 26-June 3, 1864. Baton Rouge: Louisiana State University Press. 2007, 259; PR Perez Eldridge; Chipman to Wife June 8, 1864.
5. *Cape Cod Republican* of Harwich, MA, "From the 58th Mass Regiment," June 30, 1864.
6. NA. RG 94. Entry 561. Medical Officer Files (John Bachelder).
7. PR Leonard E. Howard.
8. NA. Civil War "Widow's Pensions" (James P. Atkins).
9. Buck. Fortieth Massachusetts Infantry; Fortieth Massachusetts Regimental Book, Vol. 3; Carded Medical and Pension Records John M. Perry.
10. Deane Diary 234-35; Chipman to Wife June 19, 1864.
11. Chipman to Wife June 28, 1864.
12. Alvah Beach to Sister May 4th, 1864.
13. ORA III, 4, 246; *Boston Courier*, "Military," May 4, 1864.
14. *Boston Daily Globe*, "Joseph W. Phinney Dies," December 29, 1934; Roe. Fifth Massachusetts Volunteer Infantry, 273.
15. Whaleman's Shipping List, "Bark Golconda," October 18, 1859 and "Destruction of Bark Golconda," July 19, 1864; *Philadelphia Daily Evening Bulletin*, "Arrival of Valuable Prize Steamer," June 16, 1864; NA. RG 24. Muster Roll *Metacomet*.
16. Samuel Allyne to John July 3, 1864.
17. Thomas Hamm, archivist and history professor at Earlham College in Indiana, worked out the knotty family link between the Wings of Sandwich and their relatives in Montgomery County, Indiana.
18. Chipman to Wife June 29, 1864; NA. RG 94. Fourteenth NY Heavy Artillery Regimental Book, Vol. 5.
19. Daniel W. Barefoot. General Robert F. Hoke: Lee's Modest Warrior. Winston-Salem: John F. Blair. 1996, 214; PR Leonard Hinds.
20. Chipman to Wife July 25, 1864.
21. Service and Carded Medical Records Charles N. Godfrey; *New York Tribune*, "Arrived," July 14, 1864. The captain of the *Atlantic* was Oliver Eldridge of Yarmouth.
22. SR Nathaniel S. Ellis.

23. Chipman to Wife August 1, 1864.
24. Ibid.; John F. Schmutz. The Battle of the Crater: A Complete History. Jefferson, NC: McFarland. 2009, 321-22.
25. *BP*, "Company A 58th Regiment," June 27, 1865; Alan Azelrod. The Horrid Pit. New York: Carroll and Graf. 2007, 232; Schmutz. Battle of the Crater, 304; PR John W. Tinkham.
26. NA. RG 153. Office of JAG. Folder NN 3056.
27. Chipman to Wife August 7, 1864; Barnes to Mrs. Charles Chipman August 10, 1864.
28. Barnes to Mrs. Charles Chipman August 10, 1864.
29. *BP*, "Death of Major Charles Chipman," August 16, 1864 and "Major Charles Chipman," August 23, 1864; *Yarmouth Register*, "Funeral of Major Charles Chipman," August 19, 1864.
30. NA. Civil War "Widow's Pensions," Carded Medical Records and SR Roland G. Holway.
31. PR and SR Samuel J. Wood.
32. PR Samuel J. Wood and Henry B. Baker; Public Documents of Massachusetts, 1863, Vol. 4, Herring Pond Indians. 8-11.
33. Richard H. Abbot. "Massachusetts and the Recruiting of Southern Negroes 1863-1865." *Civil War History* 14, No. 3 (September 1968): 197-209; Thomas T. Moebs. Black Soldiers-Black Sailors-Black Ink: Research Guide on African-Americans in U. S. Military History 1526-1900. Moebs Publishing. 1994, 1339-1340.
34. Civil War Records. Sandwich Town Offices; *Boston DA*, "The Quotas of Massachusetts," September 15, 1864; NA. RG 94. Fourteenth U.S. Colored Heavy Artillery (First North Carolina) Regimental Book, Vol. 1; *North Carolina Times* of New Bern, "Recruiting for the Loyal States," August 5, 1864.
35. MSA. MF GSU 504. Returns of Naval Enlistments; *Boston DA*, "The Quota Full," September 6, 1864.
36. *BP*, "Substitutes," September 20, 1864; MSA. MF GSU 300. Sandwich Substitutes; Perry Family Collection. Thomas C. Perry to William August 14, 1864.
37. ORN I, 21, 407.
38. NA. RG 76. Alabama Claims. Docket 291; Nicholas Dean. Snow Squall: The Last American Clipper Ship. Gardiner, ME: Tilbury House. 2001, 197-99.
39. *Boston Herald* September 17, 1864; *BP*, "Arrest of Deserters," September 20, 1864.
40. NA. RG 94. Fortieth Massachusetts Regimental Book, Vol. 3; PR George T. Lloyd.
41. PR George T. Lloyd.

42. SR Daniel V. Kern.
43. Perry Family Collection. Thomas C. Perry to William August 14, 1864; PR Samuel Marvel.
44. Ephraim B. Nye Diary of October 4, 1864.
45. PR Edward Heffernan.
46. PR Nathaniel H. Fish and Joseph A. Baker.
47. *BP*, "Trusses," July 26, 1864; PR Horace L. Clark.
48. SR John T. Collins.
49. *BP*, "The Presidential Election," November 15, 1864; Perry Collection. My Very Dear Brother November 28, 1864.
50. SR Isaac C. Hart; Perry Family Collection. My Very Dear Brother November 28, 1864.
51. *BP*, "The Fair in Sandwich," December 27, 1864 and "Correspondence," January 10, 1865.

Chapter Eleven. It Seemed Like a Dream— 1865 and End of War

1. James Robertson Jr. "Houses of Horror: Danville's Civil War Prisons." *Virginia Magazine of History and Biography* 69, No. 3 (July 1961): 340-341.
2. PR and SR Thomas B. Bourne and William W. Phinney.
3. NA. RG 153. Office of JAG. Folder OO-0377.
4. NA. RG 24. Entry 204. Records Relating to Enlisted Men (Ansel C. Fifield).
5. PR Willard Weeks Jr.
6. PR Horace H. P. Lovell; SR Hiram B. Ellis. Ellis did not live long enough in Sandwich to be considered one of its soldiers.
7. Samuel Allyne to John January 1, 1865; *Yarmouth Register*, "Sandwich Items," February 24, 1865.
8. SR Thomas M. Gibbs; PR Charles H. Little; Civil War Box at Bourne Historical Society (Thomas M. Gibbs). Soldier Nathan C. Perry swore after the war that Little coaxed Gibbs into enlisting (PR Charles H. Little).
9. SR William W. Phinney.
10. *BP*, "Trusses," July 26, 1864; PR Horace Lee Clark (Second Mass. HA); SR Obed M. Fish.
11. PR and SR William W. Phinney, Thomas B. Bourne and James McKowen.
12. PR John W. Tinkham; John Wilson. "Seven Months in a Rebel Prison." *Cape Cod Genealogical Association Journal* XXX, No. 3 (Fall 2004): 106-107.
13. Moses M. Ordway to Brother February 23, 1865.
14. ORA I, 46, Part 1, 187.
15. *New Bedford Mercury*, "The Late Lieut. E. B. Nye," April 7, 1865;

Sandwich Independent, "I Never Surrender," April 26, 1917. Brian P. Murphy of Norwood, MA told the author some years ago that William F. Nye accompanied his brother's body home. He can no longer find the source of that information.

16. SR Joseph J. C. Madigan.
17. Robert Browning Jr. Lincoln's Trident: The West Gulf Blockading Squadron During the Civil War. Tuscaloosa: University of Alabama Press. 2015, 499-500; ORN I, 22, 71; NA. RG 24. Deck Log of *Kickapoo*.
18. *New Bedford Mercury*, "Discharge from the Draft," March 21, 1864.
19. PR Ezra Bassett.
20. PR and SR Joseph A. Baker.
21. PR and SR John W. Campbell.
22. PR Leonard Hinds.
23. *Boston DA*, "Massachusetts' Youngest," April 8, 1865.
24. ORA I, 46, Part I, 1211; James Oliver. Ancestry, Early Life and War Record of James Oliver M.D. Athol, Mass. 1916, 98.
25. ORA I, 46, Part I, 1211; Perry Family Collection. Clementine to My Dear Brother July 9, 1865. Robert L. Krick of Richmond National Battlefields Park feels that the bombardment described by Clementine Perry Hart was near the present Route Five, about fifteen miles southeast of Richmond.
26. Civil War Box at Bourne Historical Society (Thomas M. Gibbs to mother April 12, 1865); Alfred S. Roe. The Twenty-fourth Regiment Massachusetts Volunteers 1861-1866. Worcester, MA. 1907, 388. Nineteenth century Cape Codders frequently spelled father as "farther." It may indicate how they pronounced the word.
27. *BP*, "War News," April 11, 1865; ORN I, 22, 122-23.
28. *BP*, "Sandwich," April 25, 1865.
29. Keene Family Box (Warren P. Keene Memoirs).
30. Mildred Gibbs Gage. "Saved by His Own Hands." *Yankee Magazine* 39, No. 4 (April 1975).
31. NA. RG 24. Deck Logs of *Kickapoo* April 22, 1865 and *Restless* May 3, 1865.
32. Civil War Box Bourne Historical (Thomas M. Gibbs to mother April 12, 1865).
33. Ordway to Brother May 7, 1865; Roe. Twenty-fourth Regiment, 393.
34. Oliver. Ancestry, Early Life etc., 100-101. For more description of the grand review see *The Union War*, Gary W. Gallagher, Harvard University Press, 2011.
35. NA. RG 94. Entry 534. Carded Medical Records Thomas M. Gibbs and Charles M. Little; Civil War Box Bourne Historical (Charles M. Little to Miss Gibbs June 28, 1865).

36. Osborne. Twenty-ninth Regiment, 337.
37. *Salem Register*, "War Items and Incidents," June 22, 1865.
38. As with Table 3 there is no formal list of the returning men; this one seems accurate based on service records.
39. SR William W. Phinney; Perry Family Collection. Thomas C. Perry to Dear Son May 7, 1865.
40. NA. RG 76. Alabama Claims. Docket 2057.
41. Alabama Claims. Docket 808.
42. NA. RG 153. Office of JAG. Folder MM 2365; *Boston Traveler*, "Trouble in the Mass. 3d Heavy Artillery Regiment," July 11, 1865.
43. Robert E. Johnson. Far China Station: The U. S. Navy in Asian Waters 1800-1898. Annapolis: Naval Institute Press. 1979, 123-27; Deck Log of *Wachusett* February 14, 1866; *Salem Register*, "Arrivals, Clearances etc," June 14, 1866.
44. *BP*, "Celebration of the Fourth in Sandwich," July 10, 1866.

Bibliography

Manuscripts

1. Allyne Family Papers. California Historical Society. North Baker Research Library, San Francisco, CA.
2. Barlow Family Folder. Sandwich Archives, Sandwich, MA.
3. Barnstable County Probate and Superior Court Records. Barnstable County Courthouse, Barnstable, MA.
4. Beach Family Papers. St. Lawrence University Special Collections, Canton, New York.
5. Bibbins Family Papers. Bentley Historical Library, University of Michigan, Ann Arbor, MI.
6. Jonathan Bourne Correspondence. New Bedford Whaling Museum, New Bedford, MA.
7. Benjamin Butler Correspondence. Library of Congress, Washington, DC.
8. Charles Chipman Papers and Letters. U.S. Army Heritage and Education Center, Carlisle, PA.
9. Civil War Box. Bourne Historical Society, Bourne, MA.
10. Civil War Boxes, Sandwich Historical Society, Sandwich, MA.
11. Civil War Document Collection. U.S. Army Heritage and Education Center, Carlisle, PA.
12. Civil War Records. Sandwich Town Offices, Sandwich, MA.
13. Thomas F. Darby Letters. Virginia Historical Society, Richmond, VA.
14. Dorothea Dix Folder. Schlesinger Library. Radcliffe Institute of Advanced Study. Harvard University, Cambridge, MA.
15. George H. Freeman Diary. Sandwich Historical Society, Sandwich, MA.
16. Charles I. Gibbs Folder. Sandwich Archives, Sandwich, MA.
17. George L. Haines Letters. Sandwich Archives, Sandwich, MA.
18. Eben T. Hale Letters. University of North Carolina Special Collections Library, Chapel Hill, NC.
19. Howes Family Papers. Cape Cod Community College Nickerson Archives, West Barnstable, MA.
20. Samuel W. Hunt Diary. Private Collection Scott D. Hann
21. Robert E. Jameson Diary and Letters. Library of Congress, Washington, DC.
22. Keene Family Box (Warren P. Keene Memoirs). Bourne Historical Society, Bourne, MA.
23. Kern Family Folder. Sandwich Archives, Sandwich, MA.
24. Daniel McAdams, A Short History. Houghton Library, Harvard University, Cambridge, MA.

25. Ephraim B. Nye Diary. Private Collection Brian P. Murphy, Norwood, MA.
26. Moses M. Ordway Letters. Library of Virginia, Richmond, VA.
27. Perry Family Collection. Bourne Historical Society, Bourne, MA.
28. Rebellion Record Town of Barnstable. Barnstable Town Hall, Hyannis, MA.
29. Oliver Ricker Diary. Massachusetts Historical Society, Boston, MA.
30. Henry H. Robbins Letters. Antietam Battlefield File of Twenty-ninth Massachusetts Regiment, Antietam, MD.
31. Sandwich Academy Folder. Sandwich Archives, Sandwich, MA.
32. Sandwich Antislavery Collection. Sandwich Archives, Sandwich, MA.
33. Sandwich Massachusetts Citizens to Abraham Lincoln (Petition Endorsed by Seth Ewer). Library of Congress, Washington, DC.
34. Stearns Family Collection. Virginia Tech University Special Collections, Blacksburg, VA.
35. Isaac Henry Taylor Letter. Massachusetts Historical Society, Boston, MA.
36. Henry F. Wellington Letters. Massachusetts Historical Society, Boston, MA.
37. Eben S. Whittemore Diary. Yale University Law Library Rare Book Collection, New Haven, CT.
38. Eben S. Whittemore Civil War Draft Documents. Gilder Lehrman Institute of American History, New York, NY.
39. Whittemore Folder. Sandwich Archives, Sandwich, MA.
40. George H. Winchester Journal. Connecticut Historical Society, Hartford, CT.

National Archives, College Park, MD

RG 76. Records Court of Commissioners Alabama Claims.

National Archives, Washington, DC

MF 1523. Proceedings of U. S. Army Court Martials and Military Commissions of Union Soldiers Executed by U. S. Authorities 1861-1866.
RG 24. Deck Logs and Muster Rolls of Ships.
RG 24. Entry 204. Records Relating to Enlisted Men.
RG 52. Entry 22. Medical Journals of Ships.
RG 52. Entry 31. Certificates of Death, Disability, Pension and Medical Surveys.
RG 92. Entry 1403. "Vessel Files."
RG 94. Entry 534. Carded Medical Records.

RG 94. Entry 561. Medical Officers Papers.
RG 94. Entry 800. Correspondence of the New England Soldiers Association.
RG 94. Regimental Books.
RG 111. Entry 14. Orders of Signal Corps.
RG 111. Entry 17. Synopses of Military History of Officers.
RG 153. Records of the Office of JAG.
RG 204. Entry 1A. Pardon Case Files, Papers of Abraham Lincoln.
Civil War Pension Records.
Civil War Service Records.
Civil War Widow's Pensions.

Massachusetts States Archives

1. Letters Sent to Governor John Andrew.
2. Executive Letters Governor John Andrew.
3. MF GSU 300. Sandwich Substitutes.
4. MF GSU 504. Returns of Naval Enlistments.

Newspapers, Massachusetts

1. *Barnstable Patriot*
2. *Boston Daily Advertiser*
3. *Boston Daily Courier*
4. *Boston Daily Journal*
5. *Boston Columbian Centinel*
6. *Boston Emancipator and Republican*
7. *Boston Evening Transcript*
8. *Boston Globe*
9. *Boston Herald*
10. *Boston Pilot*
11. *Boston Traveler*
12. *Berkshire County Whig*
13. *Cape Cod Advocate and Nautical Intelligencer* of Sandwich
14. *Cape Cod Republican* of Harwich
15. *Liberator*
16. *Middleboro Gazette*
17. *New Bedford Daily Mercury*
18. *New Bedford Mercury*
19. *New Bedford Standard*
20. *Salem Register*
21. *Sandwich Independent*
22. *Sandwich Mechanic*

23. *Sandwich Observer*
24. *Wareham Transcript and Advertiser*
25. *Whalemen's Shipping List* of New Bedford
26. *Worcester National Aegis*
27. *Yarmouth Register*

Newspapers, non-Massachusetts

1. *Charleston Courier*
2. *Honolulu Friend*
3. *Milwaukee Sentinel*
4. *New York Herald*
5. *New York Times*
6. *New York Tribune*
7. *New York Weekly Herald*
8. *North Carolina Times* of New Bern
9. *Philadelphia Daily Evening Bulletin*
10. *Philadelphia Inquirer*
11. *Sacramento Daily Union*
12. *Washington Daily National Intelligencer*

Primary Source Books and Periodicals

1. Barnard, Sandy, ed. *Campaigning with the Irish Brigade: Pvt. John Ryan, 28th Massachusetts.* Terre Haute: AST Press, 2001.
2. Buck, George H. *A Brief Sketch of Company G Fortieth Massachusetts Infantry 1862-1865.*
3. Crowninshield, Benjamin W. *A History of the First Massachusetts Cavalry Volunteers.* Baltimore: Butternut and Blue, 1995.
4. Deane, John M. *Civil War Diaries.* Freetown, Massachusetts Historical Society, 2005.
5. Deyo, Simeon. *History of Barnstable County.* New York: H. W. Blake, 1890.
6. Emilio, Lewis F. *History of the Fifty-fourth Regiment of Massachusetts Volunteers.* Boston, 1894.
7. Erle, John M. *Report of the Governor and Council Indians of the Commonwealth.* Boston, 1861.
8. Garner, Stanton, ed. *Mary Chipman Lawrence. The Captain's Best Mate: The Journal of Mary Chipman Lawrence on the Whaler Addison 1856-1860.* Providence: Brown University Press, 1966.
9. Gordon, George H. *A War Diary of Events.* Boston: James R. Osgood, 1882.
10. Harrington, Thomas F. *The Harvard Medical School: A History, Narrative*

and Documentary. Lewis Publishing, 1905.

11. Hayes, John D., ed. *Samuel Francis DuPont: A Selection from his Civil War Letters*. Ithaca, NY: Cornell University Press, 1969.

12. Hennessey, John J., ed. *Fighting with the Eighteenth Massachusetts: The Civil War Memoir of Thomas H. Mann*. Baton Rouge: Louisiana State University Press, 2000.

13. Herberger, Charles F., ed. *A Yankee at Arms: The Diary of Lieutenant Augustus D. Ayling*. Knoxville: University of Tennessee Press, 1989.

14. *History of the Fifth Massachusetts Battery*. Boston: Luther E. Cowles, 1902.

15. *History of the Thirty-sixth Regiment Massachusetts Volunteers 1892-1865*.

16. Little, Henry F. W. *The Seventh New Hampshire Volunteers in the War of the Rebellion*. Concord, NH, 1896.

17. McKee, James H. *Back "In War Times." History of the 144th New York Infantry*, 1903.

18. Mettendorf, Ernest. *Between Triumph and Disaster: The History of the Forty-sixth New York Infantry*. Eden, New York, 2012.

19. Oliver, James. *Ancestry, Early Life and War Record of James Oliver M.D. Athol, MA*, 1916.

20. Osborne, William H. *History of the Twenty-ninth Regiment of Massachusetts Volunteer Infantry*. Boston, 1877.

21. Roe, Alfred S. *The Fifth Massachusetts Volunteer Infantry*, 1911.

22. ─────────. *The Twenty-fourth Massachusetts Volunteers 1861-1866*. Worcester, MA, 1907.

23. Smith, John L. *Antietam to Appomattox with 118th Penna. Vols. Corn Exchange Regiment*. Philadelphia: J. L. Smith, 1892.

24. Symonds, Craig L., ed. *A Year on a Monitor and the Destruction of Fort Sumter*. Columbia: University of South Carolina Press, 1987.

25. Tobey, Edward P. *History of the First Maine Cavalry 1861-1865*. Boston, 1867.

26. Woodbury, Augustus E. *Major General Ambrose E. Burnside and the Ninth Army Corps: A Narrative*. Providence: S.S. Rider, 1867.

27. Wesley, Dorothy Porter and Uzelac, Constance Porter, eds. *William Cooper Nell Selected Writings 1832-1874*. Baltimore: Black Classic Press, 2002.

The Homeopathic Physician

Massachusetts Historical Society Proceedings

Monthly Nautical Magazine, and Quarterly Review

The American Neptune

Secondary Source Books and Periodicals

1. Alotta, Robert L. *Civil War Justice: Union Army Executions Under Lincoln.* Shippensburg, PA: White Mane Publishing, 1989.
2. Armstrong, Marion V. Jr. *Unfurl Those Colors! McClellan, Sumner and the Second Army Corps in the Antietam Campaign.* Tuscaloosa: University of Alabama Press, 2008.
3. Azelrod, Alan. *The Horrid Pit.* New York: Carroll and Graf, 2007.
4. Barbour, Harriet. *Sandwich The Town That Glass Built.* Augustus M. Kelley, 1976.
5. Barefoot, Daniel W. *General Robert F. Hoke: Lee's Modest Warrior.* Winston-Salem: John F. Blair, 1996.
6. Barlow, Raymond E. and Kaiser, Joan E. *The Glass Industry in Sandwich.* Kaiser Barlow Publishing, 1999.
7. Bourne Historical Society. *From Pocasset to Cataumet,* 1988.
8. Browning Jr., Robert. *Lincoln's Trident: The West Gulf Blockading Squadron During the Civil War.* Tuscaloosa: University of Alabama Press, 2015.
9. Burgoin, Raymond B. *The Catholic Church in Sandwich 1830-1930.* Boston: E. L. Grimes, 1930.
10. Dean, Nicholas. *Snow Squall: The Last American Clipper Ship.* Gardiner, ME: Tilbury House, 2001.
11. Ellis, Alden C. Jr. *The Massachusetts Andrew Sharpshooters: A Civil War History and Roster.* Jefferson, NC: McFarland, 2012.
12. Grover, Kathryn. *The Fugitive's Gibraltar: Escaping Slaves and Abolitionism in New Bedford, Massachusetts.* Amherst: University of Massachusetts Press, 2001.
13. Johnson, Robert E. *Far China Station: The U. S. Navy in Asian Waters 1800-1898.* Annapolis: Naval Institute Press, 1979.
16. Kittridge, Henry C. *Shipmasters of Cape Cod.* Hyannis: Parnassis Imprints, 1963.
17. Lovell, R. A. Jr. *Sandwich. A Cape Cod Town.* Town of Sandwich, MA, 1996.
18. Mallinson, Fred M. *The Civil War on the Outer Banks.* Jefferson, NC: McFarland and Company, 1996.
19. Marquis, Greg. *In Armageddon's Shadow: The Civil War and Canada's Maritime Provinces.* Montreal: McGill University Press, 1998.
20. Miller, Richard F. *Harvard's Civil War: A History of the Twentieth Massachusetts Volunteer Infanry.* Hanover, NH: University Press of New England, 2005.
21. Moebs, Thomas T. *Black Soldiers-Black Sailors-Black Ink: Research Guide on African-Americans in U. S. Military History 1526-1900.* Moebs Publishing, 1994.

22. Rhea, Gordon C. *The Battles for Spotsylvania Court House and the Road to Yellow Tavern May 7-12, 1864*. Baton Rouge: Louisiana State University Press, 1997.
23. ———. *Cold Harbor Grant and Lee May 26-June 3, 1864*. Baton Rouge: Lousiana State University Press, 2007.
24. Rice, James Montgomery. *Peoria City and County Illinois*, 1912.
25. Samito, Christian B. *Commanding Boston's Irish: The Civil War Letters of Colonel Patrick R. Guiney, Ninth Massachusetts Volunteer Infantry*. New York: Fordham University Press, 1998.
26. Schmutz, John F. *The Battle of the Crater: A Complete History*. Jefferson, NC: McFarland, 2009.

1. The Acorn, Journal of the Sandwich Glass Museum
2. Cape Cod Genealogical Association Journal
3. Civil War History
4. Massachusetts Historical Review
5. Virginia Magazine of History and Biography
6. Yankee Magazine

Master's Thesis

Marcus R. Erlandson. Guy V. Henry: A Study in Military Leadership, 1985

Index

Abbott, Jacob J. 145
Abbott, Samuel 133
Abby Bradford, schooner 35
Abigail, whaler 146
Adams, Elizabeth B. 37
Adams, Isaiah 37, 78
Adams, Watson 37, 46, 103, 118
Adeline Gibbs, ship 87
Alabama
  Mobile Bay 131, 140-41, 143
Alabama, raider 74
Alecto, ship 22
Allen, Jesse 37, 46, 61, 65-66
Allen, Jules 94
Allton, Abel 13
Allyne, Helen 23, 149
Allyne, Joseph W. 23
Allyne, Mary H. 14
Allyne, Samuel H. 14, 23, 28, 57, 123 137, 149
Allyne, Samuel H. Jr. 23, 37, 53, 105 110
Allyne, Sophronia 23
Allyne, John W. 23
Alton, John 74, 93, 132
Alton, Joseph 74, 93
Alton, Melissa 132
Alton, Samuel 16-17
Alton, Samuel T. 92, 94
Amelia, brig 23
Ames, Adelbert 99
Andrew, John 18, 29, 56, 68, 80, 46, 91
Apaches 53
Apple Grove School 11
Arizona Territory
  Fort Stanford 53
Armstrong, Mary 152
Armstrong, Robert 129, 131
Atherton, James 21, 44, 52, 63, 65, 77, 98, 104, 115-16, 149
Atkins, George 6
Atkins, Helen D. 122
Atkins, James P. 106, 112, 122
Atkins, Thomas F. 6
Atlantic, steamer 125
Avery, Gilbert 26
Avery, Reliance 68
Avery, Rodman 26, 145
Avery, Watson D. 26, 68
Ayling, Augustus 44, 52, 55-56, 63, 71, 106-107, 115, 117
Bachelder, John B. 10, 120
Badger, George W. 116
Badger, Gustavus 61, 77
Badger, John M. D. 24, 61
Badger, John M. L. 9
Badger, Mary A. E. 87
Baker, Anna 153
Baker, Henry B. 128
Baker, John F. 140-41
Ball, James 106-107, 139, 150
Baker, Joseph A. 104, 133, 141
Baker, Thomas 141
Ball, Edward 16-17
Ball, Michael A. 38, 61
Ball, Thomas 15, 51, 63
Ball, Thomas A. 63, 99
Barlow, Bathsheba H. 122
Barlow, Louisa N. 27, 125
Barlow, Solomon N. 48
Barnes, Joseph H. 36, 45, 51, 65, 71, 107, 128, 150
Barnstable Patriot 102, 105, 118, 147
Bassett, Ezra 140-41
Bassett, Gorham F. 22
Bates, Lucy 49

Baxter, Benjamin 47
Beckerman, John F. 7
Beecher, Henry B. 51, 119
Belle Isle, schooner 24
Benson, Henry 59, 71, 91
Benton, gunboat 82, 91
Black Troops and Sandwich
   Robert H. Chadbourne 70, 126
   Hartwell Freeman 77, 91
   Giles M. Pease 97
   John T. Collins 110
   Southern recruiting 129
Blackwell, Arabella 87
Blackwell, Frederick A. 88
Blackwell, Henry 132
Blackwell, Joseph 9
Blackwell, Samuel 9
Blackwell, Susan 49-50
Blackwell, Thomas 50
Blake, David A. 27, 47
Blake, Thomas D. 27
Booth, Edwin 27
Booth, John Wilkes 143
Boston and Sandwich Glass Company 4, 41, 43, 52
Bourne, Charles 6, 84
Bourne, Hannah 84
Bourne, Henry A. 53, 112
Bourne, Jerome 25
Bourne, John 6, 84
Bourne, John H. 25
Bourne, Jonathan 2nd 7, 25
Bourne, Joshua T. 25
Bourne, Joshua W. 25, 33, 42, 81
Bourne, Mary C. 25
Bourne, Melatiah T. 25
Bourne, Samuel C. 48
Bourne, Thomas B. 112, 114, 126, 128, 133, 135, 138
Bowes, Sarah 18
Bowman, Benjamin 10
Boyd, Belle 66
Boyden Livery Sandwich 107
Boyden, Robert R. 123
Boyden, William E. 30, 35, 123, 137
Boyer, Henry 20
Boyer, James 20, 104
Boyer, Ophelia 20
Brady, Charles 21, 30, 37, 43-44, 52, 54, 62, 128
Brady, Edward 18, 65
Branch, William H. 131
Breckenridge, John 21, 39-40, 96
Breese, William 61
Brooks, Alfred O. 52, 63, 77
Brown, Moses 13, 47, 57
Brown, Thomas W. 137
Bruce, George F. 107
Bryant, Josephine 22
Bumpass, Frank G. 116
Burbank, Luke 145
Burbank, William H. F. 18
Burgess, Frank H. 86, 129
Burgess, Howard 29
Burgess, Seth S. 7
Burgess, Thornton W. 86
Burnside, Ambrose 70
Burnside Expedition 37, 44, 46-47
Burr, Jonathan 11
Butler, Benjamin 31-32
Butler, Bradford 97
Butler, James D. 6, 14
Cady, Charles F. 25
Cahill, Thomas 22, 49
Cahoon, Freeman 13
California
   San Francisco 23, 37, 152-53
California troops
   First Cavalry 37, 53
Cambridge, steamer 31
Campbell, Catherine 69, 150
Campbell, John W. 62, 65, 69, 141, 150
Cape Cod Advocate 9

Cape Cod Express 137
Cape Cod Glassworks 18, 43, 52
Cape Cod Railroad 6, 106, 128, 140
Carleton Hall Sandwich 104
Caroline, brig 22
Cass, Thomas 28, 34
Catskill, steamer 53
Central House Hotel 8
Ceylon, ship 21
Chadbourne, John 18, 38, 93, 103
Chadbourne, Robert H. 70, 126, 150
Chadwick, Joshua T. 7
Chamberlain, Benjamin 118, 131-32, 145, 153
Chamberlain, George A. W. 21
Chamberlain, George N. 9
Chapman, A. A. 12
Chapman, L. F. 12
Chapouil, Anthony 9
Cheval, Alfred 46, 51, 77
Childs, Braddock R. 9, 25
Childs, William H. 25, 131, 140
Chipman, Charles
  early life 20
  1860 delegate 21
  Sandwich Guards 21
  politics 21
  signs volunteers 29
  elected captain 30
  discipline 31
  contraband attitude 33
  Eldridge sentence 37
  wife's pregnancy 39
  denounces Breckenridge 39
  receives clothing 41
  selected for major 41
  Chamberlain girl scandal 44
  meets Deming Jarves Jr. 45
  orderly Swift 47
  reaction to political message 49
  Heywood friendship 50
  shell from ironclad 51
  abolitionist attitude 51
  attitude toward commander 52
  complaints from Sandwich 54
  at Antietam 65
  political and Lincoln attitude 68
  lauded by Meagher 70
  in Sandwich 77
  short of money 83-84
  sends money to Sandwich 90
  hears of Gettysburg 92
  Vicksburg comment 96
  Sandwich carpenters 99
  Copperheads in Sandwich 101
  politics and Charlotte Freeman 102
  Sandwich 1864 departure 115
  Black Troops comment 116
  retrieves colors 122
  Petersburg trenches 124
  critical of Black troops 126
  wounded 127
  funeral 128
Chipman, Elizabeth G. 151
Chipman, George 21
Chipman, Hettie N. 37
Chipman, Isaac K. 7, 35
Chipman, James 92, 94
Chipman, Jonathan 15, 19, 21
Chipman, Sands 123
Chipman, William C. 7
Chipman, William N. 38, 47
Christ, Benjamin 70-71
Clancy, Patrick 84
Clarence, brig 7, 83, 131
Clark, Edward 115
Clark, Evelyn Freeman 115
Clark, George H. 20, 104, 108
Clark, Horace L. 134
Clarke, Ann B. 33
Clarke, Charles 123
Clarke, Franklin R. J. 33, 123
Clarke, John 33
Clarke, Josiah F. 14

Clarke, William F. 123
Clement, Alonzo 123
Cogswell, George 51, 65
Colclough, John 86
Cole, Mary S. 134
Coleman, David 37
Collins, John T. 18, 41, 76, 110, 134, 151
Collins, Mary 41
Collins, Patrick 17
Collins, Reuben Jr. 53
Colorado, frigate 34
Colored Troops 70, 77, 91
Commodore, steamer 107
Congress, frigate 37, 50
Connecticut, steamer 112
Connor, Justin 19
Connor, Mary 19, 64
Cook, James 65, 69, 88, 110, 115-16
Copperheads in Sandwich 101
Cordell, Edward 72
Corps D'Afrique Ninth Reg't 91
Cosmopolitan, steamer 108
Covell, John N, 129-30
Cox, James 19, 62, 116
Cox, Robert 19
Crocker, Alexander 22
Crocker, Asa Jr. 88
Crocker, Asa Sr. 88
Crocker, Heman 88
Crocker, Horace 88
Crocker, Loring 22
Crocker, Temperance 88
Cumberland, sloop 37, 50
Dalton, Christopher 16-17
Dalton, Christopher B. 10, 18, 38, 65, 116
Dalton, James 103, 118
Dalton, James Henry 10, 41, 86, 117
Dalton, John W. 89
Dalton, William B. 10, 38, 46, 61
Daniel Webster, steamer 76

Darby, Thomas 43, 46, 51, 54, 64, 73, 77, 83, 89, 100
Davis, Allen 124
Davis, Benjamin 19
Davis, James 88
Davis, Thomas 64, 117
Day, Joseph M. 30, 41
Dean, Cornelius 57, 132
Dean, Warren P. 62, 69, 76
Delaware
  Christiana 141
  Wilmington 141
Delaware Troops
  First Infantry 141
Delware, Mary Jane 150
Devens, Charles 142
Dickey, William H. 126
Dillaway, George 52, 55
Dillingham, Charles 19, 41, 104, 114
Dillingham, Isabella 41
Dix, Dorothea 76
Dolan, Bridget 18
Donegal, blockade runner 123
Donnelly, Edward 116
Donovan, Cornelius 19, 117
Doran, Sarah 19
Draper, ship 87
Duffy, Rosanna 11
Dunham, Lucy 22
Du Pont, Samuel 48, 82
Eaton, Joseph
Edwards, Spencer 20
Elder, Josiah 63
Eldridge, Cyrenius 87
Eldridge, Nancy 41
Eldridge, Perez 31, 36, 41, 106, 120, 151
Ellen Barnard, brig 53
Ellis, Abner 145
Ellis, Charles E. 118, 151
Ellis, Eleanor 41
Ellis, Eliza 137

Ellis, Hiram B. 137
Ellis, Josiah 46
Ellis, Nathan B. Jr. 70
Ellis, Nathan S. 129
Ellis, Nathaniel S. 125
Ellis, Stillman 143
Ellis, Thomas 57
Emory Hospital Washington 62
Ewer, Benjamin 23, 37, 46, 103, 118
Ewer, John 74, 99
Express, steamer 37
Fagan, Alice 17, 36, 43
Fagan, John 17-18, 43, 65, 116
Fagan, Patrick 88
Fagan, Peter 17
Falmouth, sloop 25
Fernandina, bark 38
Ferraro, Edward 111, 116
Fessenden, Benjamin 75
Fessenden, C.B. H. 20
Fessenden, George L. 41
Fessenden, Mary 41
Fessenden, Sewell 8, 20, 41
Fessenden, William 8
Fifield, Ansel C. 23, 93, 97, 136
Fifield, Watson 59
Fillmore, Millard 20
Fish, Elizabeth M. 12
Fish, Henry 92
Fish, John F. 37
Fish, Nathaniel 42, 79, 93, 133
Fish, Obed M. 111, 114, 126, 133, 135, 138
Fish, Sumner B. 29, 36
Fisher, Calvin G. 33, 42, 91, 96, 100-101
Fisher, Daniel F. 83
Fisher, Francis A. 66, 100-101
Fisher, Joanna 146
Fisher, Levi 22
Fisher, Lucinda 101
Fisher, Martha 100-101

Fisher, Nathan 146
Fisher, Nathan B. 24, 146-47
Fisher, Sarah 11
Fisher, Theodore 15
Fletcher, Maria 13
Fletcher, Thomas 13
Florida
  Fernandina 48
  Fort Jefferson 150
  Jacksonville 108
  Key West 53, 75
  St. Augustine 103
Florida, raider 75, 83, 123, 131
Fogarty, Ann 16-17
Fogarty, Daniel 16
Forest City, steamer 89
Forest King, schooner 7
Forman, Jacob G. 13, 21, 76
Forrest Hill Prison 100
Foster, Christopher 131
Foster, John D. 69, 72
Foster, Josiah 69
Foster, Josiah Jr. 29, 35
Fowler, Dr. 52
Freeman, Charlotte 102
Freeman, Ezra B. 35
Freeman, Frederick 11, 57
Freeman, George H. 28
Freeman, Hartwell 57-59, 77, 91
Freeman, Watson Jr. 102
Freeman, Watson Sr. 101-102
Free Soil Party 14
Fuller, Benjamin 22, 107
Fuller, Cordelia 22, 52
Fuller, Dorcas M. 22, 107
Fuller, Nathaniel 22
Gaffney, Bridget 18
Gaffney, James 18, 114, 126, 133
Galvanized Yankees 142
Garner, Stanton 151
Garrison, William Lloyd 10
Geisler, Francis 20

Geisler, Francis C. 20, 70
Geisler, Elizabeth 20
Georgia
  Andersonville 126, 128
  Brunswick 151
  Fort McAllister 74
  Macon 133, 138
Gibbs, Ann Maria 137, 145
Gibbs, Bradford 22
Gibbs, Charles I. 21, 131, 140
Gibbs, Elizabeth F. 20-21
Gibbs, Emily F. 125
Gibbs, Excie 151
Gibbs, Freeman B. 80
Gibbs, George F. 80, 123, 146, 151
Gibbs, Paul C. 131
Gibbs, Pelham 32
Gibbs, Phineas 103, 118, 142-44
Gibbs, Russell 143
Gibbs, Seth F. 80, 123
Gibbs, Thomas M. 137, 142-45
Gibbs, William R. 131
Gifford, Daniel S. 25
Gilmore, Quincy 108
Gilson, Helen 103
Glasgow, steamer 140, 143
Godfrey, Charles N. 124-25
Godfrey, John W. 27, 34, 48, 74, 83
Godfrey, Josiah Jr. 7, 27
Godfrey, Louise 48
Golconda, bark 87, 123
Golden Eagle, ship 23
Goodspeed, Sarah 53
Gordon, George 81
Grant, U. S. 47, 110, 118, 144
Greenport, sloop 7
Guiney, James 116
Gurney, Deborah 13
Gurney, Samuel B. 13
Hacker, Francis 9
Hackett, Mary Ann 18
Hackett, Thomas 18, 19, 71-72

Haines, Benjamin 14, 19, 37
Haines, Edward 18
Haines, George F. W. 19, 24, 73-74, 93, 97
Haines, George L. 19, 41, 52, 59 71-72, 80-81, 104
Haines, James G. B. 19, 40-41, 52
Haines, Sarah 52
Hall, Charles B. 10, 43, 84, 102, 104, 116, 134
Hamblin, Ezra 79
Hamblin, Nathaniel 7, 23
Hamlen, Benjamin 37, 51, 55, 71
Hammond, Luther T. 103, 105
Hammond, Zilpha 105
Handy, Francis D. 7
Handy, Pliny B. 87
Harewood Hospital Washington 76
Harmon, Persia 46
Harney, William S. 33
Harper, Mary 104
Harper, William H. 9, 56-57, 77, 104, 116
Harpers Hotel 9
Harpur, John 10
Harriet Lane, steamer 25
Harris, Russell 25
Harrison, Alexander M. 153
Harrison, Emily 87
Harrison, Mary 87
Hart, Clementine Perry 142
Hart, Isaac C. 134, 142
Hartford, Joseph W. 40
Hartford, Maria 40, 53
Hartford, sloop 131
Hatch, Albert D. 85, 89, 139
Hathaway, James 25
Haviland, Emma 19
Haviland, Jacob 19
Haze, steamer 65
Heald, Abel S. 41, 67
Heald, Hiram H. 7

Heald, James 54-55, 67-68
Healey, Abraham 145
Heffernan, Abigail 17, 133
Heffernan, Edward 17, 57, 132-33
Heffernan, Lucy 49
Heffernan, Mary Ann 49
Heineman, Elizabeth 20
Herring Pond Tribe 13, 20, 128-29
Hewins, Joseph S. 88
Heywood, Charles 50-51, 74, 131
Heywood, Cynthia 50
Heywood, John D. 9
Hinckley, Nathaniel 85
Hinds, Heman S. 7, 27
Hinds, Leonard 27, 29, 124, 141-42
Hobson, George 42, 49, 79
Hollis, Thomas 19, 64, 152
Holway, Bethia 128
Holway, Edward W. 89, 141
Holway, Elizabeth 141
Holway, Hepsa 141
Holway, John 128
Holway, Roland 112, 128
Hooper, Foster 85
Horace, schooner 13
Hosmer, George W. 20
Howard, Charles L. 74-75, 122
Howard, Elizabeth 139
Howard, James 19
Howard, Leonard E. 120
Howes, Alvin C. 24, 123
Howes, Charles A. 24, 46, 93, 100
Howes, Daniel W. 25
Howes, Nathaniel P. 24
Hoxie, Charles A. 22
Hoxie, Charles H. 22, 152
Hoxie, Charlotte 41
Hoxie, David 22, 106-107, 152
Hoxie, Nathaniel C. 22
Hoxie, Rebecca 22
Hoxie, Zenas 22
Huddy, John T. 145

Hume, schooner 27, 34
Hunt, Henry 100
Hunt, Louisa 22
Hunt, Samuel 54, 65, 96, 100, 115, 149, 152
Indiana
  Madison 107
  Montgomery County 60
Indiana Troops
  Seventh Cavalry 123
Illinois
  Morrison 48
  Peoria 25
Illinois, steamer 23
Illinois Troops
  Twelfth Infantry 47
Irish Brigade 54, 63, 70
Jackson, Clement 99
Jacob Bell, ship 75
Jameson, Robert 95
Jamestown, ship 23
Jarves, Deming 4, 6
Jarves, Deming Jr. 45, 82
Jarvesville 4-6, 10-11, 17-18
Johnson, Anthony 20
Johnson, John F. 145
Johnson, Persis 151
Jones, Charles E. 47
Jones, Emily M. 149
Jones, Francis F. 151
Jones, James T. 78
Jones, Solomon H. 72, 74, 83, 99
Kansas
  Atchison 152
Keene, Martha 10
Keene, Warren P. 72, 143
Keith, Isaac 6-7
Keith, Isaac N. 137
Kelley, James 34, 55
Kelley, William 92
Kensington, steamer 48
Kentucky

Paris 83
Camp Nelson 99
Somerset 83
Kern, Daniel V. 132, 149
Kern, Francis 14-15
Kern, Henry A. 30, 42-43, 52, 128
Kern, Martin Jr. 95, 100, 104
Kern, Rebecca 41
Kern, Theodore 18, 41
Kern, William E. 18
Kerr, Robert 105
Kickapoo, ironclad 140-41, 143
Kimball, Henry 14, 49, 56
Kingfisher, bark 38
Knippe, Henry 19, 59, 79, 104, 114, 126, 128, 133
Knippe, Isabella 19
Lackawanna, sloop 131
Lane, Andrew 61, 92
Lapham, James L. 24, 87
Lawrence, Edward D. 103
Lawrence, Edward J. 103
Lehigh, ironclad 99
Leonard, Jonathan 10, 28, 59, 84, 133-34
Lincoln, Abraham 34, 36, 56, 76, 89, 108, 111, 134, 137, 143
Lincoln Hospital Washington 76
Linnell, Sarah S. 23
Little, Charles H. 97, 137, 142, 145, 152
Little, Francis 38
Little, Sarah 145
Lloyd, Hannah D. 132
Lloyd, George T. 19, 118-19, 132, 145
Lloyd, James D. 19
Lloyd, Samuel 19
L.N. Godfrey, schooner 27
Long, Patrick 66
Long, Thomas 67
Loring, William 9, 13
Louisiana

Port Hudson 91
Louisiana Troops
   Third Louisiana Native Guards 70
Lovell, Horace 21, 46, 66, 93, 97, 112, 114, 126, 128, 133, 135, 137, 152
Macomber, Perry G. 6
Madigan, Joseph 43, 106-107, 122, 139, 140
Magoon, Davis 25, 76
Magoon, Freelove 25, 76
Maine
   Sumner 67
Maine Troops
   First Cavalry 47
   First Heavy Artillery 120
Manley, William 108, 145
Manimon, Barzillai 145
Marsh, Joseph 14, 18
Marston, Eugene 87
Marston, Jonathan B. 87
Marston, Louise T. 8
Marston, William H. 8, 87
Marvel, Eliza 132
Marvel, Samuel 112, 120, 132-34
Maryland
   Annapolis 37, 66, 110-111
   Antietam 64-65
   Berlin 97
   Frederick 62, 97
   Hagerstown 35
   Perryville 47
   Point of Rocks 82
Mason, Thomas 58
Massachusetts
   Boston 42
   Brewster 23
   Cambridge 4
   Centerville 122
   Dedham 88
   Dennis 25, 86, 131
   East Boston 150
   East Sandwich 6-7, 11, 23, 78, 141

Harwich 132
Hyannis 47
Lancaster School 110
Marston's Mills 85
Monument 6-7, 10, 20, 25, 34, 48, 59, 72, 76, 84, 132
New Bedford 80, 85, 134, 139
North Sandwich 6, 13, 27, 47
Orleans 23
Plymouth 14
Pocasset 6-7, 26-27, 38, 44, 47, 56 68, 96
Reading 94
Salem 92
South Sandwich 7, 23, 72, 88
Spring Hill 6, 18, 52, 60
West Sandwich 6-7, 10, 13-14, 41, 57, 87, 92, 143
Massachusetts Troops
  First Cavalry 42, 49, 69, 79, 93, 104, 108, 114, 133
  First Infantry 51, 55
  Second Cavalry 100, 116
  Second Heavy Artillery 111
  Second Infantry 92, 94
  Third Cavalry 132
  Third Heavy Artillery 146
  Third Infantry 28, 30
  Fourth Cavalry 139
  Fifth Cavalry 117, 129
  Fifth Infantry 29, 36, 123
  Fifth Light Artillery 74, 94, 96, 132
  Ninth Infantry 34, 55, 70, 93, 114
  Ninth Light Artillery 74, 94
  Eleventh Infantry 54, 92-93
  Fourteenth Light Artillery 139
  Eighteenth Infantry 46, 66, 93
  Twentieth Infantry 61-62, 64, 70, 92
  Twenty-second Infantry 89
  Twenty-fourth Infantry 37, 103, 118, 143
  Twenty-eighth Infantry 38, 46, 49, 51, 61-62, 71, 93
  Twenty-ninth Infantry
    formation of 42
    Company D and 45
    Army of Potomac proximity 51
    Suffolk to White House 53
    departure Harrison's Landing 61
    Antietam 64-65
    Falmouth and transfer 69-70
    Fredericksburg 71
    fraternization 73
    to Kentucky 77
    at Paris, KY 83
    at Somerset, KY 83
    ordered to Vicksburg 90
    Jackson campaign 95
    march to Knoxville 99
    winter in Tennessee 104, 106
    re-enlistment 106
    to Cincinnati 109
    return to Boston 110
    return to Sandwich 116
    at Cold Harbor 119
    to Petersburg 122
    march on Broadway 145
  Thirtieth Infantry 70
  Thirty-second Infantry 93
  Thirty-third Infantry 92, 94
  Thirty-sixth Infantry 106, 110-111, 114
  Fortieth Infantry
    Sandwich soldiers in 57
    arrival Washington 63
    at Fort Ethan Allen 68
    "hanger-on" at camp 77
    to Suffolk, Virginia 79-80
    to West Point, Virginia 81
    Frederick MD train 96
    at Berlin, MD 97
    witnesses execution 97
    at Folly Island, SC 98
    illness at Folly Island 103

   Florida and Olustee expedition 108
   to James River campaign 117
   Drewry's Bluff battle 118
   to Cold Harbor 119
   at Chapin's Farm 139
   enters Richmond 142
   muster out 145
Forty-first Infantry 58
Forty-fifth Infantry 59, 69, 71, 78, 80, 91
Fifty-fourth Infantry 20, 97, 103-104, 108
Fifty-fifth Infantry 104
Fifty-eighth Infantry 112, 120, 125, 132
Sixty-first Infantry 137, 142
Massachusetts Battalion 36, 41
Massachusetts Sharpshooters 70
Matilda, steamer 132
Maxim, Seth F. 131
McAlaney, Ann 110
McAlaney, John 19, 30, 37, 46, 110-111, 114, 116
McAlaney, Sarah 52
McAlaney, Susan 30
McCabe, John 38
McClellan, George 64
McDermott, Thomas 16-17
McDermott, William 18, 37, 99, 116
McElroy, Patrick 54, 61
McGirr, Catherine 34
McGirr, Edward 34, 62
McGirr, Margaret 34
McGirr, Patrick 16-17, 34, 55, 61, 75
McKowen, Catherine 153
McKowen, Francis 100
McKowen, James 58, 132-33, 135, 138, 153
McLaughlin, Sarah T. 11
McMahon, Patrick 145
McManus, Owen 18
McNulty, James 58, 116, 136

McNulty, Margaret 41
McNulty, Peter 42, 61
McNulty, Thomas R. 4, 19
Meade, George 92
Meagher, Thomas 70
Merrimac, ironclad 50-51
Metacomet, steamer 123
Midnight, bark 61
Miller, John Q. 121, 131
Milwaukee, ironclad 141
Minnesota
   Fort Ridgeley 142
Minnesota, frigate 33
Mississippi
   Vicksburg 81-82, 90-91, 94, 96
Mississippi Marine Brigade 91
Missouri
   Sedalia 42
   St. Louis 25, 33
Missouri Troops
   Seventh Infantry 33, 41, 81-82
Monahan, Martin 31
Mondamin, bark 7, 131
Monitor, ironclad 50
Montague, James P. 144
Montague, John 16-18, 115
Montague, Sarah 17-18, 52, 115
Moody, Loring 132
Moran, William 4
Morning Star, bark 75
Mount Wollaston, whaler 153
Nahant, ironclad 72, 82, 99
Nebraska
   Dixon County 150
Neiter, Andrew 86
Neiter, Peter 86
Nell, William C. 14
New Bedford City Guard 28
Newbold, William A. 141
New Hampshire Troops
   Seventh Infantry 108
   Eleventh Infantry 124

New Ironsides, ironclad 82-83
New Jersey Troops
  Fifteenth Infantry 124, 141
New Mexico
  Socorro 105
Newton, Isaac 89
New World, ship 120
New York
  New Columbus Harbor 20
  Governor's Island 46
New York Troops
  Fifth Infantry (Zouaves) 34
  Twelfth Infantry 29, 35
  Fourteenth Heavy Artillery 122
  Forty-sixth Infantry 109
  Fiftieth Infantry 97
  Seventy-ninth Infantry 109
  One hundred-fourth Inf. 65
  Ullman Brigade 77
Nichols, Mary A. 152
Nickerson, Cranston W. 87, 123
Nickerson, John 83
Nightingale, Charles W. 48
Nightingale, Joseph 13
Norris, Benjamin 13, 80
Norris, Benjamin A. 88
Norris, Frederick 80, 123
North Carolina
  Elizabeth City 27, 29
  Kinston 71-72
  New Bern 69, 71, 78-80, 129
  Plymouth 110
  Portsmouth Hospital 78
  Roanoke Island 37
  Salisbury 133
North Carolina Troops
  First Colored Heavy Artillery 129
  Seventeenth Infantry 124
Nye, Charles 13
Nye, David D. 96
Nye, Ebenezer F. 7, 146, 153
Nye, Ephraim 74, 93, 96-97, 132, 139

Nye, Ezra 75
Nye, Joanna G. 153
Nye, Lemuel 18
Nye, Nancy 23
Nye, Nathan 131
Nye, William F. 96, 139, 146
Ocean, bark 24, 87
Ohio
  Cincinnati 77
Ohio, ship 72, 83
Oklahoma
  Enid 151
O'Neill, James 34, 55, 93, 97, 114
O'Neill, John G. 137
Orrell, John 13
Ottawa, gunboat 48
Packard, Charles 29, 80
Pardey, Priscilla Baker 141
Parker, Charles W. 87
Parker, Erastus O. 6
Parkinson, Joseph O. 10, 84
Parks, Henry 31
Parry, John 86
Patapsco, ironclad 136
Pease, Giles 14, 27
Pease, Giles M. 27, 97, 103, 108, 153
Pembroke, steamer 30
Pennsylvania
  Gettysburg 92-94
Perry, Caleb H. 111
Perry, Clementine 134
Perry, Elijah F. 83
Perry, George W. 59
Perry, Henry 97, 145
Perry, John M. 122
Perry, Joseph M. 34
Perry, Nathan C. 103, 108, 145
Perry, Susan E. 10
Perry, Thomas C. 7, 53, 59, 134, 136, 145
Perry, William 59
Phelps, John 37

Phinney, Abram 7, 83, 131
Phinney, Betsy 69
Phinney, George E. 34
Phinney, George O. 137-38
Phinney, Isaac H. 80, 119
Phinney, Jabez 34
Phinney, Jesse F. 34
Phinney, Joseph 123
Phinney, Lucinda 7
Phinney, Sylvanus 30, 147
Phinney, Sylvester 29
Phinney, William W. 29, 42, 69, 108, 114, 126, 128, 133, 135-38, 145
Pierce, Deborah 57
Pierce, Ebenezer 45, 52
Pierson, George 13
Pinkham, Matthew 10
Pioneer, gunboat 37, 44, 46
Pope, Abby 41
Pope, Elisha 8
Pope, John 61
Pope, John W. 86-87, 149
Pope, Sarah 8
Pope's Hotel 8-9
Porter, Burr 77
Powhatan, frigate 34
Quinn, Charles 43
Quinn, Dianna 57
Quinn, Ellen 114
Quinn, Matthew 57
Quinn, Susan 43
Quinnell, Sophia 104
Ranger, steamer 143
Rebecca Simms, ship 20
Red Rover, steamer 91
Regan, Bartholomew 93
Restless, bark 144
Rhode Island
   Portsmouth Grove 66, 76
Rhode Island troops
   Eleventh Infantry 80
Richardson, Israel B. 65

Richmond, sloop 131
Ricker, Oliver 76
Riley, Ann 110
Riley, Phillip 37, 103, 110, 118
Riordan, George 54, 92-93
Riordan, Titus P. 17, 93
Robert Edwards, ship 20
Robbins, Caleb T. 65, 116, 153
Robbins, Verilo H. 65
Rogers, John H. B. 86
Rogers, Sarah 86
Runnells, Andrew J. 10, 134
Runnells, Susan P. 134
Russell, Henry 10-11, 13
Russell, Mary 11
Russell, Peter 116
Russell, William H. 13
Ryder, George G. 35
Sabine, frigate 74-75, 99
Sandwich abolitionists 33
Sandwich Academy 11, 20
Sandwich Antislavery Society 13-14
Sandwich Catholic Relig. Society 134
Sandwich Collegiate Institute 11
Sandwich Female Academy 11
Sandwich Guards 21
Sandwich Mechanic 9
Sandwich Observer 9, 14
Sandwich Society of Friends 13, 89, 123-24
Sandwich Tack Factory 7
Sangamon, ironclad 102
Santee, clipper 147
Savannah, frigate 37
Saxon, steamer 83
Scargo, ship 25
Schuster, Abraham 86
Scobie, George 97
Scott, Jane 41
Sea Breeze, bark 87
Sears, Augustus 10
Sears, Barzillae 101

Sears, Isabella 151
Sears, Lucy Smith Gibbs 101
Shaw, Colin 92-94
Shaw, Neil 92-93
Shenandoah, raider 146
Sheridan, Philip 114, 132
Sherman, Andrew F. 86
Sherman, Daniel P. 86
Sherman, Thomas C. 137
Sherman, William T. 95, 134
Shevlin, James 93, 97
Sigel, Franz 33
Signal Corps 45
Simpson, Thomas 91
Skiff, Ebenezer 13
Small, Laura 152
Smith, Alfred E. 58-59, 77
Smith, Henry G. 7, 24
Smith, James W. 71, 84
Smith, Lucy A. 107
Smith, Sabin 8
Southack, Mary 41
South Carolina
  Beaufort 103, 105
  Charleston 27, 82
  Columbia 134
  Folly Island 98
  Hilton Head 51, 53, 108
  Morris Island 97
  Port Royal 48
Southfield, gunboat 111
Sportsman's Retreat 8
Spring Hill School 11
Spring, William C. 57
Stanford, Josiah 23, 149
Stanford, Leland 23, 149
Stearns, O. H. 106
Stephania, ship 87
Strickney, Anna 150
Stone, Lucy 14
Stowe, Harriet Beecher 51
Substitutes 89, 130, 141

Sumner, Edwin 70
Sunflower, steamer 75
Swasey, Isaac N. 10, 14, 28, 49, 56
Swasey, Lucy 10, 41
Swift, Abram 131
Swift, Betsy 146
Swift, Charles E. 96, 145
Swift, Clark 88
Swift, Cynthia B. 50
Swift, Dean 118
Swift, Ellis M. 6, 146
Swift, Francis C. 40, 47, 88, 99, 112
Swift, Francis H. 26, 153
Swift, Mary 88
Swift, Nancy W. 151
Swift, Noble P. 87
Swift, Sarah S. 88
Swift, Seth 146
Swift, Shadrach F. 88
Swift, Thomas 14, 40
Swift, William H. 26, 145
Swift, Ward F. 7
Swift, Wayman 27
Tacony, tender 83
Teasdale, Harriet 8
Teasdale, William 8
Tennessee
  Fort Donelson 47
  Knoxville 90, 107
Tennessee Troops
  Tenth Infantry 137
Texas
  Franklin 105
  Indianola 152
  San Elizario 105
Thatcher, Henry 140
Thomas Powell, steamer 132
Thompson, David 8
Tillie, steamer 53
Tinkham, John W. 82, 91, 104, 112, 125-26, 133, 135-36, 139
Tobey, Charles W. 7, 87

Tobey, Thomas 87
Tobey, Watson 87
Turner, Joseph 19, 63, 77
Turner, Mary C. 64
Umpire, brig 83
United States Hotel Boston 100
United States Troops
    First Colored Heavy Art. 110, 134
    First U. S. Volunteers 142
    Fourth Artillery 51, 80, 119
    Seventh Infantry 93
    Eighty-fourth Colored 126
Valetta, bark 22
Vanderbilt, steamer 61
Vermont, ship of the line 48
Virginia
    Alexandria 36, 61, 145
    Appomattox 143
    Bermuda Hundred 117
    Boulware's Landing 139
    Bristow Station 112
    Burkeville 144
    Camp Butler 37, 40, 47, 50-51
    Cedar Creek 133
    Chapin's Farm 139, 142
    City Point 100, 139, 144
    Culpeper 61, 89, 97
    Craney Island 61
    Danville 126, 136
    Drewry's Bluff 117
    Fair Oaks 53-54
    Falmouth 69-70, 72, 92
    Fisher's Hill 133
    Fort Ethan Allen 63, 68
    Fortress Monroe 28, 31, 36, 39
    Fort Steadman 139
    Fredericksburg 70-71
    Gaines's Mills 55
    Glendale 55
    Harper's Ferry 66
    Harrison's Landing 55
    Kelly's Ford 79
    Laurel Hill 114
    Libby Prison 66
    Martinsburg 36
    Miner's Hill 68
    Petersburg 126, 142
    Richmond 142, 144
    Rip Raps Island 36, 42-43
    Savage's Station 55, 67
    Shepherdstown 66
    Spotsylvania 114
    Suffolk 53, 79
    Warrenton 69, 97, 103
    West Point 81
    White House Landing 53
    Wilderness 112
    Winchester 66, 92, 133
Vixen, steamer 72
Voorhees and Bell 39
Wabash, frigate 48
Wachusett, sloop 146-47
Wallen, Joseph K. 13
Ward, James 115
Ward, John 115
Weeks, Eunice 38, 57, 137
Weeks, Henry W. 146
Weeks, John 38, 52, 57, 67
Weeks, Stephen 66, 76
Weeks, Willard 38, 57, 137
Weeks, Willard Jr. 56-57, 137
Western Sanitary Commission 76
Weston, William H. H. 104, 117
Wheeler Jr., Thomas 38, 49, 62
White, Francis B. 88
White, John G. 88
White, Mason 80, 104
White, Thomas F. 47
Whittemore, Eben S. 28, 52, 55-56, 59, 67, 110
Whittemore, Mary 52
William S. Schmidt, ship 101
Willis, William F. 122
Winchester, George H. 13-14

Wing, Elizabeth D. 124
Wing, Eliza G. 11
Wing, Gideon 60, 123-24
Wing, Henry 35, 83
Wing, Isaac H. 7
Wing, Lauretta W. 12
Wing, Mary C. 146
Wing, Paul 2nd 14, 23, 35, 123
Wings Neck Light 103
Wisconsin
  Camp Reno 142
  Milwaukee 142
Wood, Love 128
Wood, Phebe L. 45
Wood, Samuel J. 128
Wood, William H. 33, 45
Woods, Bernard 38
Woods, Delia 18
Woods, Francis 38, 65, 99, 114, 116
Woods, James H. 18, 116
Woods, John 58, 69, 77
Woods, Sarah 58
Woodward, Emeline 70
Woodward, Ezekiel 70
Woodward, William H. 107, 116
Wright, Anderson 44, 77, 116
Wright, Noah 44
Wright, Stillman 59
Wright, Zenas W. 7

Made in the USA
Columbia, SC
06 July 2025

60387759R00136